Poitou-Charentes

& the Vendée

D0307716

Poitou-Charentes and the Vendée made to measure

Poitou-Charentes and the Vendée à la carte

Contents 13

THE COUNTRYSIDE AND NATURE 14

THE BEACHES 28

CRAFTS 36

HISTORY AND HERITAGE 50

PICTURESQUE VILLAGES 60

RESTAURANTS 66

FOOD AND DRINK – LOCAL SPECIALITIES 70

WINES AND SPIRITS 76

FESTIVALS AND CULTURAL EVENTS 86

EXCURSIONS 90

SPORT AND LEISURE 94

Poitou-Charentes and the Vendée in detail

A weekend in La Rochelle

A weekend spent in La Rochelle will make you realise just how much there is to see in the capital of the Charentes. The city has a rich historical heritage and wonderful museums, and the harbour is perfect for romantic moonlight walks. All the more reason to grab the opportunity of spending time in what has been rightly called the 'Pearl of the Charentes'.

Saturday is the day for window-shopping in the streets of the town, sheltered from sun and rain under the wide arcades. Those who love the sea and old ships should make for the port. Wander along the Quai Duperré and the Quai Vavin, to the Quartier du Gabut, a former fishing village lined with picturesque, brightly painted wooden huts. You will then find yourself in the trawler dock, where you can visit one of the most original maritime museums in the world where old working boats form the the exhibits, ranging from a frigate to a modest fishing dinghy. Lovers of regional cuisine should visit the Vieux Marché (old market) to taste *mouclade* (mussels), *farci* (stuffed boiled chicken) or *cagouilles à la charentaise* (snails). Take your children to the Port des Minimes to see the sharks, jellyfish, giant squid and turtles in the Aquarium. In summer, when the city suffocates in the heat, or if it is raining, you can take shelter in the Musée du Nouveau Monde (New World museum), which is dedicated to the pioneers of the Americas, unless you prefer to admire the works of Eugène Fromentin in the Musée des Beaux-Arts (art museum). If you have time on Sunday, take a boat trip to the Île de Ré to sample the delicious local seafood for lunch.

A cycling weekend on the Île de Ré

The Île de Ré is a favourite haunt of French stars trying to go incognito, as well as cyclists. So, if you're not into star-spotting, try a family biking holiday in this most Mediterranean of the islands off the coast of the Charentes.

The Île de Ré is a long, narrow island with a succession of different types of beach.

There are salt marshes and oyster-beds, varied landscapes and villages of white houses, whose gardens are full of rambling roses. Pine forests line the huge beaches and coastal sand dunes. Follow the salt marsh path all around the Fiers d'Ars then cycle up to

the lighthouse of Baleines to the north of Saint-Clément. Alternatively, peddle down to Saint-Martin and explore the Fort de la Prée in the south. Enjoy a weekend of sun, sand and cycling.

A weekend around Angoulême

Spend a weekend in the Angoulême region and you'll be surprised at the variety and number of activities that this part of the Charentes region has to offer.

It will take you at least a day to explore Angoulême. Begin by walking through the town on foot. From the Place des Halles, you can wander the narrow streets to the Palais de Justice (courthouse) then you will emerge at the Hôtel de Ville (town hall). From there, continue up to the Place de New York and sit down at a pavement café. Don't miss the magnificent cathedral of Saint-Pierre, a masterpiece of the local Romanesque style. Or you could spend the afternoon poring over the

cartoons which are something of a national institution in the Centre National de la Bande Dessinée. Angoulême pottery is also worthy of attention and the Musée des Beaux-Arts (art museum) has the finest examples. If you want to buy some, Renoleau has the best selection of local

faience for sale. Don't leave Angoulême without having tasted the local delicacies in the Marché Victor Hugo, which is open on Sunday mornings. Continue the weekend by relaxing in the countryside near Angoulême on the banks of the Charente. Visit the Fleurac mill, where you can learn the art of paper-making as practised in the 18th C. Wander behind the mill and you'll see little wooden bridges and tiny islands covered in vegetation in the middle of the river. Continue towards Trois-Palis, where a delicious chocolate treat is waiting for you at the Chocolaterie Letuffe.

Three or four days on the Cognac route

Spend a long weekend travelling around Cognac and sampling this brandy of world renown. The name of the town has become synonymous of course with the warming spirit which it has manufactured for centuries.

The first stop is Cognac, brandy capital of the world. The largest distilleries invite you to see their ancient *chais* (cellars), many of which are several hundred years old. Don't miss the opportunity of visiting the Château des Valois, the birthplace of king François I. The Valois family owns the Otard firm. From Cognac go to Jarnac, then drive from Segonzac to Châteauneuf-sur-Charente. Here, the vines extend as far

as the eye can see, covering the limestone slopes of the growing areas known as the Grande and Petite Champagne. These are the best brandy-producing slopes in the world. It is time to stop and visit the cellars and taste some of these famous wines and spirits. You can also learn about the various occupations connected with the wine trade – coopers, glass-makers, label-printers, *chai* master –

which have helped this cognac to become the greatest brandy in the world. At Château-Bernard visit the Saint-Gobain glassworks, where the bottles are made.

Drive on to Villeneuve de Chassors to be initiated into the secrets of making the oak barrels. At Segonzac experts at the Cognac University will explain some of the secrets of blending. The trip ends at Jarnac, home of Courvoisier, exclusive supplier of brandy to Napoleon himself.

The real thing

All Cognac brandies originate from Cognac itself and the surrounding area. This may seem obvious, but in fact the name 'Cognac' is tightly controlled. Only brandy made from these particular grapes, eaux de vie from this specific area and adhering to the regulated distillation and ageing methods are permitted to use the name Cognac. Thus all Cognacs are brandy, but not all brandy is Cognac!

A week on the Vendée coast

From the marshes south of Brittany to Saint-Gilles-Croix-de-Vie, from Saint-Jean-de-Monts to Les Sables d'Olonne, the Vendée coast has something for everyone, from the salt marshes in the north to the wide beaches of golden sand in the south. There are dunes and pine forests, farmland and vineyards – as many different landscapes as you could wish for.

Start in the north with the lonely and rugged Breton marshes, ideal for long walks along the dykes, and visit the

locks on the estuaries and the little oyster-fishing ports. At low tide take the Passage du Gois and walk out to the island of Noirmoutier. It's a unique trip across a landscape of sky, sea and wet sand. Saint-Jean-de-Monts lies between 12½ miles (20 km) of fine sand and a dense forest. It's an ideal place for taking a walk through the forest or lazing on the beach. Spend

the rest of the week on the Côte de Lumière (Coast of Light) at Saint-Gilles-Croix-de-Vie on the Corniche Vendéenne, a rocky patch of coast between sandy dunes. Stop at Brem-sur-Mer to taste the local wines (especially the whites and rosés) of the *fiefs vendéens* (the Vendée estates). Continue southwards to Les Sables d'Olonne, the Vendée's biggest and most popular seaside resort. Here you can visit the old fishermen's bars, where the locals hang out, in the district known as the Quartier de la Chaume – authenticity guaranteed! How about a day in the country?

Visit the bird sanctuary in the Bay of Aiguillon or take a trip

into the forest at La Tranche-sur-Mer. There is so much to see and do in this unspoilt part of France.

A week on the coast of the Charentes

Take a week to explore the coast of the Charentes and the 'islands of light'. Salt marshes and ancient forts dominate the forests of pines and the golden sand dunes. It's the perfect place for a healthy, refreshing, seaside break.

Start the week with a stop in Châtelaillon, one of the largest and safest beaches in the whole region. It covers nearly 2 miles (3 km) and is perfect for families with young children. Then leave

the mainland for the Île de Ré, just off the coast. This island, which was the location for a famous prison, has more than 6 miles (10 km) of sandy beaches and is a paradise for windsurfers and lovers of shellfish. If you're interested in birds visit the sanctuary at Lilleau des Niges. The Île d'Oléron, just to the south, is much larger and is also well worth a visit. You can bike around the island and see its sandy coastline, salt marshes and white villages surrounded by lush vineyards. Taste the many wines made on the island, of which one of the best is Colombard, which goes particularly well with seafood, another local speciality. Seafood takes you to Marennes, almost a synonym for oysters. While you are there, climb to the top of Fort Chapus to admire the view out to sea. Continue on to the Fouras peninsula and the Île d'Aix, with its coves and moorland. Further south, on the Arvert peninsula, naturists will find a beach all

to themselves on the Côte Sauvage, where they can surf amid the Atlantic breakers. Don't miss the Phare de Cordouan, one of the oldest lighthouses in France, off the coast at Royan, another famous seaside resort. At Royan stop for some refreshment at a pavement café. A stone's throw away there is the Zoo de la Palmyre, an open-air zoo, whose attractions include polar bears and Siberian tigers. Complete your visit with a trip to the Gironde estuary, stopping at Talmont, where you can admire the Romanesque church, which is built right at the edge of a precipitous cliff, overlooking a long drop.

A week in Deux-Sèvres

From the gateway to Anjou in the north to the marshes of Poitou in the south, you can explore the Deux-Sèvres region, with its rich architectural heritage framed in lush valleys criss-crossed by streams.

The gateway to the region is the town of Niort, which is surrounded by marshes. Begin by visiting the *donjon* (castle keep) by the river Sèvre. From the top you will have an excellent view of the town. Don't forget to visit the market halls on Saturday morning, the busiest day of the week. This is the place to stock up on angelica, which has been grown and preserved here since the Middle Ages. Don't leave without strolling through the botanical garden on the banks of the Sèvre, whose green waters run through the heart of the city. Then leave Niort for Arçais, the largest village on the marshes, which has more than 25 miles (40 km) of navigable canals. Continue on to Melle, where the silver mines, which are among the oldest in Europe, can still be visited. Stop to see its lovely Romanesque churches. Continue northwards via Parthenay, an ancient medieval fortress of tall towers and narrow, winding streets. The citadel of Thouars, perched on a rocky spur and dominating the valley of the Thouet, is the next stop. It is the gateway to Anjou and is surrounded by vineyards as far as the eye can see. Stop here and wander through the picturesque streets with half-timbered houses. Then visit Bressuire, whose rich farmland and narrow valleys will enable rock-climbers and water-sports enthusiasts to enjoy climbing and kayaking in unspoiled countryside.

Finally, return south, to Gâtine, apple-growing country, famous for the Clocharde

dessert apple. At Vasles children will love the Mouton Village, dedicated to sheep and sheep-farming, an important industry in these parts.

A week in the Charentes countryside

From Confolens in Charente-Limousine, to the shores of the river Charente at Aubeterre-sur-Dronne, the Charentes countryside, with its oak forests, brandy-producing vines and valleys dominated by imposing châteaux, is an ideal location for a holiday combining visits to monuments and places of interest with sporting activities.

Begin by spending a few days in the Confolens district. You'll see many châteaux and fortresses perched high in the crags above the valleys of the Charente and the Tardoire. Don't forget to visit the Gallo-Roman baths at Chassenon, which are amazingly

well preserved. The fishermen among you may wish to tickle a few pike in the tributaries of the Charente, or you may prefer to see the countryside on horseback. Continue your stay in the gentle countryside surrounding the small town of La Rochefoucauld. You can visit the town's

château, or you may prefer to take a canoe on the nearby river Tardoire. The last day of your trip should be dedicated to a visit to Aubeterre-sur-Dronne, one of the prettiest villages in the Charentes. After an apéritif under the linden trees in the Place Trarieux, leave the fresh air for a few moments and go down into the church of Saint-Jean, an extraordinary underground sanctuary. If you prefer fresh air to cellars, you can visit the Musée du Papillon (butterfly museum p. 190). The collection has of some 12,000 butterflies and 6,000 other insects.

A fortnight in the Vendée

This land of marshes, meadows and sparkling, sandy seashores merits a lengthy visit. The coves, inlets and island beaches, the mildness of the climate and the canals of the Poitou marshes will ensure your stay is a memorable one.

If you're a history buff, you'll enjoy visiting the haunts of the Chouans, who were at the heart of the Vendée military. Important Chouan sites include the memorial at Les Lucs-sur-Boulogne and the Logis de la Chabotterie, the manor house where Charette, one of the leaders, was arrested. At Puy-du-Fou, there's a *son et lumière* show, which explains and brings to life the turbulent times at the turn of the 19th C. and the Chouannerie uprising. For those who prefer warm sand and the wind in their hair, the Côte Lumineuse (luminous coast), extending from Saint-Jean-de-Monts to Les Sables-d'Olonne, has salt marshes, oyster-beds, pine forests, secret inlets and golden sandy beaches. Take a trip to the offshore islands of Yeu and Noirmoutier. It's not far from here to the Poitou marshes, where you can take a boat trip on the canals. Spend two nights camping in the water-meadows, then stock up on local foods at the market in Coulon. Maillezais is the place to buy honey, and you can also see the remains of its Romanesque abbey.

An active fortnight in the Charentes countryside

The Charentes has much to offer in the way of unspoiled countryside and there are many sporting activities. Here are a few ideas for things to do and places to visit.

The Charentes countryside, with its meadows and forests, is the perfect place to hike or ramble, or even ride on horseback. You can canoe or kayak down its rivers and rock-climb in the valley of the Tardoire. Anglers will find plenty of sport in the tributaries of the Charentes, where there are pike and eels to be had. Water-sports enthusiasts will prefer the seashore and the off-shore islands, where the Atlantic breakers are an superb for surfing and windsurfing.

The Charentes is flat enough to make a cycling tour an option. On the Île de Ré follow the paths through the coastal marshes, those of the Coubre forest on the Arvert peninsula, and on the Île d'Aix those that lead to the Pointe Sainte-Catherine. The Côte Sauvage is a beautiful spot, and the beach offers a great setting for horse riding. If you are by the coast, you can learn about the local fishing industry by visiting a mussel-farm at Charron, and sampling a few of the *fines de claires* oysters at Marennes and tasting the **sel auxalgues** (salt with seaweed) from the salt-marshes of the Île de Ré. Birdwatchers should not miss the bird sanctuaries at Lilleau des Niges, Moëze and L'Aiguillon bay.

Poitou-Charentes and the Vendée à la carte

The countryside and nature

Between the farmland and marshes, countryside and seashore, you will see a vast array of flora and fauna.

Nantes

Cholet

Sèvre nantaise

DT63

A87

① *Argenton-Château*

Lac d'Hautibus
p. 135.

②③ Île de Noirmoutier

②②

②①

Marais breton-vendéen

②④

Île d'Yeu

②⓪

La Roche -sur-Yon

A83

Forêt de Mervent

③

②*Neuil-sur-Argent*

Parc de Tournelay
p. 134.

①⑨

Les Sables-d'Olonne

Fontenay-le-Comte

Marais Poitevin

④

③ *Forest of Mervent*

Forest and zoological park
p. 152.

④ *Poitou marshes*

Drained marshes and wetlands
p. 146.

①⑧ ①⑦

Île de Ré

La Rochelle ①⑥

Baie de l'Aiguillon

N11

⑤ *Melle*

Hundreds of species of trees from temperate climates and a rose collection
p. 165.

⑩ *Moëze*

Moëze Nature Reserve
p. 209.

①⑤

Île d'Oléron

①③ **Rochefort** ①④

A837

①⓪

⑥ *Forest of Chizé*

Forest and zoorama
p. 166.

⑪ *La Palmyre*

Zoological park
p. 234.

①②

Forêt de la Coubre ⑪

⑦ *Forest of Horte*
p. 184.

⑫ *Port-des-Salines*

Fisherman's village, small exhibits about salt marsh workers and oyster farmers
p. 230.

Royan ●

⑨

⑧ *Aire de Beau Vallon*

Swimming and walking in the forest
p. 193.

Estuaire de la Gironde

⑬ *Île d'Oléron*

Forest, wading birds and salt marshes
p. 228.

⑨ *Saint-André-de-Lidon*

Chaillaud botanical gardens
p. 239.

⑭ *Rochefort*

Conservatoire du bégonia
p. 207.

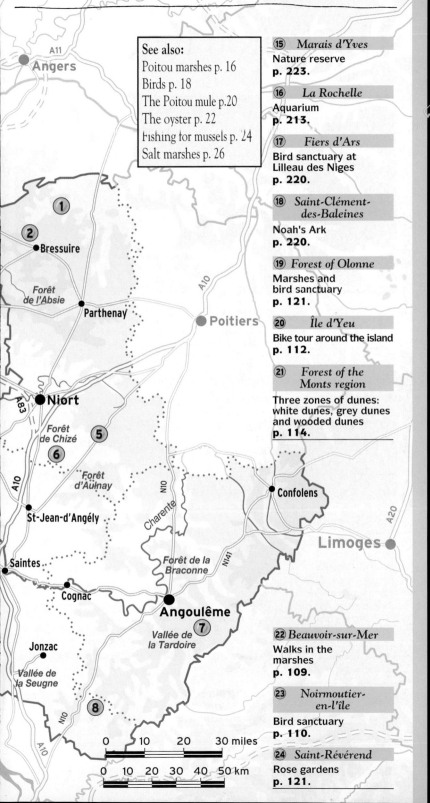

See also:
Poitou marshes p. 16
Birds p. 18
The Poitou mule p. 20
The oyster p. 22
Fishing for mussels p. 24
Salt marshes p. 26

⑮ Marais d'Yves
Nature reserve
p. 223.

⑯ La Rochelle
Aquarium
p. 213.

⑰ Fiers d'Ars
Bird sanctuary at
Lilleau des Niges
p. 220.

**⑱ Saint-Clément-
des-Baleines**
Noah's Ark
p. 220.

⑲ Forest of Olonne
Marshes and
bird sanctuary
p. 121.

⑳ Île d'Yeu
Bike tour around the island
p. 112.

**㉑ Forest of the
Monts region**
Three zones of dunes:
white dunes, grey dunes
and wooded dunes
p. 114.

㉒ Beauvoir-sur-Mer
Walks in the
marshes
p. 109.

**㉓ Noirmoutier-
en-l'île**
Bird sanctuary
p. 110.

㉔ Saint-Révérend
Rose gardens
p. 121.

The Poitou marshes
a world of their own

The Poitou marshes cover an area of 237,220 acres (96,000 ha), from Niort and Fontenay-le-Comte to the Atlantic Ocean. The landscape is striking and varied. There are two major areas, the coastal area, where the marsh has been drained, and the interior wetlands. Each has its own special landscape. The fragile ecological balance depends on the regulation of the water table through a complex network of canals.

The legacy of the monks

The marshes are the results of the Herculean labours of monks in the Middle Ages. Once covered by the sea, the area became silted up with deposits from the river estuaries, resulting in a foul-smelling swamp. This

changed in the 11th C. when the monks of the neighbouring abbeys of Nieul, Maillezais, Saint-Michel-en-l'Herm, Saint-Maixent and Absie decided to drain it and

make it habitable. They dug canals, installed locks, built mills and drained the swamp to create land that could be cultivated.

The drained marshland and bay of Aiguillon

The drained marshland is protected by dikes and sluice-gates and looks something like the Dutch polders. The

canals drain water from the land in winter and irrigate it in summer. The pasture obtained through reclamation is best suited to animal husbandry. The high salinity of the marshes explains why they consist exclusively of grassland and why trees and shrubs, with the exception of tamarisks, do not thrive. At the seaward end of the marshes is the bay of Aiguillon, which has a rich shellfish population and is thus full of migratory birds.

Ancient mussel beds

The drained marshes are ideal for rearing *pré salé*, the delicious salt-marsh mutton so sought after by gourmets. The spring lambs are a particular delicacy. The mussel-beds in the bay of Aiguillon have been cultivated since the 13th C.

escaped convicts and other fugitives from justice. There are many small plots called *mottes*, surrounded by water, on which vegetables are grown. Nothing goes to waste. Willow is used for basket-making, wood for clogs, dandelions for salad, plantain leaves for wrapping goat's cheeses and so on.

The wetlands

This is the floodplain around the Sèvre at Niort. It is known as the 'green Venice' because of its canals, which are lined with ash trees and pollarded willows. Plantlife

includes wild irises and angelica, and there are coypus and otters, eels, marsh frogs, wild swans and ducks. Fortunately thanks to the presence of numerous dragon-flies, mosquitoes are rare.

Mojettes and *lumas*

The inhabitants of the Poitou marshes were largely self-sufficient. They grew their own food, fished and hunted. *Mojettes*, large white haricot beans with a thin skin, were their staple food, and were eaten with Vendée ham. *Lumas* (snails), which love the damp, were very numerous and were also eaten, as they still are. They are usually gathered after rain.

The waterways

All the waterways have local names. The canals and their levels are state-owned and are the widest waterways. The *rigoles*, which are 50-66 ft (15-20 m) wide and 6 miles (10 km) long and the *conches*, which are 20-33 ft (6-10 m) wide, are owned by the commune. There are a few *fossés* (moats), which belong to a couple of local land-owners. The waterways were once the only highways and were used for taking children to school, family outings, going to church, as well as for transporting sheep and cattle. The maze of waterways was also an excellent refuge for

HOW TO MAKE ANGELICA LIQUEUR

This plant grows wild in the marsh and can be made into a delicious liqueur. Trim about 4 oz (100 g) of fresh stems and place in a jar with a pinch of cinnamon and a clove. Cover with 1¾ pints (1 l) of vodka or eau de vie, and leave the jar in the sun for 2 hours a day for 8 days. Make a syrup with 12 oz (350 g) of sugar and 12 fl oz (350 ml) of water. Add to the angelica preparation and leave to mature for 3 months. Filter before drinking.

Birds and birdwatching

The white-spotted bluethroat (see p. 221)

The marshes of Bouin, the Gironde, the coast and the immediate hinterland are all migratory routes for birds flying to Africa. Many sites have been created in order to protect these birds and make it possible for ornithologists to observe them.

A natural stop

The mudflats contain plenty of food, especially shellfish and worms. La Brière and the Lake of Grand-Lieu in the north and the bay of Aiguillon in the south form the boundaries of a fertile area at the crossroads of the migration routes. The mouths of the rivers Loire, Charente and Gironde are warmed by the Gulf Stream (p. 38.) and contain many different fish, so are also popular with birds.

Careful programming

Migration is triggered by the shortening of the days. When this happens, birds begin to eat more to increase their stores of fat, which will serve as reserves of energy for the long flights of 6-8 hours a day at speeds that can exceed 60 mph (100 kmph) for some species, such as teal. The main seasons for birds flying over France are autumn and spring. The number of birds passing overhead at these times has been estimated at between 500 million and 600 million. Some birds, such as the tern, cover impressive distances of more than 9,320 miles (15,000 km) and do so twice year. A stork can easily fly between 6,220 to 12,500 miles (10,000 to 20,000 km).

Where and when to see them

The best places to watch bird migrations are the **bay of Bourgneuf**, between the mainland and the **Île de Noirmoutier**, the lakes and ponds in the woodlands of Vendée, midway between the banks of the Loire and the marshes of the southern Vendée, the marshland of **Brittany** and the **Vendée**, the **bay of Aiguillon** and the drained marshland. Bring along some powerful

A young gull

THE BEST TIME FOR BIRDWATCHING

Learn the habits of the species that frequent the sites. There is no point in looking for migratory species, such as brent geese in July. That's when they'll be in Siberia. The best times of day are early in the morning or in the evening. April–May and September–October are the best times for watching migrations, and in the cold months you can see the birds that overwinter in France and leave when the weather improves. It is at high tide when the spectacle is most impressive, particularly in the Aiguillon and Bourgneuf bays where birds fly in in their thousands, skimming over the mudflats.

binoculars or choose a reserve that rents them out. You will need to be very patient and quiet; amateur photographers should be prepared to spend many hours in a hide, in order to capture the perfect shot of the fledglings as they leave the nest for the first time.

Birds of passage

The brent goose is one of the first birds to arrive, in September, departing again for the north in February. The elegant avocet, with its long, black, upcurved beak, mallards, pintails and shovellers, as well as the oystercatchers, grey plovers, stone curlews, black-tailed godwits and lapwings follow the same pattern. Ringed plovers and turnstones keep to the shores, dashing along beside the water in search of tiny worms. By the end of March the white-spotted bluethroat is a common sight on the salt marshes.

(For further details, contact the bird society, Ligue Protectrice des Oiseaux ☎ 01 53 58 58 38.)

Resident birds

Some birds hardly migrate at all or have settled down in the reserves and sanctuaries in which they are protected. To the north on the island of Noirmoutier you will see the shelduck, a large, noisy duck with a red band across its white body, a black head, and a thick, bright red bill. The tall, elegant heron fishes for frogs, fish, eels and even small mussels, and can be seen on the Breton-Vendée marshes The little egret shares the same habitat. Both species tend to gather in large numbers at the end of the day.

A lapwing

The Poitou mule

This charming animal with its extraordinary appearance is known in France as le baudet de Poitou. Nicknamed 'the peasant's moped', it almost became extinct with the mechanisation of farm work. It is really a large, woolly donkey, which is willing and able to undertake the most back-breaking work. Thanks to the efforts of the National Donkey Sanctuary at Dampierre-sur-Boutonne, the breed is now being saved.

An ancient breed

The first precise description of this ancient breed dates to 1717, by which time the baudet du Poitou was already very well known. Although its exact origin is unknown, it is believed to have emerged in the time of the Gauls. In 1884 the first stud book was created in Niort for the baudet du Poitou. Even today, each animal is carefully recorded and identified by an implanted electronic chip.

Mule stud farms

The baudet was originally used for heavy labour, such as draining the Poitou marshes. But in addition to its strong constitution, the baudet du Poitou cross-breeds well. Breeders in the Melle district cross carefully selected baudet stallions with equally carefully selected mares in order to produce the incredibly strong and hardy Poitou mules.

The spread to Europe

The Poitou mule soon became a valuable draught animal and was used for ploughing and other farm work. They were exported throughout the whole of Europe, ensuring prosperity for the region. Buyers flocked to the traditional Melle fair, and each year, some 20,000 mules were traded, all of them with such stamina and strength that they were much sought after over, particularly in Spain and even as far afield as India. Army corps used mules extensively as pack animals, including the Chasseurs Alpins and the Zion Mule Corps.

Looking for the extinct baudet

In the 1950s farmers began to replace donkeys and mules with tractors. As the animals became less useful, interest in keeping and breeding them waned, and the numbers of baudets began to decline to a

worrying extent. By 1980 only about 60 specimens were left. A tremendous effort was needed to save this, the oldest pure-bred donkey in the world. It resulted in the Asinerie Nationale de Dampierre-sur-Boutonne, a national donkey sanctuary (see p. 227), formed in 1980. It set about introducing a breeding programme and created an inventory of thoroughbred animals. A research programme was also launched in order to investigate the biology of this breed of donkey. They even went to the lengths of creating a special sperm bank for it!

Foreign fillies to the rescue

Because of the small number of *baudets* available, inter-breeding became common, weakening the breed still further. In order to introduce new blood, females were sought outside France. Their offspring were bred with genuine *baudets*, and the fillies from these unions were mated in turn with genuine Poitou *baudets* until finally the breed could be said to be saved. By 1994 there were 200 *baudets* scattered throughout the world, of which a third were in Poitou, a third in the rest of France and the rest elsewhere, including the USA.

(see p. 227)

AN OFF-ROAD DONKEY

The *baudet du Poitou* is a donkey like no other. First of all, it is tall, standing 4½-5 ft (1.4-1.5 m) at the withers, and its weight varies between 38 and 65 st (250 and 430 kg). But what distinguishes it above all is its thick, woolly coat of long, reddish-brown or dark-brown hair. The muzzle, nose and eye area are silvery-white. It is equally resistant to heat and cold and is as

much at home in the marshes as in the mountains. The mare is much smaller, but her coat is just as thick, and she carries her foal for a whole year, suckling it for 7-8 months. The little foal, which is generally very affectionate, matures at the age of three years.

The oyster
the pearl of the Charentes

The oyster is to Charente-Maritime what olive oil is to Provence – its very soul. A delight to the tastebuds and believed to be a boost to male fertility thanks to its trace elements and mineral salts, it is also very important to regional prosperity.

From seabed to plate

Breeding oysters requires patience – it takes four years for an oyster to reach a suitable size for eating. Oysters lay their eggs in the summer; the tiny seeds are fixed to other shells or roof-tiles, known as collectors, and develop for 18 months. The young oysters are then separated and placed in oyster-beds where they are allowed to grow into adults. They are then matured in special pools, *claires*, where they develop trace elements and mineral salts, and grow larger and turn green. They are then placed in clear water to make them expel any sand and mud which they may contain. Finally, they are rinsed before being packed into special lidded baskets, *bourriches*.

How to choose the best oysters

Fines de claires are oysters that have matured for two months at a concentration of 20 oysters per square yard (metre). **Spéciales** are finer and have been matured for 6 months with only 5-6 a square yard (metre). Oysters are graded according to size – the largest are no. 1, and the smallest are no. 4, but the tastiest are the sizes in between. If you don't like 'milky' oysters don't buy them in spring or summer.

When to eat oysters

Contrary to traditional beliefs, oysters can be eaten all year round. They are fattest in the mating season, from May to August, when they retain all their nutritional goodness. The misconception derives from an edict issued by King Louis XV, who did not ban the consumption, but only the transportation of oysters during months that did not contain an 'r', because these are the hottest of the year. In an era where refrigerated lorries were far in the future, it could be dangerous to eat oysters far from where they grew. Look carefully at the *bourriches* in the fishmonger, the labels will tell you the origin, size and freshness of the product.

Oyster-eating: a matter of taste

Oysters are usually eaten raw, so they should be kept in a cool, well-ventilated, place at a temperature of 41-50 °F (5-10°C). If they are moist inside and tightly closed they should keep for 10 days. They should only be opened immediately before they are eaten. To be sure they are alive when eaten, touch the edge of the oyster with the tip of a knife. If it reacts, go

OYSTER CULTIVATION

1. Seed oysters, suspended in the water, attach themselves to a collector.

2. After a year or two, the oysters are detached from the collector and placed on oyster beds where they grow for several years.

3. When they are fully grown, the oysters are taken from the beds to the refining basins, where they are left to fatten before being sorted, scraped and rinsed in fresh water so that they expel any sand and impurities they may contain.

ahead and swallow it, if not, discard it immediately. Raw oysters are eaten as they come, sprinkled with a little pepper, little lemon juice or shallot vinegar and accompanied by rye bread with salted butter. To eat them cooked,

they should be poached quickly in a white wine and herb sauce and eaten hot. Don't make the sauce too spicy or you'll mask the subtle flavour.

Fines de claires from Marennes-Oléron

In this part of the Vendée, oyster cultivation began in the former salt marshes in the mid-19th C. The *fines de claires* are the exclusive privilege of the Marennes-Oléron basin, the heart of oyster production in France, and the local people guard their prize carefully. Each year, the basin produces 45% of France's deep-shelled oysters, about 58,000 tonnes a year. Their beautiful greenish colour

makes Marennes-Oléron oysters the pride of the region and easy to distinguish from others.

Colourful oyster-farmers' huts

The coastal marshes are greatly enhanced by the brightly coloured or lime-washed wooden huts of the oyster-farmers. Their tiled roofs are covered in moss, and the windows are small. The doors are frequently painted in brightly contrasting colours. These are in effect fishermen's workshops and are situated close to the basins, being used for storing equipment and for taking a rest between visits to the oyster beds and the *claires*.

HOW TO STORE OYSTERS

To store oysters all you need to do is to stop them from opening, which you can do by packing them down and covering them with a heavy weight. Keep them in the bottom of the refrigerator or, in winter, on a window ledge. You can open and eat your oysters up to 10 days after they left the water without any fear. It's advisable to reject oysters that contain no water and those whose mantle (the darker edge) does not react when touched with the point of a knife. If you buy a whole basket (*bourriche*), don't open it until just before you are going to eat the contents.

Fishing for mussels

The mussel is a bivalve mollusc, which likes water that is rich in plankton and algae, such as that found in the bay of Aiguillon. The female mussel produces around a million eggs at each laying, ejecting the embryos into the water. The larvae then attach themselves to a support, such as rope. A minute shell forms within a month, which is attached to the support by the filaments, known as the byssus.

A long history

Huge piles of mussel shells have been found at many prehistoric sites, including that of Saint-Michel-en-l'Herm in the Vendée, proving that the taste for mussels is nothing new. The Romans were particularly partial to mussels, and throughout the Middle Ages people living along the coast exploited this rich resource, although they confined themselves to natural beds. It was not until the 13th C that mussels began to be cultivated.

Pearl mussels

The mussel reached its heyday in the 18th C. when a few shells were found to contain some very beautiful pearls. Along the banks of the river Charente divers and fishermen set out to look for pearl mussels, hoping to make their fortune by selling their treasures to the ladies of the French court.

Unfortunately, this activity proved to be less profitable than anticipated and was eventually abandoned.

An Irish genius

In 1235 an Irishman, Patrick Walton, was sole survivor when his ship ran aground at Esnandes. He settled in the region and one day, when he was tending his fishing nets at low tide, he noticed that stakes in the water were covered with young mussels, and that they were fatter than those he picked out of the sand haphazardly. This was the beginning of the *bouchots* system.

> ### MUSSEL RECIPES
> One of the most popular ways to eat mussels is *Moules Mariniéres*, where they are cooked and served in a sauce of white wine. They can be also be cooked plain, or with a little chopped parsley, onions, sprig of thyme and butter. You can eat a many mussels as you like as each mussel contains hardly any calories, yet they are full of minerals and trace elements.

The capture

In February and March, when the water temperature begins to rise, the support ropes are made ready. A line of posts is erected in the sand at the low-tide mark and ropes are stretched horizontally between them, forming a taut network, like a fence 16 ft (5 m) long. The rising tide covers the posts, bringing in a cloud of mussel larvae, which attach themselves to the ropes. At Noirmoutier, for example, more than 250 miles (400 km) of rope are used every year! In May tiny black dots, the size of pinheads, the miniature mussels, finally begin to appear on the ropes.

Cultivation

As soon as the tiny shells have formed, to help them develop properly, the ropes with their bunches of 'baby mussels' are cut from the posts and wrapped around oak stakes, 20-26 ft (6-8 m) high

planted in spaced rows, 65-82 ft (20-25 m) long. These are known as *bouchots*. The mussel spats, which by June are no bigger than a fingernail are placed on *bouchots* furthest from the water's edge. As they grow, they are transferred to *bouchots* nearer to the shore.

The harvest

The space left between the rows of *bouchots* forms an 'avenue' through which the flat-bottomed mussel boats can pass. These boats are called *boucholeurs*. No matter how low

the tide, the boats can easily gain access to the *bouchots* to repair, replace them and move and harvest the mussels. Harvesting is performed either by hand with a crescent-shaped mesh landing net or by machine. A mussel is large enough to eat when it is around 18 months old.

How to eat mussels

Mussels that are sold commercially are subject to strict health checks and must be labelled with the date on which they left the production site. They can be stored in a cold place for several days if covered with a damp cloth. In this way, they will remain tightly closed, and therefore alive. They will also retain the seawater they have stored (which will form delicious cooking juices). Never place mussels in liquid. The old tradition of only eating them in months that contain an 'r' is no longer valid. In fact, they are at their best from May onwards and right through the summer.

MUSSELS GROWN ON *BOUCHOTS*

1. Ropes are stretched between oak posts to which the mussel larvae, floating in the water, attach themselves.

3. Mussels grow for at least two years before they can be harvested, which is carried out by hand or by machine.

2. Once the tiny mussels have been formed, the ropes are rolled around stakes (bouchots) planted at the low tide line.

The salt marshes
white gold of the coast

For centuries salt was the only means of preserving savoury food. From prehistoric times onwards coastal peoples obtained it by heating brine in sheets of clay. Over the centuries extraction methods gradually improved. In the Middle Ages monks reclaimed a lot of land from the sea, and as a result, the coast of Poitou and Charentes, as well as the Guérande in Brittany, attracted many buyers of salt from Europe. Salt continues to be extracted today from the marshes of the Île de Noirmoutier, Beauvoir-sur-Mer, Saint-Gilles-Croix-de-Vie, Olonne-sur-Mer and the Île de Ré.

A complex chequerboard

Seen from the air, the salt marshes form a network of geometric patterns. This chequerboard of basins and canals carefully channels and directs the flow of seawater through the salt marshes; the successive compartments or pans decant and evaporate the salt. The pans have rounded corners and are arranged in parallel rows (see p. 27).

The water circuit

The inlet or *étier* for the seawater is regulated by a sluice-gate, the *coef*, which is opened to the high tide every fortnight. Water flows over

the **mudflats** into the decantation reservoir and starts to warm up and evaporate. A succession of gentle gradients and the careful regulation of

> ### BASS IN A SALT CRUST
> Gut and clean the bass and wash it but don't remove the scales.
> Lay it on a baking sheet or in an ovenproof dish on a ¾ in (2 cm) bed of coarse salt. Season the fish with herbs (thyme, bay leaf, tarragon etc), and cover with another thick layer of coarse salt, which can be bound with a little egg white to keep it in place. Bake for 45 minutes for a bass weighing about 2½ lb (1.2 kg). To serve, break open the crust. Eat with butter and lemon juice.

the flow bring the brine to the *métières*, then the *tapes* and the *brassious*, as the various pans are called, which decrease in size and depth. Through the combined effect of wind and sun, the concentration of salt in the pans increases. The salt finally crystallises in the *œillet* (eyelet), the final pan from which it is harvested.

Working the salt pans

A salt marsh worker is called a *saulnier* in Poitou-Charentes and a *paludier* in Guérande in Brittany. He walks barefoot around the *œillet* because the little clay walls of the pans are very fragile. The fine layer of white crystals that float on the surface in large sheets is called *fleur de sel* (flower of the salt). It is gently raked in with an implement called a *lousse* and tipped into a basket. Each *oeillet* can yield only 11 lb (5 kg) of white salt a day. The coarse grey salt crystallises in the bottom and is recovered with an *ételle*, a sort of toothless rake with a 16½ ft (5 m) long handle. The piles are drained before being removed in a wheelbarrow. In season an *œillet* can produce 110-155 lb (50-70 kg) of coarse salt a day.

Seasonal work

Salt is harvested from June to September and only in fine weather. The salt marsh

worker is at work from dawn until dusk. When summer is over the soft mud is removed from the mudflats, and they are cleaned of vegetation. As soon as the weather turns cold, the salt marsh is flooded to protect it from rain and frost. In March the work of drying and cleaning begins. The edges of the pans are built up again and cracks are repaired. Just before the seawater is let in again at the start of the season, the whole marsh is drained. The salt pans are emptied and the clay on the bottom is checked to ensure that it is immaculate. Two days later, the first salt is harvested.

Salt pan dictionary

Each salt marsh has its own vocabulary. In Noirmoutier, Olonne and Ré the worker is called a *saulnier*, but he is a *paludier* in Guérande. There are various names for the different salt pans. The implements also change their names. The *ételle* becomes a *tas* or *simoussi*, the *lousse* becomes an *ouvron*. The little promontory on which the coarse salt is heaped is called a *ladure* in Guérande and a *table* or *foyer* in Poitou. The ancient craft has its own terminology, which is part of the local dialect, and different words are used at each marsh.

THE SALT MARSH

Seawater enters the salt pans via a little channel, which is subsequently closed. By a series of gradients the water flows from pan to pan, each shallower than the last, and the water evaporates. The residue of liquid becomes much saltier and the salt finally crystallises in the last pans.

The beaches

Whether you are on the coast or on the islands, want somewhere exposed or sheltered, are a naturist or prefer to be fully clothed, some of the most beautiful beaches in Poitou-Charentes are listed here.

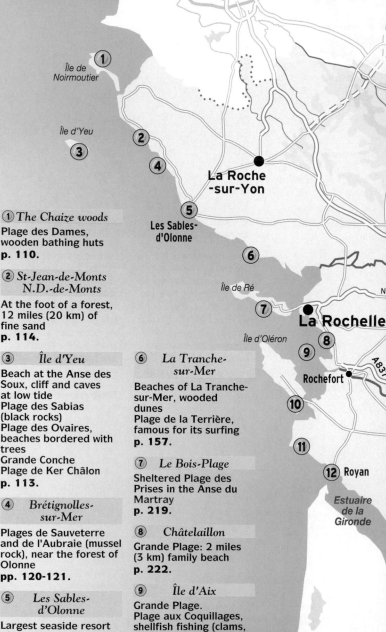

① The Chaize woods

Plage des Dames, wooden bathing huts
p. 110.

② St-Jean-de-Monts N.D.-de-Monts

At the foot of a forest, 12 miles (20 km) of fine sand
p. 114.

③   Île d'Yeu

Beach at the Anse des Soux, cliff and caves at low tide
Plage des Sabias (black rocks)
Plage des Ovaires, beaches bordered with trees
Grande Conche
Plage de Ker Châlon
p. 113.

④   Brétignolles-sur-Mer

Plages de Sauveterre and de l'Aubraie (mussel rock), near the forest of Olonne
pp. 120-121.

⑤   Les Sables-d'Olonne

Largest seaside resort of Vendée
p. 122.

⑥   La Tranche-sur-Mer

Beaches of La Tranche-sur-Mer, wooded dunes
Plage de la Terrière, famous for its surfing
p. 157.

⑦   Le Bois-Plage

Sheltered Plage des Prises in the Anse du Martray
p. 219.

⑧   Châtelaillon

Grande Plage: 2 miles (3 km) family beach
p. 222.

⑨   Île d'Aix

Grande Plage.
Plage aux Coquillages, shellfish fishing (clams, razor-shells and limpets)
p. 210.

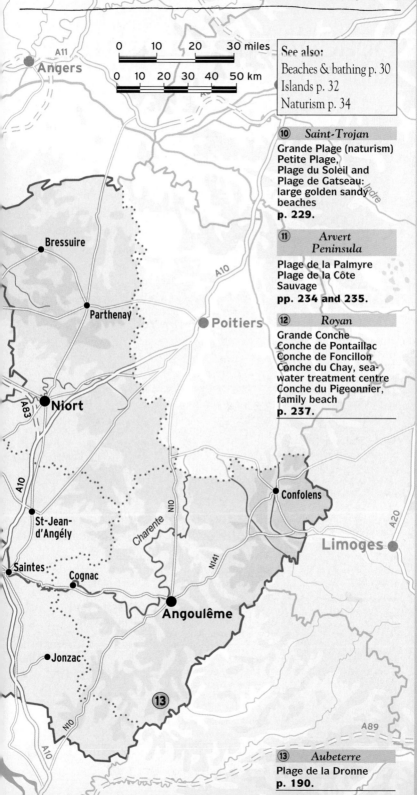

0 10 20 30 miles
0 10 20 30 40 50 km

See also:
Beaches & bathing p. 30
Islands p. 32
Naturism p. 34

A11
Angers

Bressuire

A10

Parthenay

Poitiers

A83

Niort

A10

St-Jean-d'Angély

Charente

N10

Confolens

A20

Limoges

Saintes

Cognac

N141

Angoulême

Jonzac

N10

A10

A89

⑩ *Saint-Trojan*

Grande Plage (naturism)
Petite Plage,
Plage du Soleil and
Plage de Gatseau:
large golden sandy
beaches
p. 229.

⑪ *Arvert Peninsula*

Plage de la Palmyre
Plage de la Côte
Sauvage
pp. 234 and 235.

⑫ *Royan*

Grande Conche
Conche de Pontaillac
Conche de Foncillon
Conche du Chay, sea-
water treatment centre
Conche du Pigeonnier,
family beach
p. 237.

⑬ *Aubeterre*
Plage de la Dronne
p. 190.

Beaches and bathing
caring for the coastline

The coast of Poitou and the Charentes is one of the most popular with French holidaymakers, known for its long stretches of fine sand and good weather. Although some parts of the coastline are built up, much of it is still in its original state and the Conservatoire du Littoral (society for conservation of the coastline) regularly adds to the number of protected sites.

Operation clean water

A major concern for everyone on the beach is whether the water is clean and safe. The French Ministry of Health publishes analyses of the water at resorts. As a result, most have made an effort to improve the quality and cleanliness of their beaches. Every year, the Blue Flag of the European Union is awarded to the communes that offer the best beaches and cleanest water. And, as far as safety goes, if you happen to come into contact with a jellyfish in hot weather, don't panic. You may have a temporary, superficial feeling of burning, but they are really not dangerous.

LES SABLES D'OLONNE
VENDÉE

The ravages of pollution

There is nothing more unpleasant than to find your feet and towels stained with tar or to have to wade through a slimy carpet of rotting seaweed before you can get to the sea. The pollution caused by tankers running aground or washing out their holds while at sea has left the unpleasant sight of dirty coastlines and dying birds. But we must all do our bit to keep the coast clean. Plastic bags, bottles and other detritus washed up by the tide underline the need not to leave rubbish and clutter behind on the beach.

Fragile and breakable

The dunes are tempting places for picnicking and

walking, and they also make a pleasant campsite. But camping in the wild and lighting fires are strictly forbidden here and are subject to heavy fines. Comply with these rules and make sure they are followed. The dune is a living, moving, fragile environment, which is threatened by being visited too often. It is only held together by plantations of pines, evergreen oak and marram grass, which guarantee its stability.

Supervised bathing

Busy beaches will usually have a life-guard. A green flag means no danger; an orange flag means caution; a red flag means that bathing is forbidden. But where there is no life-guard on duty an apparently calm sea may conceal treacherous currents. In general, beaches where the waves form large breakers or rollers are exciting, but are dangerous for children and inexperienced swimmers. It may be difficult to get to safety between two rollers and you will quickly tire. If you happen to get carried away on the current, don't try and fight it directly, but try to swim at an angle to it to try to reach the shore. Never swim in channels reserved for shipping, water-skiing or sailboarding.

Weather forecasts

Take note of weather forecasts if you intend to go out on the water. They will tell you the wind speed, state of the sea and any potential changes. Wave height is measured between a peak and its following trough, out at sea, where the swell forms. Even a *belle* (beautiful) sea has troughs of between 4 and 20 inches (10-50 cm), *forte* (strong) from 8 to 13 ft (2.5 to 4 m), *grosse* (heavy) from from 20 to 30 ft (6 to 9 m).

Wind speed is measured on the Beaufort Scale which ranges from 0 to 12. Landlubbers would say that a force 3 is windy, force 5 to 8 is a storm and beyond that they would have difficulty keeping upright!

No dogs allowed

In the summer dogs are not allowed on the beach, even on a lead, and stereos are forbidden on many beaches. Horses are allowed on to the sands only in certain places and at certain times, at low tide. The same applies to kites since they could hurt someone on a sudden dive to the ground.

TREASURE TROVE

If you've had enough of baking in the sun, don't forget that the beaches are a goldmine for every kind of beachcomber. Just look in the shops that sell marine objects, and you'll get some ideas for collecting what the sea has left behind. There are shells, driftwood, polished glass, pretty pebbles and dried seaweed. In winter these treasures will remind you of your days at the beach.

Islands
a taste of paradise

Large or small, busy or quiet in season or out, the islands are paradise. Some can only be visited by boat, others can now be reached by bridge, much to the disgust of some of the locals, and each has its own individual character.

Climate
The islands off the Poitou-Charentes coast are warmed by the Gulf Stream, the current that flows out of the Gulf of Mexico, and benefit from a mild microclimate. The thermometer hardly ever dips below freezing, as can be seen from the mimosa, palm trees and other exotic species. The Vendée even boasts a similar number of hours of sunshine to those of the Côte d'Azur, but the sea breeze prevents the heat from becoming excessive in the summer.

When to go
The crowds come in July and August. The narrowness of the islands and their streets cause nightmarish traffic jams, so avoid these periods if you don't like crowds. For a more relaxing stay, try visiting the islands in spring or autumn, when you'l still find the weather very pleasant. You could even try coming in winter, when the sea is high and the sky is overcast. It never gets very cold.

How to get there
Only Yeu and Aix have remained true islands only accessible by boat. The trip to the Île d'Yeu is long enough for poor sailors to experience seasickness, so take that into account, especially out of season when the seas are rougher. The other islands – Oléron, Ré and Noirmoutier – are attached to the mainland via a bridge, which makes them easier to get to but spoils some of the charm.

Oléron

At 19 miles (30 km) long, this is the largest of the islands. Previously there was a toll on the bridge, but this has now been abolished. The island is flat, but has a varied landscape. Next to the oyster-beds and fishing grounds are many fine sandy beaches, bordered with pine forests, which are perfect for families, and even in summer some are secluded. It's a paradise for rockpool fishers. The interior of the island is quite a surprise

DON'T FORGET THE ISLETS

Fort-Boyard is the best known. It lies off the Charentes coast in the channel between Oléron and Aix. Like **Fort de Louvois**, situated on an islet at Bourcefranc, it is part of the chain of massive

fortifications of the département of Charente-Maritime. The less well-known **Île Madame** is accessible at low tide by the Passe aux Bœufs. It is spoiled by an invasion of campers in the summer, but out of season it is a lovely place to walk in unspoilt countryside.

as there are market gardens and vineyards from which wine and Pineau are made.

Ré

The uproar caused by the building of the bridge linking the island with the mainland still refuses to die down, as in July and August the island suffers more traffic jams than the Paris ring road on Friday night. The only solution is a bicycle – Ré is 19 miles (30 km) long, but narrow. Cycling is easy, even with children, and less dangerous as the cycle paths are well maintained. You can wander through quaint villages and see the vineyards.

Yeu

The rocky island of Yeu is quite wild and windswept. Its cliffs are reminiscent of those in Brittany. Don't try to bring a vehicle to the island because the roads are too narrow. It can easily be crossed by bicycle, although young children will have difficulty

on some of the steeper parts of the island. Fortunately, the beaches that face the mainland are very safe. If you intend to visit out of season, bring raincoats and warm clothes. You are several miles from the mainland here.

Noirmoutier

This island, known for its salt and potatoes, is best visited in February when the mimosa is in flower. It is very flat and a large part of the land is below the level of high tide. There are plenty of activities for the visitor, but the island suffers from being split in half by an ugly main road. Fortunately, some of the villages and beaches have retained a secret, insular charm. As in all other cases, avoid the high season.

Aix

This tiny island is not very well known but is absolutely delightful. Best of all, it can be toured on foot in only three hours using the circular coastal path. Access is by boat from Fouras and the best time to visit Aix is in late spring when the hollyhocks are in bloom.

Naturism
the art of living 'au naturel'

The French have a much more relaxed attitude to the naked body than many races, and naturism is widely practised in France. The Île d'Oléron, the Arvert peninsula and the coasts of the Vendée, with their long beaches and white sand dunes, are much loved by naturists.

In harmony with nature

Naturism is the art of living in harmony with nature by practising nudity in a communal environment. Naturists exercise the right of self-respect, respect for others and the environment. The naturist and the nudist are both naked but the resemblance ends there. Nudism is restricted to occasional undressing and spending a day naked on the beach, while naturism is a way of life. British naturists have long endured being the subject of some mirth in their own country, and will welcome the opportunity to practise their way of life in a relaxed and accepting atmosphere. Alternatively, if you are a novice but have always wanted to try it, a sandy beach in the warm French sun presents the perfect opportunity.

A million and a half naturists

The Fédération Française de Naturisme has 78,000 members, but France welcomes thousands of naturist tourists. They

come from the Netherlands (37%), Germany (21%), Belgium (24%), the United Kingdom and Switzerland, and no fewer than 1.5 million naturists spend the summer under the French sun. There are also more occasional nudists who want to swim or sunbathe naked in a quiet cove or on a secluded beach. The profile of the average French naturist is said to be that of a city-dweller, married with a child and fairly well-off and usually a business person, teacher or professional person of some kind. So now you know!

Being a naturist

Naturist centres and beaches usually have a few basic rules. The first rule is informality to encourage friendship. To ensure that everyone gets along well, political, religious and philosophical discussions are sometimes banned. The emphasis is on healthy living and eating, so naturists are encouraged to have a healthy and natural diet, to eat and drink in moderation, and to refrain if possible from alcohol and tobacco.

Naturism on the beaches

The local authorities designate certain areas of beaches for naturism. They are clearly signed and often supervised by local police. The French do not reserve areas of their beaches especially for naturists – it is simply that naturism is permitted in certain areas. This means that naturist beaches are open to everyone, even to the coyly clothed. The French naturists call those who refuse to remove all their clothing '*textiles*'. You can probably guess why. However the naturists are very tolerant and by no means chase the '*textiles*' away; perhaps the naturists are hoping to add to their numbers. On the other hand, voyeurs are always given short shrift! If you are only an occasional naturist or just want to swim without a costume, choose beaches specifically reserved for the purpose or find out about the 'nudist spot' in your area.

Naturist beaches in the region

The Poitou-Charentes region has a good number of naturist beaches. In the Vendée, La Faute-sur-Mer and La Tranche-sur-Mer (p. 157) have space reserved for naturists. On the Île d'Oléron (p. 228), the Saumonards beach at Boyardville, the Plage de la Chaucre (Saint-Georges d'Oléron) and the central part of the Grand Plage at Saint-Trojan are all available to naturists. The beaches of the Arvert peninsula along the Côte Sauvage, which are the largest in France with 2½ miles (4 km) of white sand, and those of Saint-Palais, are a paradise for naturists. In addition to these clearly identified and marked beaches, there are lots of little ones that are not so well known, as well as plenty of inlets and coves that are quiet and secluded (although some may be difficult to reach) and where you will be able to throw off your costume and expose yourself fully to the sun without attracting any unwelcome attention from passers-by.

THE LAW IN FRANCE
Naturism in France was a victim of 19th C. morality and the Napoleonic Code. Under the former Article 330: '*Any person who shall have committed a contempt of morality shall be imprisoned for between three months and two years and shall be fined between 500 and 15,000 francs*'. Under the reformed penal code of the late 1980s, Article 222 specifies that there is only a public contempt of morality if there is a sexual display. Since 1983, the Fédération Française de Naturisme has been recognised by the French government as an 'educational youth movement'.

Crafts

Ceramics, earthenware, sailing accessories and, of course, the famous
Charentaise slippers – there are lots of ideas for presents.

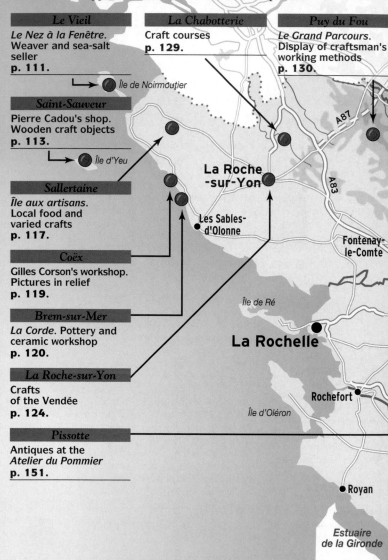

Le Vieil

Le Nez à la Fenêtre.
Weaver and sea-salt
seller
p. 111.

La Chabotterie

Craft courses
p. 129.

Puy du Fou

Le Grand Parcours.
Display of craftsman's
working methods
p. 130.

Île de Noirmoutier

Saint-Sauveur

Pierre Cadou's shop.
Wooden craft objects
p. 113.

Île d'Yeu

Sallertaine

Île aux artisans.
Local food and
varied crafts
p. 117.

La Roche
-sur-Yon

Les Sables-
d'Olonne

Fontenay-
le-Comte

Coëx

Gilles Corson's workshop.
Pictures in relief
p. 119.

Île de Ré

Brem-sur-Mer

La Corde. Pottery and
ceramic workshop
p. 120.

La Rochelle

La Roche-sur-Yon

Crafts
of the Vendée
p. 124.

Rochefort

Île d'Oléron

Pissotte

Antiques at the
Atelier du Pommier
p. 151.

Royan

Estuaire
de la Gironde

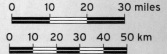

0   10   20   30 miles

0   10   20   30   40   50 km

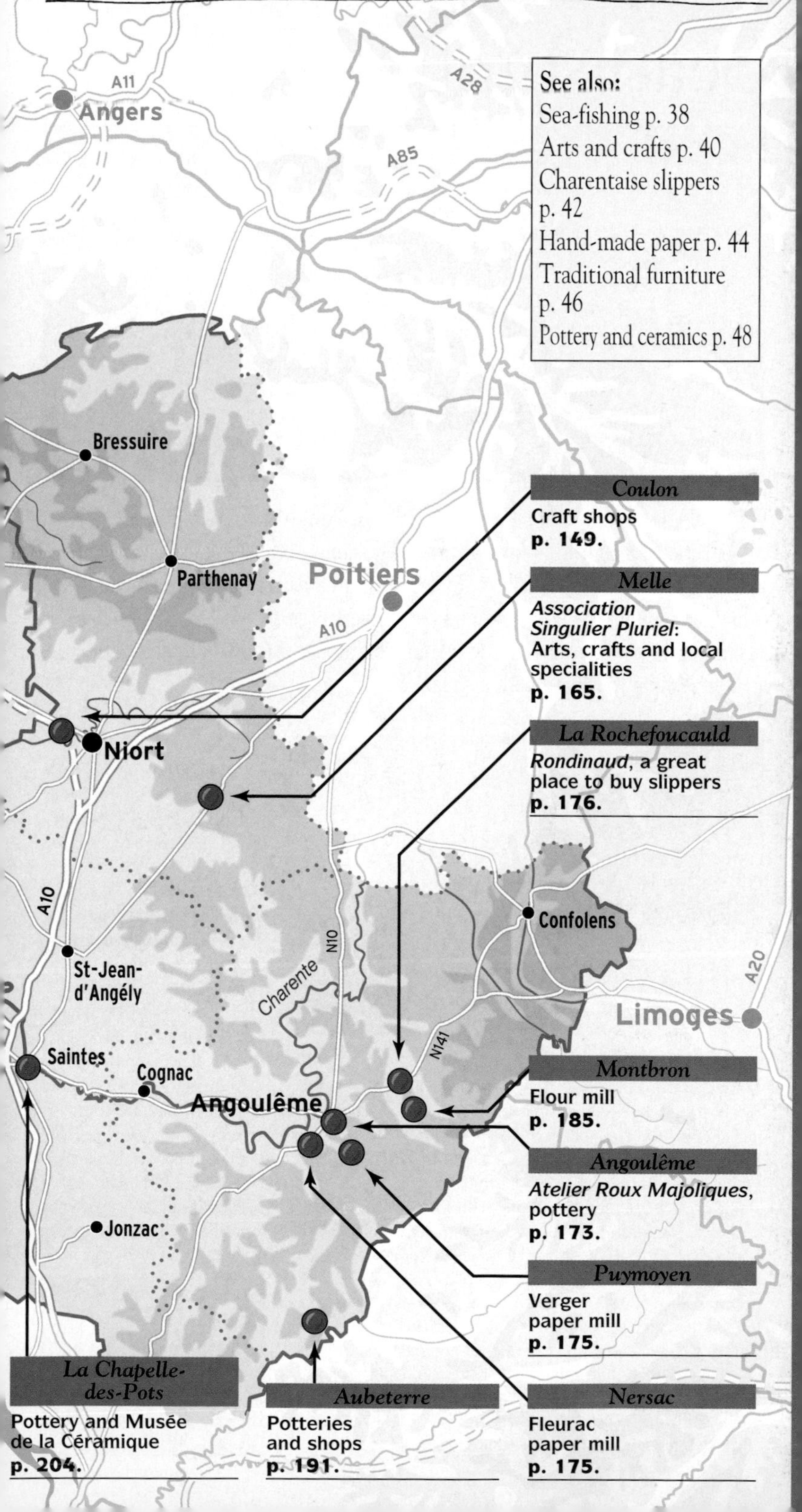

See also:
Sea-fishing p. 38
Arts and crafts p. 40
Charentaise slippers
p. 42
Hand-made paper p. 44
Traditional furniture
p. 46
Pottery and ceramics p. 48

Angers

A11

A28

A85

Bressuire

Poitiers

Parthenay

A10

Coulon
Craft shops
p. 149.

Melle
*Association
Singulier Pluriel*:
Arts, crafts and local
specialities
p. 165.

Niort

La Rochefoucauld
Rondinaud, a great
place to buy slippers
p. 176.

A10

Confolens

Limoges

A20

St-Jean-
d'Angély

N10

Charente

N141

Montbron
Flour mill
p. 185.

Saintes

Cognac

Angoulême

Angoulême
Atelier Roux Majoliques,
pottery
p. 173.

Jonzac

Puymoyen
Verger
paper mill
p. 175.

La Chapelle-
des-Pots
Pottery and Musée
de la Céramique
p. 204.

Aubeterre
Potteries
and shops
p. 191.

Nersac
Fleurac
paper mill
p. 175.

Sea-fishing

The diversity of sea-beds off the coast of Poitou and Charentes has encouraged fishing for centuries. The main ports are Saint-Gilles-Croix-de-Vie, Les Sables-d'Olonne and La Rochelle, and the fleets, which are among the largest in France, are very diverse. The catch varies, according to the seasons and the fishing techniques used, which range from inshore fishing to fishing with a square net and fish-traps.

Deep-sea fishing

Few of the fishing fleets still include the huge 1000-tonne fishing boats. Most deep-sea fishing is now from trawlers, whose average size is between 20 and 50 tonnes and which stay at sea for two to three weeks. The trawl is a huge net, more than 500 ft (150 m) long, which drags the bottom. This is how sardines, mackerel, hake, burbot, monkfish and crayfish are caught. Tuna fishing is a speciality of the fishermen of the Île d'Yeu, who fish further out to sea in the Gulf of Gascony.

Inshore fishing

Inshore fishing is practised from all the ports along the coast. Smaller vessels, which can be used for many different types of fishing, put to sea for between one and three days. They may trawl or put down lobster-pots to catch a variety of crustaceans (spider crabs, edible crabs, lobsters, crayfish, etc.), or may use seine nets, which can be up to 3 miles (5 km) long to catch skate, sea bream, monkfish and hake. They also use a line covered with multiple hooks to catch bream, pollack and conger eel.

Amateur sea-fishermen

Amateur sea-fishermen use three main techniques. Fishing with a **rod and line**, from a boat at anchor, fishing with a **trailing line,** where the ship moves forward very slowly, trailing the lines behind it and **laying nets** in the evening, which are hauled in early the next day. In rough waters dedicated fishermen look for bream, sought after for its delicious flavour and the sport it gives to anglers.

From the shore

Some fishing methods are centuries old. The fish-traps on the Île d'Oléron, which are called *écluses à poissons* (fish locks) in French, are laid in the north of the island on the strand in the area between the low- and high-water marks along a row of breakwaters. Mesh-covered openings allow the outgoing tide to escape but trap the fish. The traps are privately owned.

Family fishing-huts

The *pêcheries* are rudimentary huts perched on stilts with a system of cables and pulleys for hauling in the large

square nets known as *carrelets*. They are sited on publicly owned land by the sea and cannot be sold. Permission to operate one is issued by the Service Maritime, and the licence is valid for five years at a time, although it is renewable. Generally speaking a family

that owns the licence will operate the hut for generations.

In the estuaries

The mouth of the Gironde, as the mouth of the Loire, is suited to seasonal fishing for a special catch such as that of **elvers** (baby eels). The elvers are caught in January and February when they swim up the estuaries in search of fresh water. Elvers are caught in very fine nets stretched in rigid circles.

Fish-farming

Fish-farming in a natural environment is an activity that is very much on the increase, especially on the islands of Oléron, Ré and Noirmoutier. Scientific organisations are encouraging a new type of fish-farming,

which makes it possible to raise deep-sea fish without having to depend on factory fishing. Bream, turbot, sea-trout and burbot are now finding their way from these fish farms onto the fishmonger's slab, a welcome development, in view of the crisis in sea-fishing.

BRINGING BACK
THE CATCH

In all the fishing ports along the coast, **bringing back the catch** in the evening is a very special moment. Old people wait on the quay. The fish are unloaded onto trays, which are taken to the auction. The nets are spread out, the decks washed, there is lots of bustle and a smell of fish and salt in the air. The **fish auction** that follows is impressive, with rows of bidders shouting out their bids at a rate of knots.

Arts and crafts
a continuing tradition

A longside the traditional crafts, such as cabinet-making, glass-making and cooperage, other less common skilled occupations still manage to flourish. Fishermen's nets are made on the Île de Ré and boats are still constructed according to age-old designs at Noirmoutier. Craftsmanship is still important in the region.

Boats and ships

The craft of **boatbuilding** is still practised at Noirmoutier and at Marans by ship's carpenters working in wood who know their material perfectly. They work in solid oak, mahogany without knots and pine, which is seasoned and dried for years on end for maritime use. The flat-bottomed boats of the Poitou marshes, called *plattes*, old-fashioned sailing dinghies and different types of fishing boat are difficult to construct. They are built to order and to the specifications of the customer. Nowadays, the profile of the hull is created on a computer and a small-scale model of the half-hull is built before constructing the final craft.

Caught in the net

On the Île de Ré, where fishing is one of the main sources of income, **making nets** remains an important activity. Once made from natural fibre, fishing nets today are all made of nylon yarn. Mounting the nets on the ropes and adding the floats are still done by hand, and vary depending on the type of net – purse-net, trawl net, straight net, seine net etc. The size of the mesh is determined by the type and size of fish being caught. These nets also have other less serious uses, such as for sports and games and even for decoration.

Building a flat-bottomed boat at Marans, in the Vendée.

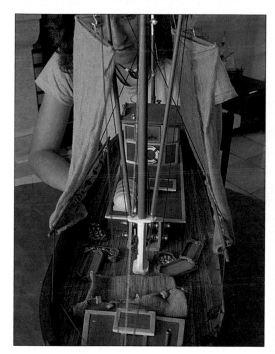

purpose from all over the world and cleaned, scraped, polished then cut, pierced and glued in order to create beautiful, delicate objects.

Baskets of all kinds

The country craft of **basketry** is one that is practised in all rural societies. In the marshes of the northern Vendée, around Challans, and in those of Poitou, the locally grown **osier** is the preferred material. It is cut in winter and the bark peeled in early summer and then left to dry for a year. It is then soaked for two hours to make it supple before being worked. In woodland areas of the region, baskets are made from **chestnut wood**. Young slender trees are felled in winter and are trimmed and soaked for 6 weeks. They are then baked to make them supple and cut into slats. The baskets made from these slats are very strong and sturdy.

Dream-boats

Models of old ships are based on contemporary plans or engravings. This painstaking work (some of the parts are no bigger than a pinhead) requires hours of preparation to make the calculations and assemble all the materials. The best woods are seasoned for five years and the finish requires hundreds of hours of work. The painting and varnishing and the sewing of the sails are all done by hand. Gold leaf and delicately braided and knotted ropework add the finishing touch.

Fortunately, some models of modern ships, such as trawlers or the famous *Pen Duick*, are simpler to create.

A world of shells

One of the last workers in mother-of-pearl left in France has his workshop on the island of Aix. Working with mother-of-pearl is an ancient craft. It was obtained from shells and used for making buttons, toilet articles and even knife handles, as well as in marquetry and jewellery. These days mother-of-pearl shells are imported for this

WIND IN THE WEATHER-VANE

The craft of **metalworker** covers a wide range of products, from wrought iron gates and balustrades to hand-made locks and bolts, shop signs, and more. But it is the weather-vane that has captured the imagination of the people along this windswept stretch of coastline, and you'll see them everywhere. The metal-workers' imagination runs riot and you'll see some most original shapes, from the outline of a salt-marsh worker to a sailing ship or mermaid.

La Charentaise
the most comfortable slippers in the world

The charentaise is famous throughout France and loved and cherished everywhere in the world as the best-made, most comfortable slipper in existence. The upper is traditionally covered in a wool tartan pattern but there are hundreds of different styles, which tend to vary according to current tastes.

The art of recycling

The slipper traces its origins back to the reign of Louis XIV. The French navy of the time was revitalised thanks to Colbert and Turgot, and this brought many industries to Rochefort, including woollen mills for weaving jackets for the sailors. But what was to be done with all the rejects for which the navy refused to pay? The Charentais, who hate waste, had the bright idea of combining the wasted cloth from the jackets with felt, and began making slippers.

How the slippers were made

The upper was made of woollen cloth, whilst felt from the paper-mills, which had soaked up water, paper pulp and glue, was used for the soles. Once it had been left to dry for a long time, it was both rigid and waterproof. Although the picture below shows a man at work on the slipper last, it was women who traditionally made the parts for the slippers and assembled them. They joined the uppers to the soles using a cross stitch which has

An old poster promoting the supposed merits of the slippers

become known as 'slipper stitch' (*point de chausson*). The slippers are supple and simple in shape, and do not have separate shapes for the left and right foot.

A court slipper

The whole of France was soon wearing these comfortable slippers. The duke of La Rochefoucauld even tried to introduce them to Versailles, although history does not say whether Louis XIV himself wore them. At the court of Louis XVI the servants were supplied with charentaise slippers so that they could

Traditional slipper-making at the Rondinaud de Chasseneuil factory

FAMOUS FEET AND THE CHARENTAISE
According to tradition, these cosy slippers were a great hit with politicians. De Gaulle had his made to measure, like his beds. François Mitterrand often wore them, and Laurent Fabius trotted out for his early morning baguette in them. Diana, Princess of Wales, ordered them for her family, so even royal British feet have known their comforting warmth.

move about noiselessly, whilst polishing the wooden floors at the same time!

From felt to rubber

Like all items of clothing, the charentaise slipper has moved with the times. In 1850 a shoemaker from La Roche-foucauld began to replace felt soles with leather soles and sewed them on with shoe-maker's stitch. Later, the tip of the upper was reinforced with a piece of leather and a tiny heel was added. In about 1950, they started using rub-ber for the heels and finally vulcanised rubber which was baked in a mould. Seams disappeared because the sole was welded to the fabric with a strip of melted rubber.

The charentaise goes global

After a period of decline, when charentaise slippers were not considered to have

a glamorous enough image – even **Greta Garbo** is said to have abandoned hers with regret for more fashionable footwear – the charentaise

made a comeback. The wind of change was blowing once more and styles altered. The Rondinaud factory at La Rochefoucauld even became a major European producer of footwear, with branches in the United Kingdom and Canada and customers from all over Europe, South Africa, the Caribbean and even Japan.

Slippers for all

About 40,000 pairs of charentaise slippers are made every day and there are more than 500 different models manufactured by Rondinaud (p. 176) alone, the factory long since having stopped depending on the standard design. There's even a therapeutic 'doctor's' model, which is sold in pharmacies. You'll be spoiled for choice, with dozens of patterns, from spots and flowers to checks, in wool or satin, in the height of fashion or with a traditional flavour, but if you're looking for real authenticity, choose a tartan-patterned upper sewn onto a felt sole and lined with wool.

With 500 different models, you're sure to find one that fits!

Hand-made paper
from pulp to vellum

A land of water and of mills, the Charentes naturally became famous for paper-making. Since the 16th C. the mills of the Angoulême district have been churning out hand-made rag paper, made from cotton, linen or hemp, which is admired for its strength and whiteness. Today, very little paper is made although the mills of Fleurac and Puymoyen still produce paper in the same way it was made in the 18th C.

A short history

The first royal paper mill in Angoulême dates back to 1516. The industry was very export-oriented, and paper was sent to England and Holland, where Angoulême vellum was used for reproductions of the works of the Flemish painters. Colbert, Louis XIV's minister of the interior, developed the French paper-making industry further. The Angoulême mills flourished, and related industries, such as printing, felt making and metal plate-making, were developed.

The raw materials

To make paper, you need to mix together the correct quantities of linen, cotton or hemp rags, glue and river water. In the most traditional method, the rags are steeped in water in huge stone vats where they are crushed and torn to shreds with big pestles. A new method was invented in the 18th C. whereby lead vats were used in which revolving blades shredded the paper. Glue was added to the mixture, resulting in a pulp ready for paper-making.

How it's made

A sheet of paper is produced using a forme, a rectangular wooden frame covered with

Paper-makers at work, lifting the sheets on the formes. Encyclopédie by Diderot and Alembert.

The sheets are left to dry in the drying-room.
Illustration from the Encyclopédie by Diderot and Alembert.

a fine metal or wooden mesh. Tightly packed strips of brass are laid vertically over the mesh, which serve as a sieve to drain the excess water away. The formes are plunged into a vat filled with paper pulp. A skilled worker will pick up just enough pulp in each forme to make one sheet of paper. The forme is shaken to drain out the liquid and the loosely knit pulp is placed on a thick sheet of felt. Another sheet is placed on

top, and the two are pressed to squeeze out more liquid. The final drying stage is when the sheet is hung over rows of rods in a well-aired room.

This is the technique used for making laid paper (with a ribbed surface) and it is still used today for the finest quality paper.

LAID PAPER AND VELLUM

Vellum was very thin parchment, made from calf's skin or lamb's skin, which has given its name to a form of laid paper without lines. When handmade vellum is held up to the light, it looks smooth and consistent, and a little cloudy. Laid paper, on the other hand, retains the parallel lines of the forme or mould. Laid paper and vellum can be made with a water-mark, a transparent design in the paper that can be seen only in the light. From the early 19th C. hand-made paper began to disappear, replaced by machine-made paper. A few mills still make it in order to keep the skill going.

Sizes and watermarks

In the 18th C. paper sizes ranged from 12 in (31 cm) by 16 in (40 cm) to 22 in (56 cm) by 30 in (76 cm). They were identified by designs etched on copper plates and pressed on to the sheets while they were still wet – the watermark. The design could be seen if the paper was held up to the light. The design for the smallest size was a pot, a Christ figure the largest and a crown was for the intermediate size.

Long-lasting paper

Thanks to the natural materials used, hand-made paper is of exceptionally high quality and can easily last for six or seven centuries. This high quality has enabled medieval manuscripts to be preserved in perfect condition. In consequence, Angoulême has become a byword for quality and the Ministry of Foreign Affairs, the Louvre Museum and the Bibliothèque Nationale all buy their paper from Angoulême. Banknotes are also made from hand-made paper, but don't expect to see any hanging up to dry in the local paper-mills!

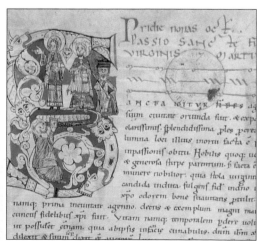

Until the invention of printing, during the Renaissance, paper was a luxury item that was heavily decorated

Traditional furniture

Sober and simple, the traditional furniture of the Vendée was plain and almost crude in design. The Saintonge, on the other hand, an area with a wine-making tradition had a richer and more varied style. The region was proud of its craftsmen, and cabinet-making and the making of fine reproduction furniture continues to be one the flourishing industries of the Saintonge region today.

The bench-chest was an important feature in early French bedrooms

Everything in its place

Houses were small so furniture had to be practical and functional. Until the 18th C. furniture consisted mainly of beds, stools and chests, which could double as seats or tables. They were made of whatever wood was locally available, **oak**, **chestnut**, **poplar** and **fruitwoods**, and shapes were very plain. Taller pieces began to appear from the 19th C. onwards, and plain styles were abandoned in favour of a more curved outline.

Chests

The **bench-chest** was the most important piece in the room. It was very simply made, straight and sturdy, without a back, although it sometimes had armrests. It was not highly decorated, apart from panels of carved diamonds or other geometrical designs. These chests were often placed at the foot of the bed and were used for storing clothes and for the owners to sit on. The *maie* was a taller chest resting on

feet, which was used as a dough-riser and sometimes as a table.

Everyday pieces of furniture

Each piece was made for a specific purpose. When living conditions improved in the 19th C., more elaborate furniture began to appear. **Cabinets**, **linen closets** and *bonnetières* were used for storing household linen. The design, consisting of two doors separated by a drawer,

TRADITIONAL FURNITURE ● **47**

SMALL ANTIQUES

Antique furniture can still be found at antique dealers or in auction houses. However, it is possible to pick up some good pieces or small items of furniture by visiting second-hand shops and fairs. You'll find a lot of pieces from the early 19th C., such as pottery and earthenware, paste ornaments and items from country life, salt cellars and butter pots. Some shops sell old lace, head-dresses, shawls and napkins and, of

course, with the sea so close, there are plenty of marine artefacts, some sold in specialist shops.

became very common. The **confiturier** was a smaller, one-door cabinet, topped by a drawer. It was used for storing preserves and other foods.

L'homme debout

This tallboy is typical of furniture in the Vendée and owes its name to incidents during the wars of the Vendée, when men hid in them to escape from the Republicans. Their pursuers were fooled because the pieces look as if they have two doors separated by a central drawer but, in fact, the drawers are false. Despite its exciting past, the *homme debout* did not come into general use until later in the 19th C.

More elaborate pieces

With the emergence of a middle class, homes increased in size and furniture became more decorative. It remained functional, but the decoration was richer and pieces were larger. **Sideboards** and **dressers** containing two to three drawers became commonplace. The Louis XV style, with turned, curved feet, brass locks or delicately worked copper decoration began to appear, replacing designs that had been traditional for centuries.

Closets

Closets and cupboards with deeply etched geometric

patterns carved into the wood are commonplace throughout the region. The decorative diamond-shaped

Louis XIII style is found in Brittany, the Vendée, Poitou and the Saintonge. Wardrobe bases are straight and the feet are flattened balls. In the 19th C. decoration became more ornate and geometric patterns, combining diamonds with (compass) roses and five-branched crosses were introduced. Curved shapes were also evolving, with mouldings, richly carved friezes, stepped cornices, inlays and floral designs in mixed woods.

Pottery and ceramics

The art of making faience is a long established one in the Charentes. Items of ancient tin-glazed ware from the Angoulême region, made by Palissy, Jucaud, Sazerac or Renoleau, are on display in the museums, and are highly prized by collectors. The heirs to these master-potters still carry on using the traditional techniques.

The origins of craft pottery

Bernard Palissy was a 16th C. glass-maker. An alliance contracted with a family of potters introduced him to the corporation of **La Chapelle-des-Pots**. Fascinated by Italian *faienza*, he dedicated himself to discovering the secret. Before doing so, he spent 16 years researching it, relentlessly trying to find out

how the glaze was applied and going as far as to burn his own furniture and even the floorboards of his home in Saintes when he ran out of wood. He created glazed earthenware figurines, bas-reliefs, modelled figures and enamelware, starting a whole industry of art potting.

The rest of the story

It was not until the second half of the 18th C. that the faience workshops began to multiply in Angoulême. The factories were influenced by the master craftsmen of the period, who worked in Rouen, Nevers and Moustiers, but they made a variety of pieces, including vases, platters, chemists' jars and holy water containers. The most famous local potter is Alfred Renoleau, who chose to follow in Bernard Palissy's footsteps and took his inspiration from the local wildlife of

Plate designed by H. Amirault in the Musée Georges-Turpin in Parthenay

the Charente. The **Faïencerie Roullet-Renoleau** is still going strong and is known as one of the best in the field. The products of this pottery are highly sought after and immediately gain in value.

Raw materials

The pottery-making regions are usually those where the local soil is suitable for firing. This is also true in the Saintonge and Angoulême districts, where the clay soils supply the raw material for the potteries, of which there are still many around La Chapelle-des-Pots. The grey or red clay from around Angoulême, or clay from the Dordogne and the Charentes supply the local workshops. It is washed to improve its consistency, then kneaded to remove air bubbles and make it

more pliable. The Faïencerie Roullet-Renoleau uses a red colour clay.

Moulding

The craftsman first designs the models on paper and then prepares a mould. There are two ways of shaping the piece. In the case of Angoulême faience it depends on the type of piece. **Calibrating** has replaced the potter's wheel and makes it possible to form round shapes on a mould, such as salad bowls, cups, plates etc. **Pouring** is reserved for more complex hollow shapes, such as vases and teapots. The liquid paste, which is called *barbotine*, is poured into plaster moulds in two halves, which fit together tightly to contain the liquid. After careful finishing to remove scratches and irregularities, the pieces

are fired in the first firing at 1,922 °F (1,050°C). The result is called **biscuit**, and it is a porous earthenware.

Glazing and decoration

Biscuit is glazed cold. The pieces are dipped in **liquid glaze** which gives them a milky white coating. They then undergo a second firing, at 1,832°F (1,000°C), after which the glaze emerges as an opaque brilliant white. The pieces are decorated with **metal oxide**, using a pen and paintbrush. The final colours are revealed and fixed by the third firing at 1,796°F (980°C). Some potteries in Aunis paint the unfired glaze and then bake the colours on during the second firing.

In the late 19th C. potters of Parthenay, such as Prosper Jouneau and Henri Amirault, created elaborate pieces inspired by Renaissance art. There is a beautiful collection of them in the Musée Georges-Turpin in Parthenay (see p. 141)

FINDING YOUR WAY AROUND CERAMICS

The term *ceramic* indicates anything made from fired clay, such as terracotta, stoneware, faience or tinware and porcelain or china. Faience is a porous ceramic with a tin glaze, which is why it is also called glazed tinware. It is fired at about 1,832°F (1,000°C). *Stoneware* is a form of earthenware, which is vitrified by being fired to a higher temperature 2,192–2,372°F (1,200–1,300°C). *Porcelain* is made from kaolin and is fired at 2,552°F (1,400°C).

History and heritage

From Romanesque churches to relics of the wars of the Vendée, explore the ancient buildings of Poitou and Charentes.

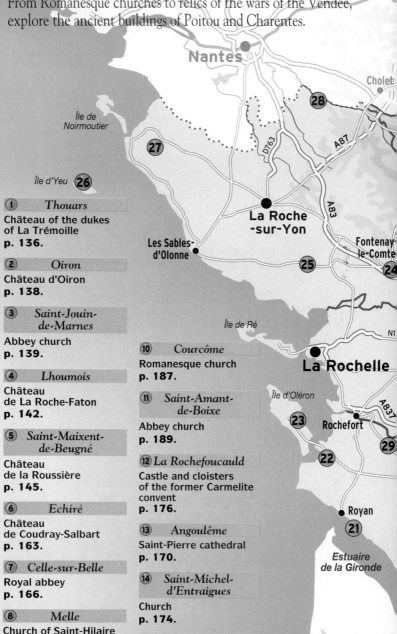

Nantes

Cholet

Île de Noirmoutier

Île d'Yeu **26**

La Roche -sur-Yon

Les Sables-d'Olonne

Fontenay le-Comte

25

24

27

28

Île de Ré

La Rochelle

Île d'Oléron

Rochefort

23

22

29

Royan

21

Estuaire de la Gironde

See also:
Romanesque art p. 52
The Protestants p. 54
The wars of the
Vendée p. 56
Local celebrities p. 58

16 *Barbezieux*
Saint-Mathias church
p. 197.

17 *Cognac*
Château des Valois
p. 201.

18 *Saint-Jean-d'Angély*
Royal abbey
p. 226.

19 *Aulnay-de-Saintonge*
Saint-Pierre church
p. 227.

20 *Saintes*
Saint-Eutrope church
p. 202.

21 *Talmont*
Sainte-Radegonde
church
p. 239.

22 *La Gataudière*
Château
p. 232.

23 *Le Château-d'Oléron*
Citadel
p. 230.

24 *Fontenay-le-Comte*
Château
de Terre Neuve
p. 150.

25 *Luçon*
Notre-Dame cathedral
p. 154.

26 *Port-Joinville*
Fort de Pierre-Levée
p. 112.

27 *Sallertaine*
Saint-Martin church
p. 116.

28 *Tiffauges*
Château
de Gilles de Rais
p. 132.

29 *Saint-Porchaire*
Roche-Courbon
p. 204.

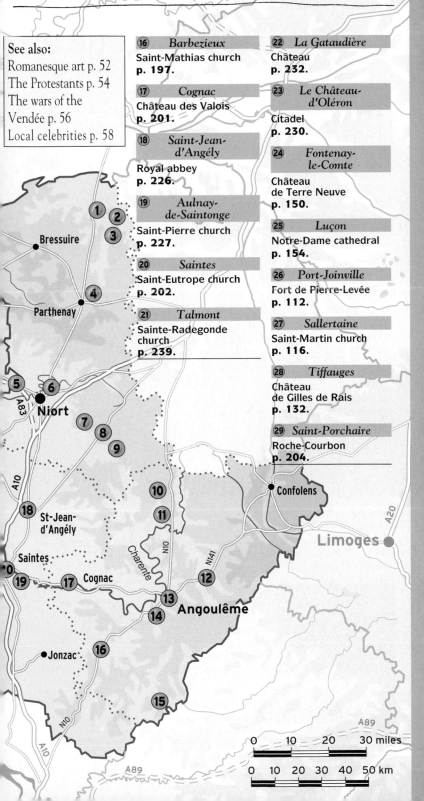

Romanesque art

Romanesque art emerged around the year 1000, triggered by a renewal of Christian faith and a general flourishing of the arts. In western France it spread from Poitou to the Angoulême region and then on to the Saintonge. Churches and chapels multiplied throughout the area, providing convenient resting places for pilgrims on their way to the shrine of St James of Compostela in Spain. The courts of the count of Poitou and the duke of Aquitaine funded much of the work.

Nieul-sur-L'Autise abbey

Architecture

In the 11th C. church builders began replacing wooden roofs, which were too easily destroyed by fire, with stone vaulting. This had notable effects on the structure. The nave had to be narrower and the side-walls needed to be thicker to support the additional weight. Apertures had to be smaller, and additional supports were often added inside. The atmosphere became more intimate. The external appearance of these churches is characterised by a balanced solidity. They frequently have a tall spire or a porch, which is also the bell tower.

At a time when few could read or write, paintings played an important role in the instruction of the faithful, as here at Notre Dame de Pouzauges (see p. 126)

Saint-Hilaire de Melle

Church interiors

Painting has an overwhelming importance in church interiors. Scenes from the Bible or the lives of the saints, geometric patterns and designs, whose colours were once very bright, created a spectacular decor, in contrast to the simplicity of the structure. The whites, ochres and reds have survived to some extent, but the blues and greens, have suffered the ravages of time. The art of the stained glass window developed at around the same time. Only sculpture, the most decorative architectural element, has survived intact to the present day.

Magnificent façades

The façades surrounding the churches' main entrances were beautifully designed, consisting of superimposed arches, framed by columns, the whole being covered in sculpture. The portal itself was deep and heavily decorated. Even the most modest church buildings possess sculptures of an astonishing richness and complexity.

Southern Vendée was strongly influenced by Poitou and has many treasures, such as the churches at Vouvant, Foussais-Payré and Fontaines in the marshes.

A wonderful world

Romanesque art allowed its church builders and craftsmen a great deal of creative freedom. The capitals of the

Detail of a bestiary in the church of Saint-Pierre d'Aulnay (p. 227)

The north portal of the church of Saint-Hilaire de Melle (see p. 164)

columns and portals are covered with figures, often representing stories from the Gospel, but there are also fantastic creatures, monsters and strange manifestations. The sculptors introduced elements of every kind – and from every culture – Graeco-Roman, oriental, Moslem and even barbarian. Memories of voyages, pilgrimages, stories and myths were combined with the Pagan memories inherited from the Celtic culture, which had swept through Europe only a few centuries before, as Roman influence began to wane.

Cloister of the Abbey of Nieul-sur-l'Autise (see p. 151)

Life and death in Saintonge

In the Saintonge decorative sculpture was used as a device for education of the people. The priests developed themes in an attempt to respond to the eternal question of human destiny and the meaning of life. Life on earth is represented by the signs of the zodiac, peasants tending crops and scenes from daily life throughout the year. Medieval man feared the torments of hell at the end of life. He was conscious of the great conflict between vice and virtue, and knew that only those who allowed virtue to triumph would enjoy eternal life.

A TERRIFYING BESTIARY

Writers of horror films could well take their inspiration from the sculptures on Romanesque churches which seem to favour the gruesome depiction of the fruits of their imagination rather than plain domestic animals. There are griffins, winged lions, fantastic birds, giant serpents, dragons devouring children, monsters with the mouths of crocodiles, people being torn to pieces, voluptuous sirens – like a cartoon strip in relief. Masks are just as expressive, with their tongues sticking out and satanic grins.

The Protestants
siege and persecution

Richelieu inspecting the sea-wall built to isolate the city of La Rochelle (1628)

Although the Vendée embraced the Reformation quite late, the city of La Rochelle soon became the focus of French Protestantism. The Reformation was supported by the city-dwellers and spread throughout the Charentes and Deux-Sèvres. The siege of La Rochelle, in 1627–8, ended the city's Protestant stance and caused many French Protestants to flee or go into exile. A large number set sail for the Americas.

Martin Luther (1483–1546) initiated the Reformation, which spread rapidly among town-dwellers

The Reformation

The Reformation was a Christian doctrine that emerged in Germany in the 16th C. which questioned the omnipotence of the Catholic church and the pope. It was started by the theologian and monk, Martin Luther. Jean Calvin introduced Protestantism into France, but the Reformation caused a deep rift between the traditional church and those who protested against it, earning them the name of Protestants. While the Edict of Nantes (1598–1685) was in force they had some respite, but before and after it the Protestants were persecuted mercilessly, culminating in the terrible St Bartholomew's Day massacre in August 1572.

Protestants in lower Poitou

The aristocracy of Poitou fervently embraced Calvin's doctrine. Catherine de Parthenay, daughter of the powerful Rohan du Parc, became a propagandist for the new form of Christianity. From her château at Parc-Soubise, deep in the forests of the Vendée, she wrote poetry and plays designed to spread the ideas of the Reformation. Her two sons became generals in the Huguenot army. The Reformation was adopted throughout the region, and Protestant communities sprang up in the villages of Saumurois and Anjou.

La Rochelle, capital of Protestantism

The Reformation came to the Charentes thanks to Calvin, who lived for several years in Angoulême and La Rochelle. The new doctrine soon attracted the wealthier and more enlightened sections of society, including teachers at the universities and noble-men, such as Chabot de Jarnac. La Rochelle, the Île de Ré and Angoulême became strongholds of the new faith. In 1568, at the height of the Wars of Religion, at the behest of Coligny and Jeanne d'Albret, La Rochelle held a meeting of all the Protestant leaders, and

La Rochelle bible, published in 1616. Musée Protestant de la Rochelle

Jean Calvin visited the region, promoting the ideas of the Reformation, which took root here

in 1570 the city became one of four strongholds given to Protestants by the Peace of Saint-Germain.

The siege of La Rochelle

After the death of the toler-ant Henri IV, who protected the Protestants, La Rochelle's

Armand du Plessis, Cardinal Richelieu

failure to submit irritated Richelieu, who claimed to be asserting the absolute power of Louis XIII. In 1627, as the threat grew stronger, La Rochelle sought help from the English, by now also Protestants, who sent a fleet of ships, which were anchored off the Île de Ré. Louis XIII besieged the town. He built a sea-wall of wood and stone, reinforced with scuttled ships, to prevent access to the port, stopping the supply of food and reinforcements. For 416 days the mayor, Jean Guiton, organised the resistance of La Rochelle, but he was beaten by starvation. Only a quarter of the population survived the siege. The town was destroyed and its privileges abolished.

Crossing the Wilderness

After the revocation of the Edict of Nantes in 1685, pas-tors were banished and every trace of the Protestant faith was banned. Driven from the towns, the Protestants had to practise their faith in the countryside, the 'wilderness'. Henceforward, the Protest-ants had no legal existence. Since the population registers were kept by the church,

Protestant births, marriages or deaths were never recorded. In order to keep their own record of events, Protestants would log them in the pages of the family Bible.

Banished from the towns, the Protestants celebrated their faith 'in the wilderness'

THE PROTESTANTS IN EXILE

Discrimination and persecution caused about 200,000 French Protestants to flee abroad, although emigration was also banned. La Rochelle became the main emi-gration port for the Low Countries, Denmark and England. Those from La Rochelle who went to America founded the town of New Rochelle, north of New York city.

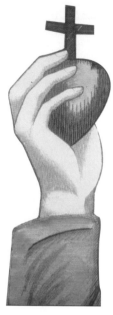

The wars of the Vendée
Blues and Whites

The story of the wars of the Vendée is important for understanding the mentality of the region. At first, the French Revolution was well received in the Vendée since here, as much as anywhere, the people dreamed of an egalitarian society. The massive insurrection in the region between 1793 and 1796 was not inspired by the turbulent upheaval and political unrest which was occurring nationwide, nor was it a counter-revolution on behalf of royalty and the clergy. What triggered the revolt was what the Vendéen holds most dear – his land.

The powder keg

Two events moved the population to rebel – the persecution of priests, to whom the faithful were devoted, and conscription. The Republic needed 300,000 men from all over France to defend its borders. But here, people preferred to die at home for their own goals rather than elsewhere for someone else's. Church bells rang out, from 10 to 15 March 1793, calling on men to rise up.

Long after the event, the insurrection in the Vendée continues to fire imaginations and inspire painters such as Charles Fortin in his melodramatic Vendéens Taking up Arms

Dieu et mon Roi!

The Vendée prepared for battle. The so-called White Army wore clogs and wielded pitchforks and clubs for weapons. They gathered around the châteaux and elected their leaders, including Charette, d'Elbée, Bonchamps, Stofflet, La Rochejaquelein and Cathelineau, who fought so bravely at Challans, Grandlieu and in the Mauges. Some 30,000 Vendéens went off to fight with the blessing of their priests, who refused to swear allegiance to the Republic. They stitched a red heart surmounted with a cross on their breasts, and their motto was *Dieu et mon Roi* (God and my King).

Raising the Chouan army, *a painting by J.H. Sauzeau (1900)*

The glorious saga

At first the rebels were amazingly successful. Between March and June local towns were captured with ease and

The Catholic and Royal Army of the West consisted of poorly equipped peasants who were ill-prepared to confront the soldiers of the Republic

little bloodshed. Once Chantonnay, Les Herbiers, Fontenay, Thouars, Machecoul, Pornic, Cholet, Chemillé and even Angers and Saumur were theirs, the peasants were satisfied and ready to go home to their farms. The Blue Army of the Republic had believed the larger threat would come from abroad in Europe, and suffered these humiliating defeats at the hands of peasants, simply by being unprepared.

IMAGES IN GLASS
Here and there, in the chapels of the Vendée, at Pouzauges, at Lucs-sur-Boulogne, and at Saint-Mars-la-Réorthe, stained glass windows record the blackest page in local history. Massacres of civilians, frantic flight and dying heroes are an authentic memorials to the bloody murders that the serenity of the place makes all the more moving.

The tide turns
Several of the leaders of the Whites had been wounded. When they tried to attack Nantes on 29 June they

Jean-Baptiste Kléber (1753–1800)

suffered their first defeat. The second, in Luçon, emphasised their predicament. This raggle-taggle army wanted nothing more than to go back to its fields and harvest the crops. Its leaders were divided and tired and had neither political agenda nor long-term strategy. The most bitter battle was fought on

17 October at Cholet. Kléber lead the 100,000 strong Blue Republican army, defeated the insurgents and recaptured the town.

The beginning of the end
The Vendéens left Cholet and regrouped on the banks of the Loire. Bonchamps died there. Eighty thousand people, men, women and children crossed the river in frantic flight for Normandy, hoping to rally English support. They were forced to turn back and had to re-cross the Loire. The death-blow was dealt at Savenay, on 23 December. Only 4000 Vendéens came home. But the worst was still to come.

The reprisals
In February 1794 the Republic sent 12 columns of infantrymen to the Vendée, which it described as 'infernal'. Their objective was to capture and hold 13 villages, but to set fire to all the rest. Almost all the able-bodied men had been killed in battle, but the women, old people and children left behind were badly persecuted. The guerrilla war lasted for two years. The last two leaders were shot in 1796, Stofflet in February, Charette in March. In all, the whole insurrection of the wars of the Vendée lasted for three years and took a terrible toll.

During the first Floréal of the 3rd year of the French Revolutionary calendar, (20 April 1795), the Vendée was conquered

Local celebrities
from François Mitterrand to Georges Simenon

Whether they were born in the region or simply have chosen to settle here, Poitou-Charentes is a popular place for many French politicians and show-business personalities. The land and sea-scapes have also inspired many writers, such as Georges Simenon. Poitou-Charentes was also the beloved homeland of François Mitterrand and Georges Clémenceau, head of the French government at the end of World War I.

Pierre Loti, exotic novelist

Pierre Loti was born in Rochefort in 1850 and was buried on the Île d'Oléron. He was a naval officer who wrote exciting novels set in the exotic locations in which he had lived, including Senegal, Japan, Burma and Tahiti. His novels include *Rarahu*, *Polynesian Idyll* and *Madame Chrysanthème*. Loti also wrote a series of novels about the sea, including *My Brother Yves* (1883), *Matelot* (1893) and *Fisherman of Iceland*, which were a huge success. His home in Rochefort (p. 217), a curious mixture of Renaissance and Turkish decor is evidence of his desire to create a blend of cultures.

Georges Clemenceau, the Tiger of the Vendée

Clémenceau was born in 1841 at Mouilleron-en-Pareds in the Vendée. He spent 50 years as a French political leader rising to fame in his defence of Émile Zola in the

Dreyfus Affair in 1898. He became prime minister in 1906, but whilst in opposition caused numerous governments to fall, which earned him the nickname of 'The Tiger'. He again led the government in 1917 during World War I, and was hailed as 'the Father of the Victory'. His government was defeated in 1920, and he retired from politics, spending his last 10 years at Saint-Vincent-sur-Jard in the Vendée. He was a

The red drawing-room in Pierre Loti's house in Rochefort

MITTERRAND AND THE CHARENTE

'Jarnac is a little town of white houses on the banks of a river. I can see the Quai de l'Orangerie, just outside my door, with the clear outlines of the houses, the linden trees whose fragrant blossom I loved to smell. I feel at home in the Charentes. The quality of the sky, the earth, the local produce and the people represent a model of civilisation for me'.
This was written by François Mitterrand for the inauguration of the trust that bears his name in the town of Jarnac.

The desk at which Simenon worked from 1941 to 1943 in the Château de Terre-Neuve

friend of the painter Claude Monet and an art lover. Clémenceau died in 1929 in the arms of one of his mistresses – at the age of 80.

Georges Simenon, creator of Maigret

Simenon was born in Belgium in 1903, but he settled in Charente-Maritime before World War II. He wrote a total of 192 novels, of which 75 featured Inspector Maigret. His books were translated into 45 languages, and 500 million copies were sold throughout the world. He was inspired by the atmosphere of the coastal villages of Charente-Maritime (Esnandes, Nieul-sur-Mer and Charron) in which he set some of the Maigret novels. From 1931 to 1934 he lived at La Richardière, on the road to Marsilly, in a huge 16th C. mansion. He claimed that he spent the happiest years of his life at La Rochelle, riding his horse right up to

Georges Simenon, creator of the famous Inspector (later Commissioner) Maigret

the Café de la Paix (in the Rue Chaudrier, under the arcades), where he would sit and take notes.

Île de Ré, island of the stars

With its salt marshes, narrow streets with white houses, gardens filled with hollyhocks and its golden, sandy beaches, the Île de Ré is a favourite retreat for French stars. They include Régine Deforges on her famous blue bicycle, the French TV personality Bernard Giraudeau, the singer Patrick Bruel and the conductor Jean-Claude Casadesus. Others don't advertise their presence, including Emmanuelle Béart, star of *Manon des Sources*, Alain Bashung, the designer Sonia Rykiel and Michel Piccoli.

A little more name dropping

Those who practise their French by studying *Paris Match*, and who know a little about French cinema and French celebrities, may be interested to know that both Laurent Boyer and Agnès Varda have chosen to settle in Noirmoutier. If you have any problems with the authorities, Philippe Marchand is the person to contact. He is a former minister and retired deputy (French member of parliament), who has chosen to live on the Île d'Oléron.

Picturesque villages

Granite houses or *bourrines*, fortified farms and mills, the villages of Poitou-Charentes contain a variety of dwellings.

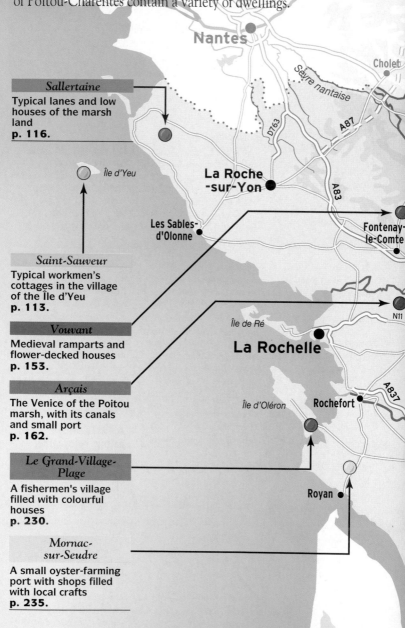

Sallertaine
Typical lanes and low houses of the marsh land
p. 116.

Saint-Sauveur
Typical workmen's cottages in the village of the Île d'Yeu
p. 113.

Vouvant
Medieval ramparts and flower-decked houses
p. 153.

Arçais
The Venice of the Poitou marsh, with its canals and small port
p. 162.

Le Grand-Village-Plage
A fishermen's village filled with colourful houses
p. 230.

Mornac-sur-Seudre
A small oyster-farming port with shops filled with local crafts
p. 235.

Nantes

Cholet

Sèvre nantaise

D763

A87

La Roche -sur-Yon

A83

Île d'Yeu

Les Sables-d'Olonne

Fontenay-le-Comte

N11

Île de Ré

La Rochelle

A837

Île d'Oléron

Rochefort

Royan

Angers

A11

A28

A85

See also:
Traditional
architecture p. 62
Mills p. 64

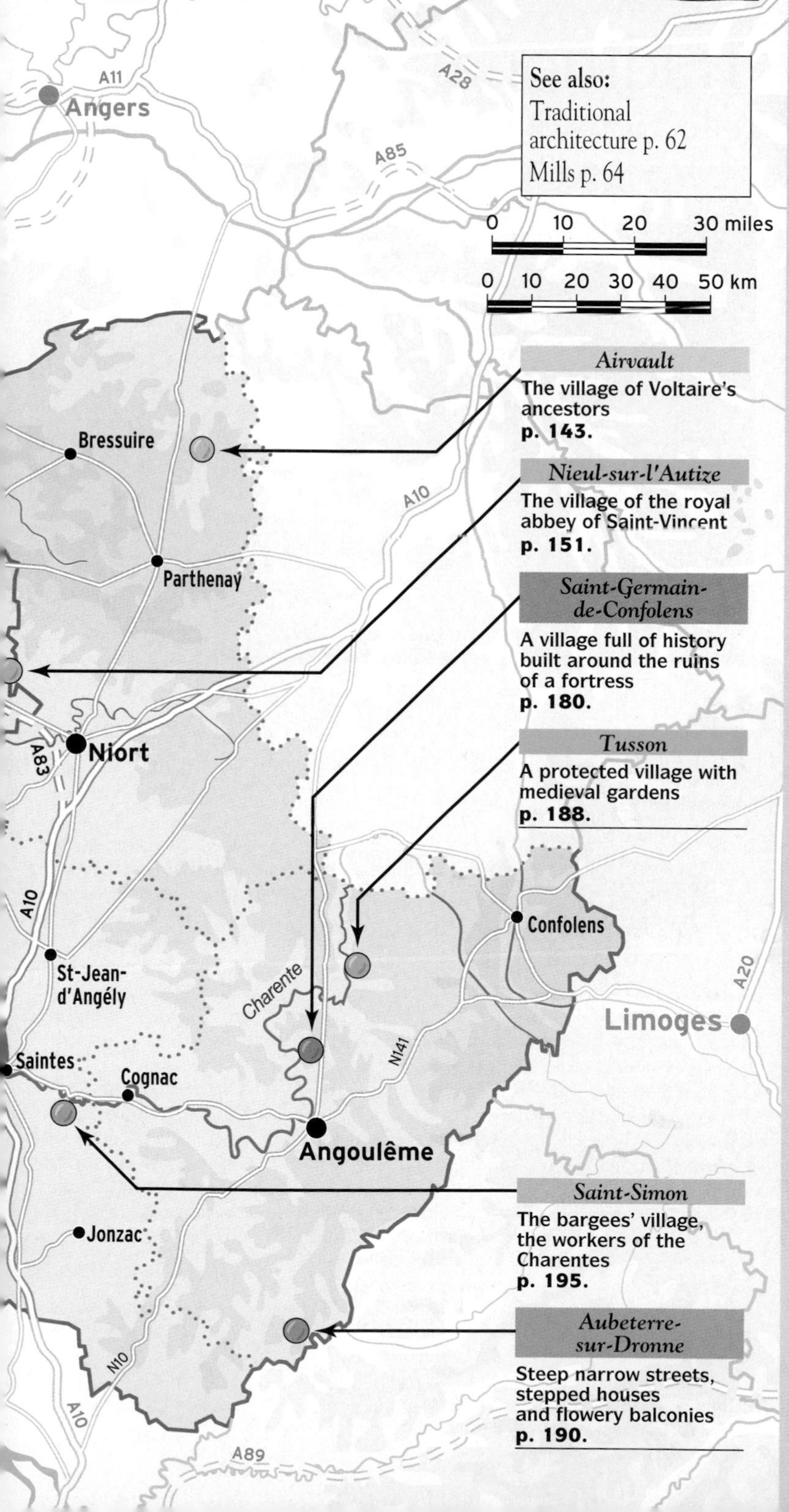

| 0 | 10 | 20 | 30 miles |

| 0 | 10 | 20 | 30 | 40 | 50 km |

Airvault

The village of Voltaire's
ancestors
p. 143.

Nieul-sur-l'Autize

The village of the royal
abbey of Saint-Vincent
p. 151.

Saint-Germain-de-Confolens

A village full of history
built around the ruins
of a fortress
p. 180.

Tusson

A protected village with
medieval gardens
p. 188.

Bressuire

A10

Parthenay

Confolens

Niort

A83

A10

Charente

N141

Limoges

St-Jean-
d'Angély

A20

Saintes

Cognac

Angoulême

Saint-Simon

The bargees' village,
the workers of the
Charentes
p. 195.

Jonzac

Aubeterre-sur-Dronne

Steep narrow streets,
stepped houses
and flowery balconies
p. 190.

N10

A10

A89

Traditional architecture
reflections of a traditional way of life

From the bay of Bourgneuf to the banks of the Gironde, from the narrow lanes of the islands to the deep valleys of the Charente river, the traditional home varies widely across the differing regions of Poitou-Charentes.

A traditional long farmhouse in the Vendée

The country home

Cottages are built of shale or granite in the northern Vendée and of limestone in the southern Vendée and Charentes. They are generally tiled, but the interior layout varies. The smallest of the cottages were lived in by landless peasants and have two rooms and an attic. Others simply depend on the size of the plot of land, and may have outhouses, such as a cowshed, barn, hayloft and additional dwelling for a farmhand.The main façade faces south and the buildings are arranged in a long line or in a square around an open courtyard.

The fortified farm

In the vine-growing country of the Saintonge there are fortified farms, where the various buildings are organised around a closed courtyard, accessible via a gate or door. This arrangement shows that the farm was once the home of a local landlord. Most of these manor farms were built in the mid-19th C. as you'll see from the dates engraved over the entrances. Detailing, cornices, mouldings and other decoration demonstrate the prestige of the owner.

The *bourrine*

This cottage, so typical of the Poitou marshes, uses natural materials. The walls are made of straw and daub, and the roofs of dried rushes, tied

A fortified farm in the Saintonge

in bunches and held in place by wooden staves. The house is long and low, with few windows, and may have a couple of small outhouses. The principal-building is lime-washed. The eves of the roof extend well out over the walls, like a hat, to protect the *bourrine* from inclement weather.

A typical house on the islands of the Charentes

A bourrine

Bourrines in the Poitou marshes

These white-painted houses have brightly coloured window frames and doors. The roofs are almost flat and covered with pink or beige tiles, which blend in with the landscape. The guttering consists of tiles laid upside down. In marshy areas, the basement area is protected from damp by a strip of tar. Sometimes the doors and windows have a brick surround. **Bourrines** on the islands have little front gardens surrounded by low walls.

Fishing huts

The huts vary according to use. Fishermen's huts are small and functional and used for storing tackle. They are mainly found on the coast and on landing stages for nets. The oyster-farmers' huts along the ditches in the north of the Vendée, on

Huts on stilts for fishing with a square net on the coasts of the Vendée

Oléron and in the Marennes basin are brightly painted and slightly larger so that several people can work in them at a time. You will also see large bathing-huts on the beaches. In some places, such as the Île d'Yeu, there are tiny little beach huts with blinds and tables and chairs, which have become a home from home.

Beach huts and villas

The fashion for sea-bathing created a cosmopolitan architectural style, inspired by literature and regional writing. The resorts of Les Sables-d'Olonne and Royan have villas in every conceivable style, from the Rococo to the Norman, and bizarre follies with turrets, ornate balconies, friezes of turned wood, tiles and pottery. Many of these quaint and interesting houses have been well preserved, despite in their seafront locations at the mercy of the elements.

A MATTER OF COLOUR

Each region of France has its own colour scheme. The islands of Noirmoutier and Yeu, and the salt-marshes favour white-washed houses and shutters in bright colours, usually bright blue. The Poitou marshes and the Charente countryside adopt softer colours, grey mortar or muted beige with lime-green or grey woodwork. The islands of Ré, Oléron and Aix prefer pale coloured wall and pastel shades of shutters, such as grey-blue or very pale green.

An oyster-farmer's hut on the Île d'Oléron

Windmills and watermills

D ating from the time when bread was the staple food, the presence of a mill in every village meant that bread was available for everyone. In addition to simply providing energy, these large and prominent buildings also served another purpose: they became rallying points and meeting places for the whole village and people from the surrounding areas.

Pivoting mill

Cellar mill

Tower mill

Windmills

There are three main types of mill. The **pivoting mill**, found in the northern half of France, consists of a rectangular wooden frame turning on a vertical pivot. The **cellar mill,** typical of Anjou, is also partly wooden, but the wooden pivot is mounted on a pointed stone tower. The **tower mill** is made entirely of stone and is cylindrical. It usually has three to five storeys and a top that turns through 360°. These are typical of the Vendée, Charentes and the islands of Noirmoutier, Ré and Oléron.

Vanes and sails

The ability of a windmill to operate depends on its capacity to turn itself towards the wind. Its four vanes are covered in **sailcloth**. The surface area can be adjusted to suit the strength of the wind, which is why the vanes are often referred to as sails. They capture the wind best when they are at a slight angle to it. The only problem is that the miller has to climb over the vanes to cover them with the cloth. In the 19th C. the **Berton system**, a set of moveable louvres that replaced the sailcloth, was installed in many mills. These have the advantage of being adjustable from inside the mill.

The Justices Mill at Saint-Michel-Mont-Mercure, in the Vendée

BUSH TELEGRAPH

Often positioned on top of a hill, mills played a part in a system of line-of-sight telegraph. The position of the sails corresponded to messages based on an agreed code. During the wars of the Vendée, the rebels would learn how close the Republicans were, if an attack was imminent or be ordered to regroup.

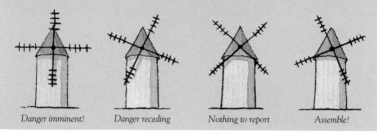

Danger imminent!   *Danger receding*   *Nothing to report*   *Assemble!*

Watermills

Watermills are operated by the action of water turning a paddle-wheel. There are two types – one in which the wheel is horizontal (more common in southern France) and the vertical kind, which has been in use since Roman times. Found mainly by fast-flowing streams, these are quite common in the Charentes and Deux-Sèvres. The oldest mills have a wooden wheel. A system of grilles prevents debris carried by the river from lodging in the wheel.

Tide mills

As you might expect from the name, these mills make use of the sea's energy. They are situated along the river or on coastlines with many inlets, such as those of Brittany. They operate by means of a millpond, which is filled at high tide, or from water directed from the marshes of Aunis and Saintonge. Most mills are now in ruins.

A hard job

Traditional milling is a dying art, although there are still a few operational mills in the Vendée. Apart from keeping the sails and wooden vanes in order, the miller has to buy grain to be milled, supervise and adjust the millstones to ensure they are correctly positioned and prepare and fill the 110 lb (50 kg) sacks of flour. He also needs to maintain the millstones and sharpen the grinding edge at least once a year. Since he is

dependent on the wind, his working hours depend on the weather and he often has to work late into the night.

How does the mill work?

Mills are predominantly used to grind grain. The rotation of the wheel or the sails drives the **millstone** by a complex system of gears. The bottom millstone is fixed, while the top one moves over it. Millstones are 3-7 ft (1-2 m) wide and made of limestone, sandstone, granite or flint. Grain is poured through a hole in the centre and as it is ground, centrifugal force moves the grain to the edge, along grooves in the stone. The distance between the two millstones determines how finely the grain will be milled.

TIDE MILLS

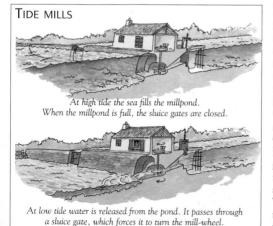

At high tide the sea fills the millpond.
When the millpond is full, the sluice gates are closed.

At low tide water is released from the pond. It passes through a sluice gate, which forces it to turn the mill-wheel.

Restaurants

Your holiday to Poitou-Charentes would not be complete without tasting the regional specialities – including the magnificent seafood – and the local wine. Bon appétit!

① Parthenay

La Truffade, traditional cuisine from Auvergne
p. 141.

② Saint-Michel-le-Cloucq

Ferme-auberge de Mélusine, country cuisine; specialities include *potée vendéenne*
p. 153.

③ Pissotte

Crêperie le Pommier, try the *galette Syracus* (made with duck cutlets and apples)
p. 151.

④ Saint-Liguaire

Auberge de la Rousille, specialities from the Poitou marshes (eels, frogs' legs)
p. 161.

⑤ Confolens

L'Auberge de la Tour, haute cuisine
p. 179.

⑥ Nieuil

Relais et Châteaux, as a dessert, try the *fromager du Ruffécois à l'angélique*
p. 182.

⑦ Angoulême

Chez Paul brasserie
p. 173.
Wine bar,
Le Tire-Bouchon
p. 173.

⑧ Chalais

Relais du Château, try the *veau Talleyrand* (served with *foie gras*!)
p. 197.

⑨ Segonzac

La Cagouillarde, local cuisine
p. 195.

⑩ Mosnac-sur-Seugne

Moulin de Marcouze, traditional cuisine
p. 193.

⑪ La Grève

Escale de l'huître, seafood specialities **p. 235.**

⑫ Île Madame

Ferme-auberge Marine, oysters and clams **p. 208.**

⑬ Surgères

Le Vieux-Puits, fish restaurant **p. 225.**

⑭ Les Portes-en-Ré

Auberge de la Rivière, seafood cuisine **p. 221.**

⑮ L'Aiguillon-sur-Mer

La Pergola, seafood specialities **p. 156.**

⑯ Givrand

Ferme-auberge du Rocher, farm specialities **p. 119.**

⑰ Saint-Gilles-Croix-de-Vie

Le Pouct'on, country cuisine and traditional music **p. 119.**

⑱ Port-de-la-Meule

La Côte Sauvage, country cuisine **p. 113.**

⑲ Bouin

Ferme-auberge du Jaunay, traditional cuisine **p. 108.**

⑳ Beauvoir

Le Martinet, fish and seafood specialities **p. 108.**

㉑ Noirmoutier-en-l'Île

Bar-cafeteria, *Iode,* country cuisine **p. 110.**

Angers

Bressuire

① Parthenay

④ Niort

St-Jean-d'Angély

Saintes

Cognac

⑩

⑨

⑦ Angoulême

Jonzac

⑧

⑤ Confolens

⑥

Limoges

Charente

See also:
Local cuisine p. 68.

| 0 | 10 | 20 | 30 miles |

| 0 | 10 | 20 | 30 | 40 | 50 km |

Local cuisine

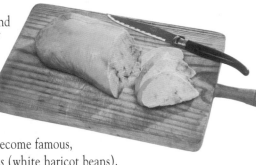

The cuisine of the region is simple and rustic, the food of peasants, but created from the wonderful local vegetables, fruits, dairy produce, meat and fish. Some traditional dishes have become famous, such as ham with *mojettes* (white haricot beans), stewed eels or *mouclade* (mussels in white wine).

It is impossible to stay on the coast of Charentes without tasting its famous oysters

Fish and shellfish

Seafood has pride of place in the food of the Vendée and Charentes. Mussels are eaten  plain or with a sauce, such as *mouclade*, a mixture of white wine, eggs and crème fraîche. Mussels are also delicious grilled on skewers or cooked in white wine. Oysters from Marennes or Vendée-Atlantique are eaten raw with a few drops of shallot vinegar or lemon juice or cooked wrapped in bacon or grilled with garlic butter. The most popular fish are Dover sole, lemon sole and bream, simply grilled with a little lemon juice.

The art of making soup

Soup has long been a staple part of the peasant diet. The regional soups are based on simple and inexpensive ingredients, such as onions, pumpkin, sorrel or haricot beans. On the coast fish soups are popular, such as mussel soup or the *chaudrée*, which is based on sole, whiting and white wine. Inland, a hearty soup, made with bacon, potatoes and green cabbage, is often served as a one-pot meal. There's also *migeot*, a cold, sweet soup, its main ingredient being bread soaked in white wine. A delicious pick-me-up after a hard day's harvesting.

Meat dishes

The various regions are proud of their special meat dishes. In the Vendée, Challans poultry is of exceptionally high quality, while *confits*, terrines and foie gras are made from duck.

SWEETS AND CANDIES

Those with a sweet tooth can buy some candied angelica in Niort, or sweets flavoured with angelica. In Charente, *marguerite* is a dark chocolate with a hint of orange, whilst the *duchesses d'Angoulême* are nougatines filled with praline (p. 173). Visit Les Herbiers (p. 127) to taste some hand-made chocolate. You can also buy interesting jams based on flowers and herbs in unusual combinations everywhere in the markets.

Gathering mojettes *in the Deux-Sèvres*

Wild rabbit pâté is a great delicacy. The marshes of the coast in northern Vendée and in Charente-Maritime are used for rearing marsh mutton, whose unique flavour is greatly appreciated by the locals. Mention should also be made of Chalais veal, obtained from calves reared in semi-darkness and fed on a diet of eggs, milk and sugar. Their meat is famous for its whiteness and unique flavour.

The Bressuire region is particularly reputed for its chicken and *andouille* (tripe sausage).

Traditional recipes

Traditional country recipes deserve to be rediscovered. Ham with *mojettes*, the thin-skinned, white haricot beans grown in the marshes, is a regional dish par excellence. *La chouée des Chouans* is a simple preparation of cabbage stewed in butter and eaten with a sprinkle of vinegar. Eels flourish in the marshes of Poitou and of the north and are eaten grilled on coals or stewed with onions, mushrooms, butter and white wine. Other favourites from the marshes are fricasseed frogs legs or garlic-stuffed snails. *Le farci poitevin* is a boned, rolled breast of pork stuffed with sorrel, garlic and cabbage, a traditional dish in lower Poitou.

The dessert menu

There's plenty of choice when it comes to sweets and cakes. The classic French brioche takes on a different shape in the Vendée, where it is plaited before being baked. It is made with unsalted butter and eaten warm as soon as it comes out of the oven (you can melt a little more butter over it before eating). The Île d'Yeu has its own speciality, a prune tart, and a hot plum tart is the pride of Saint-Georges-de-Didonne. *Le tourteau fromager*, a delicacy from Vendée and Poitou, is one of the few French cakes made with cheese. Although it's sweet, it is made with goat's cheese and is very crisp on top (see photograph p. 9). *La fouace mothaise* is a round cake made of brioche dough. A *broyé* is very hard, crunchy butter biscuit, which breaks as soon as it is cut with a knife.

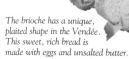

The brioche has a unique, plaited shape in the Vendée. This sweet, rich bread is made with eggs and unsalted butter.

Food and drink – local specialities

Sample the local specialities while you are in the region – from butter and cheese to charcuterie and chocolates, there is something for all tastes.

See also:
Farmhouse butter p. 72
Goats cheese p. 74

Nantes

26

25

Île d'Yeu

24

23

La Roche -sur-Yon

Les Sables- d'Olonne

Fontenay le-Comte

22

Île de Ré

21

La Rochelle

Île d'Oléron

Rochefort

19

●Royan

---

① Cakes and sweets

Vendée chocolat: sample some hand-made chocolate **p. 127.**

② Local products

Ferme des Coûts at Chambretaud: venison, duck and rabbit pâtés **p. 131.**

③ Local products

Maison des produits du terroir at Thouars **p. 137.**

④ Fruit and vegetables

Domaine de La Marchandière at Secondigny: various kinds of apples **p. 145.**

⑤ Cakes and sweets

Pâtisserie Favreau at La Mothe-Saint-Héray: speciality – the *fouace mothaise* (yeast cake) **p. 169.**

---

⑥ Cream and cheese

Fromagerie Poitou-Chèvre at La Mothe-Saint-Héray: cheese in unusual shapes **p. 169.**

⑦ Cream and cheese

Beurre d'Échiré at the *Laiterie coopérative* **p. 161.**

⑧ Cakes and sweets

Pâtisserie Angéli-Cado at Angoulême: speciality – the *angélique confite* **p. 159.**

⑨ Local products

Marché des saveurs: in a motorway lay-by at Vouillé **p. 163.**

---

⑩ Cakes and sweets

Boulangerie coopérative at Lezay: speciality – *tourteaux fromagers* **p. 167.**

⑪ Local products

Domaine de Longeville at Esse: wild boar, venison and duck pâtés **p. 179.**

⑫ Cakes and sweets

Chocolaterie Fabrice Fort at Confolens: speciality – *Kroumirs* and *éphémères*
p. 178.

⑬ Cakes and sweets

Chocolaterie Brun at La Rochefoucauld: speciality – the *Pichotte*
p. 177.

⑭ Cakes and sweets

Chocolaterie Letuffe at Angoulême: specialities – *Guinettes*, *Duchesses* and *Marguerites d'Angoulême*
p. 173.

⑮ Cakes and sweets

Chocolaterie Letuffe at Trois-Palis: specialities – *Guinettes*, *Duchesses* and *Marguerites d'Angoulême*
p. 174.

⑯ Local products

Breeding Manicot geese at Saint-Martial-sur-Né
p. 193.

⑱ Cakes and sweets

Miellerie de Maillezais
p. 147.

⑲ Fish and seafood

Établissements Razé at Grève
p. 235.

⑳ Cream and cheese

Beurre de l'ENILIA at Surgères.
p. 224.

㉑ Local products

The *Épicerie* at La Rochelle
p. 213.

㉒ Local products

Maison du sel at Loix
p. 221.

㉓ Fruit and vegetables

Le Potager extraordinaire at La Mothe-Achard.
p. 123.

㉔ Cream and cheese

Le Moulin du Puy-Gaudin at the Girouard: goat's cheese
p. 123.

㉕ Fish and seafood

Chez Gaston at Port-Joinville
p. 112.

㉖ Fish and seafood

Vendée-Atlantique oysters from the oyster-beds of the Ports de Bouin
p. 109.

⑰ Cakes and sweets

L'Arche aux fruits at Liez: jams and crystallised fruits
p. 147.

Bressuire

Parthenay

Niort

St-Jean-d'Angély

Saintes

Cognac

Jonzac

Charente

Angoulême

Confolens

Farmhouse butter

Salted or unsalted, made from whole or pasteurised milk, the butters of Surgères, Échiré and Noirmoutiers make Vendée-Charentes a butter-making region *par excellence*. The butter produced here is delicate and

tasty. When it is made from whole milk (as opposed to pasteurised) it is full of vitamins and nutritional value.

highly prized. To make pasteurised butter, the cream is heated to a temperature of 19°F (90°C) to eliminate harmful bacteria. The pasteurised butter made in France is graded *extra-fin* and *fin* (of lower quality). Of the pasteurised butters, a distinction is also made between churned butters, made in the traditional way, and others made by more modern methods. Churned butter is the best, as the aromas have been allowed to develop and it is softer and easier to spread.

Poitou-Charentes, a tradition of taste

Poitou-Charentes butter was the first to be granted an *appellation d'origine contrôlée* (AOC). This *appellation* system is similar to the one applied to French wine, in

Butter-making

Full cream from the milk is pasteurised, and then seeded with lactic ferments. The longer they have to develop, the higher the acidity, the higher the acidity of the cream, the more tasty the butter. Churning turns the cream into butter – full-cream butter contains about 82% fat and 18% water, so no wonder those on diets or with cholesterol problems

are discouraged from eating it. After churning the butter is washed in fresh water to eliminate the buttermilk, and it is then kneaded to remove any excess water.

Farmhouse butter

Wholemilk or farmhouse butter is made with cream that has not been pasteurised, which reduces its keeping qualities. However, it is by far the most tasty and the most

Butter moulds are sought after by collectors as treasured examples of folk art

that it denotes a product of superior quality and signifies that the product is checked regularly to ensure that standards are maintained. The butters of Surgères and Échiré are the best known. Always check to see that the words *beurre de Charentes-*

Poitou are written on the label to ensure you are buying the real thing.

The best butter in the world – the butter of Échiré

Deux-Sèvres also produces some of the finest butter. Échiré butter is made in wooden barrels of Vietnamese teak, which cannot rot and contain no tannin. They are traditional in the region. It takes 2½ hours of constant churning to produce, from its starting point as cream to the final lump of butter. Machine-made butter, on the other hand is made in a *butyrateur*, which produces

cream in 5 minutes. Échiré butter is made traditionally by the churning method and it has an exceptional flavour and an international reputation.

Milk cooperatives

When the vines were destroyed by the mid-19th C. plague of phylloxera, the region's peasants began to turn to dairy produce. In order to compete with large companies buying milk at low prices, a peasant from Chaillé created the first milk marketing cooperative in 1888. Other cooperatives followed, and grouped themselves into a larger

Lescure butter from Poitou-Charentes, an AOC of great repute

organisation known as the Association des Laiteries Coopératives des Charentes et du Poitou. Nowadays, only the Surgères dairy and the Saint-Jean La Ronde cooperative still remain.

Straight from the churn, delicious butter produced by the Échiré Cooperative

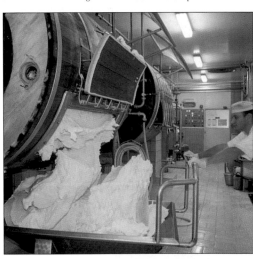

BUTTERING UP

The local cuisine makes lavish use of butter in its dishes. If you want to cook meat or vegetables use a butter that is composed of 96.8% fat, as it will reach high temperatures without spoiling. This butter also has the advantage of remaining firm at room temperature.

Churned butter is so delicious it can be eaten on its own, but it's best not to worry too much about your calories, not to mention the effects on your cholesterol levels! Try spreading it on fresh fruit, such as apples or peaches – it's absolutely delicious.

Goat's cheese

The Deux-Sèvres region is a land of rich pastures and traditional skills. It produces a wide variety of cheeses, all of which are made from goat's milk due to the number of goat herds still present in the region and its rich pastureland. If you are particularly interested in this kind of cheese, there are a number of producers you can visit (see pp. 168-169). You will usually be given the opportunity to taste some of the cheeses and perhaps meet some local people who enjoy sharing their region's specialities with others.

A Saracen heritage

When the Saracens decided to invade France they brought their own food with them, including large herds of goats. However, the French fought off the invaders and the defeated invaders returned home, leaving their goats behind. The goats flourished due to the richness of the pasture land, and the number of herds increased.

They provided exceptionally good milk from which the local people began to make cheese. There are several breeds, including the pure white Saanen, the alpine chamois, which is fawn coloured with black feet, and the Poitevine, which has a black coat.

Making goat's milk cheese

Goats usually produce milk from February to November. During this period they can give as much as 1,000 pints (600 litres). At the start of the year, while they are raising their young they are not milked, but once the kids have been weaned, the milk is used to make cheese. A fresh goat's cheese will take 3-6 weeks to make. The milk must be strained, fermented and stirred, and the cheeses drained and wiped. You can learn all about the cheese-making methods by visiting the places mentioned on pp.168-169.

Chabichou cheese from Poitou

Chabichou benefits from an *appellation d'origine contrôlée* (AOC), and is one of the most famous cheeses in France. It is manufactured in a very small district that covers the limestone soils on the threshold of Poitou. It's a whole-milk goat's cheese (45% fat), weighing about

5 oz (150 g) and is cone-shaped and about 2-3 inches (5-7 cm) tall. This cone is also known as a *bonde*.

How to recognise the different cheeses

Mothais-sur-feuille is another traditional cheese made from whole goat's milk and is shaped into a disc 4-5 inches (10-12 cm) in diameter and 1 inch (2.5 cm) thick. The weight varies from 6 to 7 oz (180 to 200 g), and the

HOW TO STORE CHEESE

Goat's cheese is soft, so don't put it in the bottom of your shopping bag. Try to store it in a cool place as soon as you can. Not all cheese should be kept at the same temperature. Fresh cheeses and cream cheeses should be kept in the coldest part of the refrigerator and goat's cheese in the intermediate area at between 37 and 43°F (between 3 and 6°C). Don't forget to protect the cheese with packaging to prevent it from drying out and losing its flavour, or being too close to other food.

cheese is wrapped in a large chestnut leaf. It's best when it's about three weeks old, when you can really appreciate its delicate, creamy taste. *La bûche de chèvre* (the log) can be made from either whole or pasturised milk and varies in its presentation, but is often found in the form of a cylinder 6-8 inches (15-20 cm) long and weighing about 7 oz (200 g). It always has a smooth white rind. Ash-coated cheeses also vary in shape and are coated with a plant ash, which gives them a unique flavour and keeps them fresh. Sainte-Maure is an example of an one such cheese. It is log-shaped and has a hollow straw running through the middle.

Fresh or dry, ash-coated or not, plain or mixed with herbs, garlic or even served with jam, the local goat's cheese can be eaten in many different ways.

The best way to eat the cheeses

Remove the cheese from the refrigerator at least an hour before you are going to eat it as the flavours develop best at room temperature. Like wine, goat's cheese is best when aged (for three weeks at most) to make it stronger. A strong cheese should be eaten with red wine. If you prefer fresh goat's cheese, accompany it with a sweet white wine. Fresh cheeses are drained and sold in pots and can be eaten lightly salted, sweetened or sprinkled with herbs.

Wines and spirits

From Cognac to Pineau, and not forgetting the local wines, you will find lots of bottles to add to your cellar here.

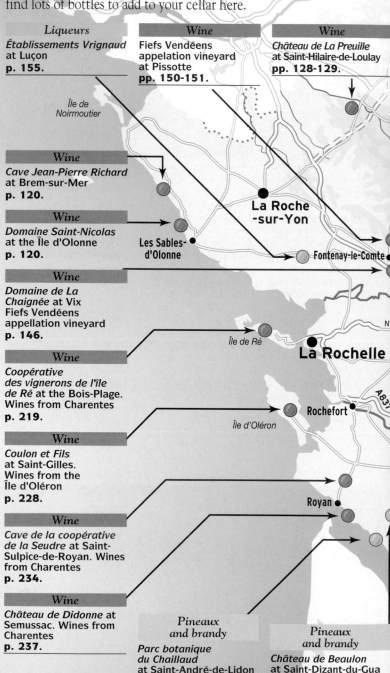

Liqueurs
Établissements Vrignaud at Luçon
p. 155.

Wine
Fiefs Vendéens appellation vineyard at Pissotte
pp. 150-151.

Wine
Château de La Preuille at Saint-Hilaire-de-Loulay
pp. 128-129.

Île de Noirmoutier

Wine
Cave Jean-Pierre Richard at Brem-sur-Mer
p. 120.

Wine
Domaine Saint-Nicolas at the Île d'Olonne
p. 120.

Wine
Domaine de La Chaignée at Vix Fiefs Vendéens appellation vineyard
p. 146.

Wine
Coopérative des vignerons de l'île de Ré at the Bois-Plage. Wines from Charentes
p. 219.

Wine
Coulon et Fils at Saint-Gilles. Wines from the Île d'Oléron
p. 228.

Wine
Cave de la coopérative de la Seudre at Saint-Sulpice-de-Royan. Wines from Charentes
p. 234.

Wine
Château de Didonne at Semussac. Wines from Charentes
p. 237.

La Roche -sur-Yon

Les Sables-d'Olonne

Fontenay-le-Comte

Île de Ré

La Rochelle

N11

Rochefort

Île d'Oléron

A837

Royan

Pineaux and brandy
Parc botanique du Chaillaud at Saint-André-de-Lidon
p. 239.

Pineaux and brandy
Château de Beaulon at Saint-Dizant-du-Gua
p. 238

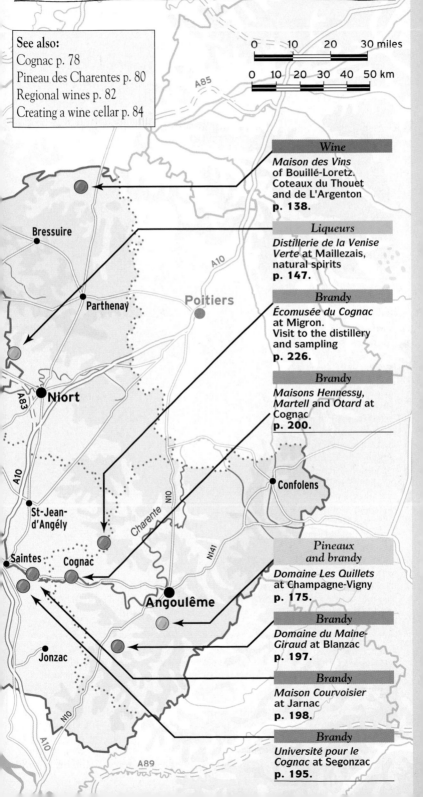

See also:
Cognac p. 78
Pineau des Charentes p. 80
Regional wines p. 82
Creating a wine cellar p. 84

0   10   20   30 miles

0 10 20 30 40 50 km

Bressuire

Parthenay

Poitiers

Niort

St-Jean-
d'Angély

Saintes

Cognac

Angoulême

Confolens

Jonzac

Charente

Wine
Maison des Vins of Bouillé-Loretz. Coteaux du Thouet and de L'Argenton **p. 138.**

Liqueurs
Distillerie de la Venise Verte at Maillezais, natural spirits **p. 147.**

Brandy
Écomusée du Cognac at Migron. Visit to the distillery and sampling **p. 226.**

Brandy
Maisons Hennessy, Martell and *Otard* at Cognac **p. 200.**

Pineaux and brandy
Domaine Les Quillets at Champagne-Vigny **p. 175.**

Brandy
Domaine du Maine-Giraud at Blanzac **p. 197.**

Brandy
Maison Courvoisier at Jarnac **p. 198.**

Brandy
Université pour le Cognac at Segonzac **p. 195.**

Cognac

The great vineyards of Cognac cover an area of around 200,000 acres (80,000 ha) and are centred around the town of the same name. It's the combination of the '*terroir*' or soil, the proximity to the sea and the hot sun which makes cognac brandy 'a happy accident of nature', as demonstrated by the great vintages of Grande Champagne, Fins Bois and Bons Bois. Many skills are involved in creating a fine cognac, including distilling, cooperage, ageing and blending.

A short history

Vines were planted extensively around La Rochelle from the 13th C. onwards, which encouraged the wine trade in the Charente basin. After salt, wine was the second most important commodity in the economy of the Charente. It was not until the 16th C. that Dutch and English merchants had the idea of distilling the wine, thus producing a stronger drink which could be shipped without risk of deterioration, and more cheaply. A terrible slump caused large stocks of this wine to be left unsold, until the day when someone happened to taste it and found to the general delight that it had vastly improved with age and could be drunk neat.

Favourable soil, enough sunshine and the gentle ocean climate give the vines of the region the qualities required for producing brandy

Traditional brandy-making equipment at Vouillé (see p. 162)

From the vineyard to the bottle

Cognac is distilled in two stages in a special vessel called an *alambic charentais*. The first distillation stage produces a liquid known as the *brouillis*, which is between 28 and 32% proof. The *brouillis* is then heated for a second distillation called *la bonne chauffe*. The brandy-maker removes all the liquid at the top and bottom of the vessel and retains only the best of the distillate. Cognac is aged exclusively in vats made of oak from the forests of Limousin and the Allier. Every year 2-3% of the brandy evaporates. This is called 'the angels' share' (and represents around 23 million bottles a year!) After a minimum of two and a half years of aging the vintages are blended to produce the final brandy. This is performed by the *maître de chais*, the master blender.

The blending laboratory at the Chaillaud estate at Saint-André-de-Lidon (see p. 239)

The art of barrel-making

The barrels play an essential role in the ageing of the vintages. Master coopers are extremely skilled workers. A barrel is made of oak staves, which are made more supple by being soaked in warm water and then bowed. They are held in place by 14-18 metal hoops and the wooden base and top. To finish off the barrel, the cooper places the frame on a saddle, on which he rounds, chamfers and trims it.

Brandy bottles

The Saint-Gobain glassworks produces traditionally shaped wine and brandy bottles on an industrial scale. With an output of some 1,500,000 bottles a day, the Charentes factory is the busiest in Europe (p. 194), and gives an idea of the scale of the French trade in wine and spirits. The clatter of its machinery contrasts starkly with the quasi-religious silence of the *chais*.

These are the cellars of Cognacs Camus, located in the valley of Cognac (see p. 200). Here the brandy ages in semi-darkness in oak barrels.

How to read the labels

The description and the price are determined by the age of the youngest brandy used in the blend. If it is less than four and a half years old, the cognac is stamped with three stars or a VS (*very superior*) label, between four and a half years and six and a half years it is known as VSOP (*very superior old pale*), VO (*very old*) or Reserve. If it is older than this, it is deemed 'Napoleon', XO, 'extra' or '*hors d'âge*' (ageless). The appellation *fine champagne* is reserved for cognacs that are blended exclusively from brandies of grapes grown in the Grande Champagne and Petite Champagne (two of the six vineyard districts).

COGNAC — A DRINK FOR EVERYONE

Cognac should be drunk from a balloon glass, which is wide at the bottom and narrow at the top. This is the purest way to drink brandy, though of course it can be enjoyed in a number of other ways – diluted with still or sparkling water as a brandy and soda, the American way, in a cocktail, on the rocks or neat at room temperature. Originally, cognac was drunk simply diluted with water and thus became the *brand-wijn* (burnt wine) of the Dutch. Cognac also works very well in cooking. Try Charentais guinea-fowl with brandy-flavoured stuffing, it's just heavenly!

Pineau des Charentes

Pineau is to the Charentes what anisette is to Provence. This happy mixture of cognac and grape juice benefits from the sunny weather of the Charentes and its fertile limestone soil. When you are visiting the region, be sure to visit some of the grape-growers who produce this legendary drink.

Accidental birth

According to legend, Pineau des Charentes, the fruit of the vine, was also the fruit of chance. During the 1589 grape harvest, a wine-maker accidentally filled a cask with grape juice, which already contained some cognac brandy. Since no fermentation occurred, he abandoned the cask in an obscure corner of his *chai*. A few years later, he discovered a limpid, delicate liquid with a mild, fruity flavour. Pineau des Charentes was born.

An *appellation d'origine contrôlée*

Two types of Pineau can be obtained, depending on the grape variety. White Pineau is made from ugni-blanc, folle-blanche, colombard and sémillon grapes. The rosé is made from cabernet franc, cabernet-sauvignon and merlot varieties. To be eligible for its *appellation d'origine contrôlée* (AOC), the cognac must come from the same

vineyard and be a minimum of 60° proof. Production must not exceed 5,875 gallons (27,000 litres) per vineyard. Pineau des Charentes is sold commercially only after it has passed a rigorous tasting committee test; it must previously have aged for a minimum of one year in oak casks.

MOUCLADE
WITH PINEAU

Put some mussels into a casserole with a glass of pineau. As soon as they open, place them on the half-shell in an ovenproof dish. Strain the cooking juice. Fry chopped onions in butter, sprinkle them with a little flour and add some black pepper. Add another glass of pineau and the strained juice. While heating gently, incorporate 3½ oz (100 g) of crème fraîche beaten with two egg yolks and sprinkle with chopped parsley. Coat the mussels with this sauce and bake them in a very hot oven for 5 minutes.

From the vine to the cask

The grapes are pressed and the juice is decanted on the same day that they are picked. Fermentation soon brings the grape juice up to a 10° alcohol content. It is at this precise moment that the brandy must be added, both to stop the fermentation and increase the alcohol content to 17 or 17.5° proof. The proportions of grape juice and brandy are about 1¾ pints (1 litre) of cognac (aged for 3 to 10 years) to 2½ pints (2 litres) of grape juice.

Reading the label

Pineau has an *appellation contrôlée*, so check that the initials AOC appear on the label. Some Pineaux are vintage, meaning that the white grape juices from which they are made all come from the same year. However, a vintage does not guarantee a good Pineau. If the year is not indicated on the label, it's a blend of several Pineaux, so that the best years balance out those that were not so good, ensuring a good Pineau. If no year is indicated, try and find the age anyway – the ideal is three years.

White or rosé?

Whether it's white or rosé, it is best to drink Pineau in a tulip glass or balloon glass to bring out the colour and bouquet. It should be drunk quite chilled at 41 and 43°F (between 5° and 6°C). It goes extremely well with Roquefort cheese, Charentais melon or strawberries. Pineau also makes an excellent accompaniment to oysters, mussels and, in particular, foie gras. Connoisseurs prefer white to rosé as it is not as sweet and its taste stays longer in the mouth, developing its fragrances better.

The wine that makes you mad!

Several years ago, Pineau was often made from noa, a grape variety that is now banned. This grape produced Pineau of excellent quality, with a very special flavour, rather like an almond. But this grape contained such a high ether content that it interfered with brain function. Hence its nickname of 'the wine that makes you mad'! Of course, a few wine-makers still make Pineau with noa, but they don't advertise the fact!

Wines of Poitou-Charentes

The vineyards of Poitou-Charentes are sandwiched tightly between their big brothers in the Loire valley and the illustrious Bordeaux region. Yet this little grape-growing region has exceptionally sunny weather and the *vins des Fiefs Vendéens* (literally, wines of the Vendée fiefdoms) have earned an *appellation d'origine contrôlée* (AOC).

White, rosé or red wines are produced by the Fiefs Vendéens

Vin de pays and *qualité supérieure*

The wines of the Vendée, Charentes and Deux-Sèvres are generally classified as *vin de pays*. These are table wines, which indicate the geographical region from which they come. The wines of Vendée and Deux-Sèvres are linked to the appellation *vin de pays du jardin de la France*, while the *vins du pays* of Charentes have their own appellation. In this higher quality there are wines described as *délimités de qualité supérieure* (VDQS) such as the *vin des fiefs vendéens*. Each of these are simple, inexpensive but distinctive wines but which have no pretentions other than to be an agreeable accompaniment to a good meal of local dishes, with which they marry particularly well.

The best local wines

There are two main regions here for VDQS wines, the **Fiefs Vendéens** and **Haut-Poitou**, which straddle the départements of Deux-Sèvres and Vienne, south of the Saumur district. North of Thouars, in Deux-Sèvres, the wines have the appellations Anjou and Saumur. The northern frontier of the Vendée, where it meets Loire-Atlantique, is the territory of **Muscadet**. The best *vins de pays* of the region are **Pays de Retz** in northern Vendée and **Vins de Pays Charentais** in Charente-Maritime.

Saint-Sornin, wine of the Charente

Vines have been grown here on the slopes of Saint-Sornin dominated by the manor of La Fenêtre since the Middle Ages. Wines of the Saint-Sornin cellar have the label

Vin de Pays Charentais. The red wines are made from gamay and merlot grapes, the whites from ugni-blanc (cognac) and sauvignon.

These minor wines still received a silver medal in 1996 in the Concours Général Agricole, which is quite an achievement. The typical cabernet that is produced can be drunk immediately, although it benefits from being kept for a few months.

Vins des Fiefs Vendéens

Vine-growing is a strong family tradition in the Vendée. Brem, Mareuil, Vix and Pissotte are the four *terroirs* (territories) of the *Vins des Fiefs Vendéens*. This small region of only 1200 acres (470 ha) produces mainly reds and rosés, from gamay, pinot noir, cabernet franc and cabernet sauvignon grape varieties. Since 1984 these wines have been granted the appellation *Vins Délimités de Qualité Supérieure* (VDQS). These light, fruity wines should be drunk young (except for exceptional vintages such as 1995 and 1996) and also chilled.

Loire Wine Festivals at Saint-Gilles-Croix-de-Vie

1st November
☎ **02 51 55 03 66.**
If you happen to be passing through this part of northern Vendée at the beginning of November, this wine trade fair is a lively, intimate affair. You can taste all the wines of the Loire (Coteaux du Layon), as well as local specialities, the *Vins des Fiefs Vendéens*. If you like them, you'll be able to buy a few bottles on the spot! To accompany the wine, the Confrérie de la Sardine (another Saint-Gilles speciality) will offer you canapés and local producers will let you taste their foie gras.

MAKE YOUR OWN VIN D'ÉPINE

Vin d'Épine is a local speciality, a type of sloe apéritif, which you can make for yourself. You will need a large crock and 20-30 wine bottles. The main ingredient is sloe or blackthorn shoots, which you can pick from bushes growing in the hedgerow. The buds need to be picked in late May. Find out from the locals where the best places are. Crush 10½ oz (300 g) of blackthorn shoots in 1¾ pints (1 litre) of plum brandy. Then add 5¼ pints (3 litres) of red or white wine and 1½ lb (750 g) of sugar and leave for 10 days. Filter the liquid and bottle it. Then wait for at least another two months before sampling the brew.

Creating a wine cellar

A few tips for buying and laying down wine

Even if the vineyards of the Vendée and Charentes are not in the same league as the great wines from other regions of France, they nevertheless produce some very pleasant wines, which go particularly well with summer dishes and seafood. The warm weather and reliability of the climate make this a region ideal for grape-growing. For the last 20 years, wines have been produced here that are still little known outside their native France, but are a very a pleasant surprise for visitors yet to discover them.

Buying wine

When buying wine you need to decide if you are buying to drink quickly or to lay down in a cellar. For wines to be drunk during the year, stick to young wines, *vin de pays* or local wines. You can even buy in bulk and bottle them yourself. But remember that the wine-maker will often keep his best wine for himself. The VDQS, which don't have wide distribution, such as those of the Vendée or Haut Poitou, should always be

Paul Rumeau in his chai (cellar) at the Domaine des Quillets, in Champagne-Vigny (see p. 175)

bought in bottles. The best of these vintages will keep very well in a wine cellar. In any event, do not drink the wine for at least a fortnight after transporting it.

Where to buy

Take advantage of your holidays to buy direct from the producer. Not only will you find wines that cannot be found any-where else, but the wine-

maker will initiate you into the art of vinification, the subtleties of the grape varieties and of wine-tasting. His knowledge and advice are worth a great deal. You can also try the local markets where wine-makers' stands will be displaying the best wines (for sale) in the region. However, if you are not sure of your own judgement you can also try the cooperatives, which are experts at selection.

Judging a good wine

The eye is the first judge. The wine must be clear and transparent and have a bright sparkle. The nuance and intensity of the colour indicate the maturity and quality of the wine. White wines range from very pale to golden, but once they have turned amber they are too old. Red wines should not be too pale; they should be a good cherry red or dark red. The next judge is your nose, to

detect over-acidity, odd odours and to let you appreciate the bouquet. An ample and complex bouquet may be floral, fruity or earthy. The wine should have a good flavour, a harmony and balance between acidity, softness and tannins.

Bringing the wine home

Visitors from the UK and Ireland who have their cars with them, can legally export as much wine as they can fit in the boot, as long as the tax is paid (i.e. that the wine has been bought from a normal retail outlet), and it is for their own personal consumption. Visitors from further

afield will need assistance with transporting their wine home, if they are planning to take more than the odd bottle back with them. Ask the wine seller for information about shipping cases worldwide. From a practical point of view, it is best not to transport wine in high summer or midwinter. Wine must always be protected from extremes of temperature, which could spoil the taste for ever. As soon as you reach your destination, put the wine in the cellar. Wine bought in bulk in a large container should be decanted into bottles without disturbing it too much. If you have bought a case of bottles, you should remove them from the packing and store them horizontally.

Cellaring

Any glass bottles can be used for storing wine, but light bottles that have no concave bottom are less suitable for rack storage. Furthermore, if you fill them too full, they could explode when you cork them. Choose heavy bottles,

of clear glass for white wine, coloured for red. Always fill them enough for the cork to be immersed when the bottle is laid on its side. When you have finished bottling, stick on the labels about 1 inch (3 cm) from the base. Taste of course is the final test. Where possible, store the white wines closer to the ground and the reds on top of them. Wine should always be stored in a horizontal or sloping position.

LOCAL FOOD AND WINE

Frogs' legs and snails call for a white Brem or a chilled red Pissotte. Crabs and prawns go well with a Sauvignon from the Haut-Poitou or a white Fief Vendéen, oysters call for a Muscadet. To accompany *mouclade Charentaise*, drink a Haut-Poitou Chardonnay. Choose a white or rosé Haut-Poitou for fish. Try a Pissotte rosé or a Mareuil red with the traditional Vendée ham. With Challans duck, drink a Mareuil red, and with lamb or mutton an Haut-Poitou Gamay. Chilled Vix rosé wines, with their strawberry flavour, are delicious poured over a red berry dessert.

Festivals & cultural events

Depending on when you visit, there may be a local festival taking place.
Enjoy the celebrations!

```
0      10     20     30 miles
0   10  20  30  40  50 km
```

Nantes

Île de Noirmoutier **(22)**

(23)

(1)

Île d'Yeu

(21)
(20)

La Roche -sur-Yon

(1) **Le Puy-du-Fou**

Son et Lumière
and *Cinéscénie*
(June–September)
p. 130.

Les Sables-
d'Olonne

(18)

Fontenay-
le-Comte **(7)**

(2) **Airvault**

Festival of world
music (July)
p. 143.

(19)

Île de Ré

N11

(17)

La Rochelle

(3) **Parthenay**

Jazz beside the waters
of the Gâtine (July)
p. 145.
*Festival des Jeux et
Opens Internationaux
d'Echecs* (early July)
p. 141.

(7) **Fontenay-
le-Comte**

*Nuits Gitanes et
d'Ailleurs,* nomadic
music and meeting with
the gypsies (June)
p. 150.
*Festival des Histoires
d'Été,* evenings with
professional storytellers
p. 150.

Île d'Oléron

Rochefort

A837

(4) **Vouvant**

*Festival des Contes
et Légendes d'Europe*
Street shows and
evening events
p. 153.

(8) **Melle**

Festival of Melle in the
Saint-Savinien church,
son et lumières
p. 164.

(11) **Roumazières-
Loubert**

Son et lumière at the
Château de Peyras
(July)
p. 182.

(5) **Nieul-sur-l'Autize**

*Les Rencontres
Imaginaires,*
evening shows about
Eleanor of Aquitaine
(July–August)
p. 151.

(9) **Confolens**

International festival
of folklore, folk music
and dance
p. 178.

(12) **Angoulême**

International festival of
comic strips (end of Jan.)
p. 170.

(6) **Magné**

Festival of painting
(July)
p. 163.

(10) **Exideuil-
sur-Vienne**

*Festival de Chants et
de Musiques du Monde*
p. 182.

Circuit des Remparts.
Vintage car race
(mid-September)
p. 172.

See also: Markets and rural fairs p. 88

⑬ Barbezieux

Comice Agricole, agricultural show (early September)
p. 196.

⑭ Cognac

Festival of detective films (early April)
p. 201.
Blues Passion, jazz festival (August)
p. 201.
Coup de Chauffe, performers, clowns and musicians roam the streets (early September)
p. 201.
Salon de la Littérature Européenne (November)
p. 201.

⑮ Montguyon

International festival of song, dance and music (end July–early August)
p. 193.

⑯ Saintes

Académies Musicales, old-fashioned musical instruments in the Abbaye-aux-Dames (early July)
p. 202.

⑰ La Rochelle

Francofolies, talent showcase (July)
p. 215.

International Film Festival, retrospectives, tributes, feature films (end June–early July)
p. 215.

⑱ Luçon

Festival des Nocturnes Océanes, romantic classical music (July)
p. 154.

⑲ La Tranche-sur-Mer

Fête des Fleurs, parade of floats followed by concerts (April)
p. 157.

⑳ Saint-Gilles-Croix-de-Vie

Festival Saint-Jazz-sur-Vie (Whit Sunday)
p. 118.

Festival de la Déferlante, all kinds of concerts in the seaside resorts (July–August)
p. 115.

㉑ Saint-Jean-de-Monts

Festival Passion Cerf-volant, kite-flying festival
p. 115.

㉒ Île de Noirmoutier

Régates du Bois de la Chaize (early August)
p. 110.

㉓ Montaigu

Printemps du Livre (May)
p. 129.

Bressuire ②

③ Parthenay

④

⑤

⑥ **Niort**

⑧

A10

St-Jean-d'Angély

Saintes

⑥ ⑭ Cognac

Charente

N10

N141

⑪

⑫ **Angoulême**

⑬

● Jonzac

⑮

N10

A10

⑨ Confolens

⑩

A20

Limoges ●

Markets and rural fairs
a riot of scents and colours

Every *commune* of any importance has its market day or days, which are excellent opportunities to learn about local foods and to buy fresh produce. Country fairs or speciality markets are less frequent but just as important. They are seasonal and make it possible to buy home-made and fresh food that you won't find at home.

Market day in the town

Every reasonably sized town has its own market. A notice board provides the relevant information at the entrance to the town. Markets are generally held weekly or fortnightly, in the mornings until about 1pm. In small towns and large villages in the country the market may even take the place of shops. You'll find local goods on sale, such as food and produce, work clothes, caps and berets, tools, grain and seeds. These markets serve local people and their needs and do not sell craft items or tourist souvenirs. Nevertheless, they are busy and lively, you'll often find stalls selling live chickens, rabbits and goats.

Tourist markets

Large markets are held regularly in the major towns and seaside resorts. A covered market, such as that at the Sables-d'Olonne, will sell perishable goods, including dairy products, cheeses, meat and fish. Sellers of fruit and vegetables usually operate in the open air, and fairs offer something for everyone – crafts, small antiques, drapery etc. You will also find locally grown fruit, vegetables and other foods, including organic produce. Many so-called 'tourist' markets are also frequented by locals.

Speciality markets

The fact that holiday-makers love to shop at markets has brought about a new kind of market. These are the speciality markets, which concentrate on organic produce and local speciality foods, flower markets, honey markets, wine markets and those specialising in onions, chestnuts and folk crafts.

Many craftsmen and small local producers use these as their shop window. You are sure to find some excellent buys. You can get details and dates of the venues from the local tourist offices.

At the fair

The tradition of fairs started in the Middle Ages, and it still remains strong in this area. The **Rouillac fair**, in Charentes, is held on the 27th of each month and is a good example. Unlike the trade fairs held in towns, a French country fair is really an enormous market, which attracts people from miles around every month. It lasts

the whole day, so there are plenty of cafés, restaurants and snack foods available, as well as a wide range of food products. Farm machinery is often displayed – tractors and other equipment – as well as livestock. In cattle-rearing areas, the cattle fair is the big event, as in Parthenay, where the so-called *foirail* is held every Wednesday. Some towns allow the fairs to follow a more touristy orientation, such as the horse fairs, the wine fair at **Cognac**, the craft fairs in the Charentes or the traditional fair at Challans in the Vendée.

Filling your basket

Choose local specialities depending on the region. The Vendée is known for its poultry and duck produce, such as pâtés, preserved duck and foies gras. In the markets of the Vendée you will also find the *Vins des Fiefs Vendéens*, sea salt from Noirmoutier, butter brioches and *mojettes* beans. In the Poitou marshes, look for honey, jams and brandy as well as goat's cheese. In Charentes keep an eye out for farmhouse butter, the so-called 'marsh lamb' (*agneau de présalé*), Charentais melons and Pineau des Charentes. Around Niort buy sweetmeats based on angelica.

Excursions

By foot, on horseback, by bicycle or on the water, here are plenty of ideas for trips that allow you to discover Poitou and Charentes at your own pace.

① Mortagne-sur-Sèvre

Bocage Express,
14 miles (22 km)
through the valleys
p. 133.

② La Réorthe

Rent a gypsy
caravan
p. 126.

③ Forest of Mervent

Mountain-biking
p. 152.

④ Champdeniers-Saint-Denis

Explore an
underground river
p. 144.

⑤ Damvix

Gypsy caravans
in the Poitou marshes
p. 148.

⑥ Ruffec

Walks, horse or
bike-rides in the
Ruffec area
p. 187.

⑦ Roumazières-Loubert

Walks, horse or
mountain-bike rides
p. 183.

⑧ Nersac

Walks on the banks of
the river Charente
at the Fleurac mill
p. 175.

⑨ Forest of La Mothe-Clédou

Arboretum du Clédou,
exotic trees
p. 185.

⑩ Angoulême

Cruises on the
river Charente,
theme cruises
p. 171.

⑪ Saintes

Boat trips on the
river Charente
with Inter-îles
p. 203.

See also:
River cruises p.92

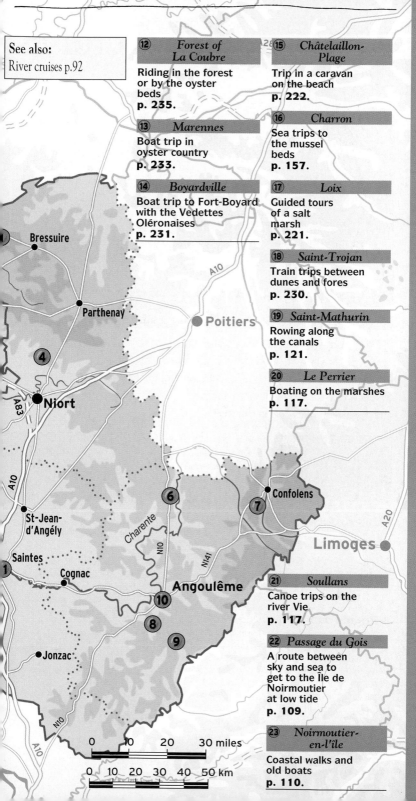

12 *Forest of La Coubre*

Riding in the forest or by the oyster beds
p. 235.

13 *Marennes*

Boat trip in oyster country
p. 233.

14 *Boyardville*

Boat trip to Fort-Boyard with the Vedettes Oléronaises
p. 231.

15 *Châtelaillon-Plage*

Trip in a caravan on the beach
p. 222.

16 *Charron*

Sea trips to the mussel beds
p. 157.

17 *Loix*

Guided tours of a salt marsh
p. 221.

18 *Saint-Trojan*

Train trips between dunes and fores
p. 230.

19 *Saint-Mathurin*

Rowing along the canals
p. 121.

20 *Le Perrier*

Boating on the marshes
p. 117.

21 *Soullans*

Canoe trips on the river Vie
p. 117.

22 *Passage du Gois*

A route between sky and sea to get to the Île de Noirmoutier at low tide
p. 109.

23 *Noirmoutier-en-l'île*

Coastal walks and old boats
p. 110.

Bressuire

Parthenay

Poitiers

Niort

Confolens

Limoges

St-Jean-d'Angély

Saintes

Cognac

Charente

Angoulême

Jonzac

0   10   20   30 miles

0   10   20   30   40   50 km

River and canal cruises

R iver trips provide a tranquil alternative to crowded roads. You don't need to be a qualified sailor to manage a longboat and exploring the countryside via its waterways is an absolute delight. If you can't afford to rent a boat for several days, try taking a short trip for a day or half a day and enjoy messing about on the river!

The river Charente at Saintes

A liquid road

Unlike traditional tourism, whose bane is the traffic jams on the roads, river tourism means travel in a completely different way. You'll have an excellent and unencumbered view of the surrounding countryside. Passing through towns will be a pleasant surprise after hours of sailing past wooded banks or grass-land. If you are a stressed-out townie you will have to adapt to a very different rhythm of life. However, you won't get seasick in these calm waters.

Houseboats

You won't need a permit to steer a houseboat that can be rented for a weekend or longer. Some instruction before you set off will enable you to master the manoeuvres without difficulty and there's a surveillance system with telephone contacts in case of breakdown. Houseboats can accommodate from 2 to 12 people depending on the model. Rates also depend

Bring a bicycle so you can explore the places where you stop

on size as well as season (from €640 per week out of season for 4, to €2,300 in summer for 10, usually starting on Saturday). The interior

DAY TRIPS

You can combine the pleasures of a river cruise with those of tourism on land if you choose a themed trip. There's a wide choice from the standard cruise with a meal on board to the more unusual idea of combining river cruising with a particular hobby. Lovers of chocolate, cognac and Pineau and crafts, such as hand-made paper, will all find a cruise to suit them, as will those who prefer night cruises or picnic cruises. Just climb aboard.

resembles a caravan, with a galley, toilet and shower. There's even onboard heating, which means that trips in winter are possible. The bridge is the best place to laze around while watching the countryside roll by.

Navigable waterways

The Charente is 225 miles (360 km) long and is navigable from Angoulême to the sea, a distance of 106 miles (171 km). Part of it is an estuary and thus tidal. The course is regulated by 21 locks between Angoulême and Tonnay-Charente. Passing through a lock is one of the highlights of a trip on the river. The lock-keeper –

often a woman – is generally a colourful character, who is fiercely proud of her river and will exchange news and gossip with you or give you ideas for places to see. It takes at least 15 minutes to go through each lock. The Sèvre Niortaise also has a lovely stretch from Marans through the Poitou marshes to Niort.

A base for excursions

Bikes are very useful for exploring areas around the canal when you stop en-route. They can easily be rented, often at the same place as you rent the boat. Take advantage of stopovers in order to take excursions into the surrounding countryside. The region is

full of quaint villages and chapels, so make sure your cruise allows for plenty of stopping places. The secret of a cruise lies in its timeless rhythm. Forget the tyranny of clock-watching and let yourself relax. There is nothing like waking to the tranquility of a country morning and taking decisions on the spur of the moment.

Places to go

One of the pleasures of river navigation is the freedom to change a plan at will. You can stop wherever you like, for a picnic, a siesta, a bike ride, or even to taste brandy in the Cognac region, or make a detour to one of the towns along the river, such as Rochefort, Angoulême or Niort. Forget parking problems. At each point of departure, you will be given plenty of literature about routes to take. There are embarkation piers at Fléac, Sireuil, Jarnac, Cognac, Chaniers and Saint-Savinien on the river Charente, and also at La Ronde on the Sèvre Niortaise.

Sport and leisure

If you want to surf the breakers, go horse riding or do a spot of fishing, here are a few suggestions for holiday activities in Poitou-Charentes.

Fishing

Shellfish at the
Pont d'Yeu
p. 114.

Kayaking

Sea kayaking at Notre-
Dame-de-Monts.
p. 114.

Water sports

Sand yachting at the
Centre Nautique at
Saint-Jean-de-Monts
p. 114.

Horse riding

Centre Équestre at
Mervent and Ferme
Équestre de la Garrelière
in the forest of Mervent
p. 152.

Île de Noirmoutier

Île d'Yeu

**La Roche
-sur-Yon**

Les Sables-
d'Olonne

Water sports

Surfing at
La Sauzaie at
Brétignolles-sur-Mer
p. 120.

Water sports

Surfing, fun-boarding
and body-boarding at
the Pointe de Grouin
p. 157.

Île de Ré

Water sports

Sand yachting, windsurfing
and fun-boarding at the
Faute-sur-Mer and at the
Tranche-sur-Mer
p. 157.

Leisure area

Parc de Pierre Brune
(bumper boats, mini-
golf, tennis)
p. 152.

Rochefort

A83

Rock-climbing

Pierre Blanche
in the forest of
Mervent
p. 152.

Fishing

In the Poitou marsh
at Damvix
p. 148.

● **Royan**

*Estuaire de
la Gironde*

Pony trekking

Riding at the Forêt
de la Coubre with
L'Écurie Tournebride
p. 235.

Fishing

In the marsh
of Saint-Sornin
p. 233.

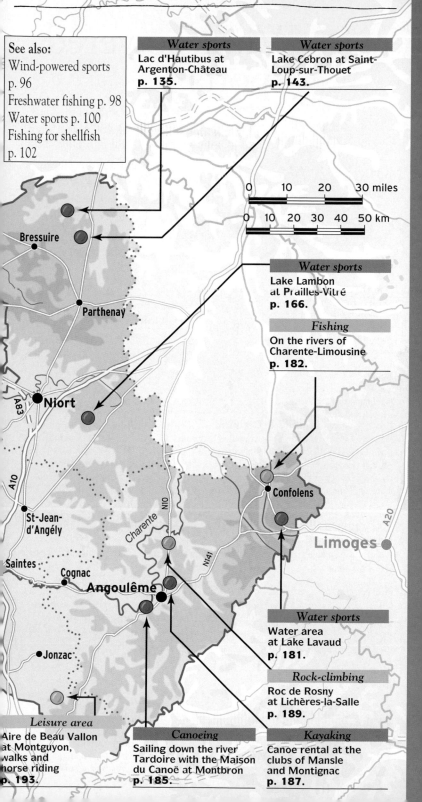

See also:
Wind-powered sports
p. 96
Freshwater fishing p. 98
Water sports p. 100
Fishing for shellfish
p. 102

Water sports
Lac d'Hautibus at
Argenton-Château
p. 135.

Water sports
Lake Cebron at Saint-
Loup-sur-Thouet
p. 143.

0   10   20   30 miles

0   10   20   30   40   50 km

Water sports
Lake Lambon
at Prailles-Vitré
p. 166.

Fishing
On the rivers of
Charente-Limousine
p. 182.

Bressuire

Parthenay

Niort

A83

A10

St-Jean-
d'Angély

Saintes

Cognac

Angoulême

Charente

N10

N141

Confolens

Limoges

A20

Jonzac

Water sports
Water area
at Lake Lavaud
p. 181.

Rock-climbing
Roc de Rosny
at Lichères-la-Salle
p. 189.

Leisure area
Aire de Beau Vallon
at Montguyon,
walks and
horse riding
p. 193.

Canoeing
Sailing down the river
Tardoire with the Maison
du Canoë at Montbron
p. 185.

Kayaking
Canoe rental at the
clubs of Mansle
and Montignac
p. 187.

Wind-powered sports

The vast coastal beaches south of the Loire lend themselves to a variety of wind sports that are available all year round. People from the Vendée even boast that they can compete with the delights of alpine skiing with their sand-karting and speed-sailing. Although windsurfing and surfing are practised wherever there is wind and water, sailing on land requires a special geography.

On the water

The best way to learn to **windsurf** is by taking a course, or you might find yourself easily discouraged. Using a beginner's board in a light wind, it will take around 3-4 hours to learn how to move. The biggest problem at first is balance, but you will soon start enjoying the sensation. However, beware of wind from the land that can push you right out to sea. The **fun-board** is lighter and more acrobatic and requires winds stronger than force 3 or 4. If you have already done some windsurfing, you will soon master the art. If not, it will probably take you at least a month.

On land

A **speed sail** resembles a windsurfing board on wheels. It's a great way of learning how to catch the wind before trying it out on the water. It's ideal for children who can usually pick it up in a few hours. If you use a small sail, you won't reach such a high speed, so if you do fall off it won't be as painful. **Sand-**karting is not for the faint hearted, because the recumbent position of the body, almost at ground level, accentuates the impression of speed. You'll find yourself moving pretty fast, so take a few lessons in order to avoid painful spills.

What about flying?

Kite-flying is a hobby enjoyed by people of all ages. It has evolved hugely from those coloured diamond-shapes that were so hard to get off the ground. Today's creations need to be handled by a professional and require both skill and strength if they are to be flown well, especially in a high wind. **Kite festivals** are great places to see a wide range of manoeuvres demonstrated. **Kite-karting** is a difficult and tricky sport. You sit on a go-kart, holding a kite and are

certain times of the day or in certain areas. The best resorts for sand-karting are Notre-Dame-de-Monts, Saint-Jean-de-Monts, Saint-Gilles-Croix-de-Vie, La Tranche-sur-Mer and La Faute-sur-Mer, which all have special facilities.

A bit of DIY

Kite-flying is more than a pastime, it's a serious sport. The specialist shops are generally owned by enthusiasts. Ask them for the addresses of associations or workshops that teach you how to make and repair kites yourself. Be sure to comply with the rules of the resort in order to prevent accidents (being hit with a kite is very painful), and note that kite-flying is often banned on the beaches after 11am.

dragged along by the wind. You will need to master the art of steering!

The equipment

Prices are high. A new surfboard or funboard costs at least €460. You could look for a second-hand board to start with (about €155). Alternatively, it's easy to rent one – all the beaches hire them for

around €15 to €25 for half a day. Speed-sail rental is comparable. Windsurfing boards cost at least €1,220 to buy new, but can be rented for between €23 and €30 for half a day. For water-sports wear a wetsuit and deck-shoes. Remember to protect your head from the sun and wear sunglasses to stop sand getting in your eyes.

Places to go

Windsurfing and fun-boarding can be done anywhere, but sand-karting and speed-sailing can only be practised on wide beaches of firm sand at low tide. Since these sports can be dangerous for bystanders, in summer many resorts only allow them to be practised at

Learning a sport

All these sports require a certain skill and an understanding of wind direction. Proper training will ensure success and stop you getting discouraged. All the sailing schools and water-sports centres offer a series of lessons. For details of each resort and more information call the **Fédération française de Voile**, ☎ 01 44 05 81 00.

Freshwater fishing
tickling trout and landing a pike

I f you enjoy fly-fishing or coarse-fishing, casting, using a spoon or other type of lure, you will find many waterways in the region which are suitable for angling. Your catch will include eels and frogs in the Poitou marshes, carp in the Bandiat and the Tardoire, pike in the Charente and trout in the Cherveux. However, you must obtain a licence, and angling in France is subject to very strict rules, so make sure you follow the guidelines.

Where to fish

France has strict regulations about where you can fish. To make your life easy, get information from the local angling federations. They will also supply you with a map of the waterways and their classification as category one or two waterways. (Charente-Maritime: La Rochelle, ☎ 05 46 44 11 18; Deux-Sèvres: Niort, ☎ 05 49 09 23 33; Charente: Le Gond-Pontouvre, ☎ 05 45 69 33 91; Vendée: La Roche-sur-Yon, ☎ 02 51 37 19 05.) Category one waterways are mainly stocked with **trout**, whereas those with a category two rating contain **coarse fish**. It is also important to realise that some rivers and lakes (including fishing rights) are privately owned. Get the owner's permission before you begin

The angler's code of honour

Lovers of trout, carp and pike will have to obtain a licence, known in France as a *carte de pêche*, before casting with a rod, or it will cost them dear. There are various types of licence. For serious enthusiasts, the *carte à taxe complète* (€49) will allow you to fish throughout the year in major and minor waterways. Most other anglers will be happy with a *carte vacances* (€23), valid for 15 days and giving the same fishing rights as the full card. For novice fishermen aged under 16, there's a special young person's card, the *carte jeune* (€11).

to fish or you may find yourself forfeiting your day's catch. In France all privately owned lakes and rivers are classed as category one, while most of the rivers in the public domain (the Sèvre Niortaise and Marans-La Rochelle canal, for example) as well as lakes and ponds are classified as category two. Fishing in reserves is strictly forbidden, with or without a card.

The right time

You are not allowed to fish earlier than half an hour before dawn and not at all after sunset. The exceptions are fishing for **eels**, which can be fished until midnight,

and for **carp**, which can be fished at any time at permitted spots. Fishing in category one waterways is usually allowed from the second Saturday in March to the third Sunday in September, but these dates may vary from year to year. In category two rivers, fishing with a rod is allowed all year round. Some species, such as pike, trout and frogs may be caught only until very specific dates.

What to fish for

As with fishing for shellfish, you must make sure that you do not catch anything below the minimum legal size. Whatever the size, you are not allowed to catch sturgeon, Atlantic salmon or sea-trout. For other species, the minimum legal size varies. If you catch a pike of less than 20 inches (50 cm)

or a trout smaller than 10 inches (25 cm), you must return it to the water, even if it is your only catch of the day! The number of rainbow trout, brown trout and freshwater salmon that you are allowed to take home

is generally fixed at six per day for each fisherman, but again, this number may vary from year to year, depending on a variety of factors. Make sure you find out the limits before you go angling.

THE BEST PLACES TO FISH

If you are looking for fresh **trout** and **eels**, the rivers around Niort and the Poitou marshes are full of them. If you fancy tackling a **catfish**, the rivers around Thouars are best. For trout, the tributaries of the Charentes (Izonne, Argentor, Péruse, Bief, Osme) are highly recommended. If you want to get the best from a fishing holiday, two ideal places for angling are the Tardoire and the Bandiat, which cross the southern Charente. These rivers are full of carp, tench, roach, bleak, gudgeon and trout. You will get the twin pleasures of great fishing and beautiful scenery.

Frog fishing in the marshes

Water sports

If you're one of those people who quickly gets bored with sunbathing, but love the sun and the excitement of watersports, why not try one of the many forms of surfing? The coastline boasts several excellent surfing beaches.

Reserved for enthusiasts

Surfing is one of the most exciting water sports, but also one of the most difficult. You will probably need to spend the whole of your first surfing summer practising, just to be able to stand up on the board,

keep your balance and ride the wave. It's best for beginnings to start with a **long-board.** This is longer than a standard surfboard and rounder at the tip, which makes it easier to balance. Whichever you choose, wear a wetsuit because you will end up spending many hours in the water.

A fun sport for all ages

You ride a **body-board** flat on your stomach or on your knees. This special board, made of firm foam, is shorter and wider than a surfboard. Lying flat on the board you swim out to the waves, then let yourself be carried back to the shore. You will be happily riding the waves after an hour or two. Even children can do it. Wear an old T-shirt to protect your stomach from

getting scratched. You must be able to swim before you try this, of course, and complex moves will require practice.

Body-surfing

Body-surfing requires no equipment at all, just a body! But it does require you to be an excellent swimmer. Body surfing consists of riding a wave and standing up at the very point that it breaks. Stand as far out as you can, and as the wave is about to break over your back, throw yourself into it on your stomach with your arms stretched straight out in front. Try this away from the shore and in waves that are not too huge.

Keeping your balance

Another new surfing technique is **skim-boarding**, using a board thinner than a surf-

SURFING IN STYLE

The surfing world is a close-knit community with its own rituals. There's a grapevine that informs everyone of the gossip, the best meeting-places and best bars, even if they tend to get a bit overcrowded. At Les Sables-d'Olonne, **Germaine's Bar** is worth a detour, while at La Tranche-sur-Mer, the **Bud House Café** in the Village des Conches is the place to be. On the Île d'Oléron the owner of **Diabolo Fun**, on the Plage des Huttes, will let you know where all the big rollers are and on the Île de Ré the **Bistrot Flottais** at La Flotte-sur-Mer is owned by a funboard champion and there's music playing every night.

The Bud House Café in the Village des Conches

board, on which you aquaplane by leaping on it at the sloping edge of a beach of fine sand. Be careful: this sport looks simple, but you could

easily fall. To make things easier, wax your skim-board with special surfing wax and always have both feet firmly planted on the board.

The equipment

Buying a surfboard can be very expensive, but you can rent one for €12 for half a day. Body-boards can be rented for between €5 and €8 for half a day. If you want to buy one, all the department stores sell models for beginners and children for around €27. Special body-surfing flippers are needed to manoeuvre, and if you don't wear them you'll end up just doggy-paddling.

Skim-boards cost almost the same price and can also be rented. If you are clever with your hands, you could make your own from plywood coated with water-resistant varnish, and then decorate it.

Where, when, how?

Some clubs organise courses that last between 2 and 4 hours a day. The **Fédération Française de Surf** will send addresses of schools and courses (☎ 05 58 43 55 88). The **Ocean Surf Report** line (☎ 08 36 68 13 60) will tell you about the wave conditions in the various spots. Real enthusiasts often exchange breaker information, and surf in summer and

winter. A good way of being in the know is to consult the 'regulars' who hang around in the surf shops.

The best spots

In general, these are all the places where the waves are well formed and start to break a long way out to sea. Many beaches are suitable for beginners as long as there are waves. There are several spots along the coast that are favourites with experienced surfers, namely La Sauzaie, Brétignolles-sur-Mer and La Tranche. Make sure that you know your limitations and avoid dangerous beaches, especially those with rocks just beneath the surface.

Fishing for shellfish
along the shore

O ne of the delights of holidaying in this region is catching and cooking your own fish. The long sandy beaches of the Poitou-Charentes coast and the ragged rocks along the rest of the coastline are rich in various types of shellfish; naturally they are best eaten fresh. As a precaution, always check to make sure there is no ban on fishing for shellfish.

For beginners
Take a fish-basket or even a potato sack to carry your catch. For shellfish you will also need a little sand-rake or a three-pronged gardening fork. If you're fishing for crabs, use a crab-hook or a metal rod with a hook at the end and wear thick gardening gloves. For shrimps, and prawns you'll need a shrimping net. Wear old trainers to protect your feet as you're climbing over the rocks.

When and where
The best season is from May to October, and the ideal time is when the tides are fullest. Fishing for shellfish is always done at low tide, so check the times of the high and low tides. Whatever you are fishing for, always go out as far possible to the water. Mussels, barnacles and winkles cling to the rocks, and you can pick out the ones that are still covered by the sea at the very edge of the

tide. Edible crabs, swimming-crabs and prawns also live in the rocks; shrimps, cockles, razor-shells and cockles can be picked up on the beaches.

On the rocks
Mussels attach themselves to the rocks by filaments, which you will have to pull out. Wash them carefully in seawater, rubbing them well. **Winkles** are easy for children to find, but don't let them pick the ones that have been uncovered for too long.

Barnacles and **limpets** cling firmly to most of the rocks along the coast, but can be detached with a knife.

Prawns swim around the rocks. Drag your net through 16-36 inches (40-100 cm) of water. Greyish in colour, they turn pink when cooked. **Edible crabs** and s**wimming crabs** also live in clefts in the rock. Put on your gloves and use your hook to detach

WHY NOT FLAMBÉ SOME SHRIMP?

Fry the shrimp in a non-stick pan in a little butter or oil over a high heat. Sprinkle them with chopped parsley, chives and garlic. Season with salt and pepper, and cook them until golden-brown and crunchy. Then sprinkle them with cognac and set it alight. This recipe is perfect for brown shrimps. You don't have to sort them, as they are eaten whole, except for the head.

them and put them in the bag. Swimming-crabs move very fast, so you will have to be quick!

On the sand

Shrimps like large, sandy beaches. Push the shrimping-net in front of you while you walk forward in the water up to your thighs. Cockles are abundant on the coast – look for places where there are lots of empty shells. Use a little rake to gather them, then rinse them thoroughly in fresh water to which you have added plenty of salt, and see them eject their sand. Razor-shells dig themselves into the sand vertically. They can be detected by the little almost-rectangular hole that appears in the wet sand at low tide. A pinch of salt will bring them up and then all you have to do is grab them. Cockles are rarer and dig themselves into the sand

to a depth of about 4 inches (10 cm). Pick them out with the fork or rake. To keep clam supplies plentiful, be careful to pick only the ones that are longer than about an inch (3 cm) or they won't be able to reach maturity and reproduce.

How to eat them

Never leave your catch out in the sun or in fresh water as it will lose its flavour. Scrape the shellfish and place in a casserole dish, cover with a lid and cook over a high heat. The heat makes them to open and they will cook in their own juices. If you want a more sophisticated flavour, add half a glass of white wine and a chopped onion to the bottom of the pot.

Crabs (10-15 minutes),

winkles (5 minutes) prawns and shrimps (2-3 minutes) should be thrown into well-salted boiling water or, best of all, filtered sea-water. Barnacles, limpets and cockles can be eaten raw, or stuffed and baked and served with a slice of buttered brown bread.

Poitou-Charentes and the Vendée in detail

Poitou-Charentes in detail

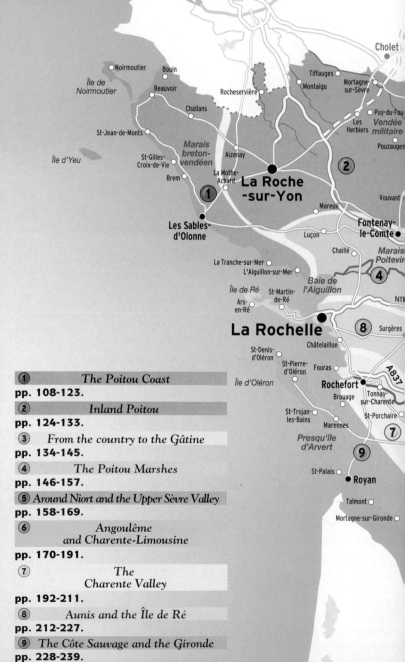

Noirmoutier
Bouin
Île de Noirmoutier
Beauvoir
Rocheservière
Cholet
Tiffauges
Montaigu
Mortagne-sur-Sèvre
Challans
Puy-du-Fou
Les Herbiers
Vendée militaire
St-Jean-de-Monts
Pouzauges
Île d'Yeu
St-Gilles-Croix-de-Vie
Marais breton-vendéen
Aizenay
Brem
La Mothe-Achard
La Roche-sur-Yon
Vouvant
Mareuil
Fontenay-le-Comte
Les Sables-d'Olonne
Luçon
Marais Poitevin
Chaillé
La Tranche-sur-Mer
L'Aiguillon-sur-Mer
Baie de l'Aiguillon
N11
Île de Ré
St-Martin-de-Ré
Ars-en-Ré
La Rochelle
Surgères
Châtelaillon
St-Denis-d'Oléron
St-Pierre-d'Oléron
Fouras
A837
Île d'Oléron
Rochefort
Tonnay-sur-Charente
Brouage
St-Porchaire
St-Trojan-les-Bains
Marennes
Presqu'île d'Arvert
St-Palais
Royan
Talmont
Mortagne-sur-Gironde

A11

● Angers

A28

A10

A85

Tours ●

Argenton-Château ○

Thouars ○

St-Jouin-de-Marne ○

(3)

● Bressuire

○ Airvault

St-Loup-Lamairé ○

On the following pages, you will
find details of the most interesting
places to visit in Poitou-Charentes.
For your convenience, these regions
have been divided into nine separate
zones. The colour code will help you
find the area you are looking for at a
glance.

Secondigny ○

● Parthenay

Est Gâtine

Ouest
Gâtine

● Poitiers

St-Maixent-l'École ○

Coulon ○

● Niort

A83

Celles ○

Melle ○

La Mothe-St-Héray ○

(5)

A10

Aulnay ○

Charente
limousine

Ruffec ○

Pays
Ruffecois

● Confolens

N10

Chabanais ○

● St-Jean-d'Angely

Chasseneuil-sur-Bonnière ○

Mansle ○

A20

Limoges ●

● Saintes

● Cognac

Jarnac ○

Champagne
charentaise

La Rochefoucauld ○

(6)

Ségonzac ○

Châteauneuf ○

Montbron ○

● Pons

(7)

Bârbezieux ○

● Angoulême

Vallée de
la Tardoire

Blanzac ○

Villebois-Lavalette ○

● Jonzac

Vallée de
la Seugne

Chalais ○

Aubeterre ○

Montguyon ○

N10

0	10	20	30 miles

0	10	20	30	40	50 km

A10

A89

Beauvoir and Bouin

and la baie de Bourgneuf

The northern end of the Breton marsh, around Beauvoir and Bouin, is protected from the sea by a system of dykes. The ditches are regulated by locks, and they open on to Bourgneuf Bay, forming little ports that are accessible at high tide. This part of the coastline is dedicated to oyster-farming. The sight of nets hanging out to dry along the canal banks gives the countryside a unique character. This part of the Vendée, from the Passage du Gois, the sea route to Noirmoutier, is off the beaten track, even for the French.

Swimming pool at the Hôtel-restaurant du Martinet

Eating in the village

In the distant past **Bouin** was an island, and it has retained the village plan of houses huddled around the church, which is worth a visit to see its altar screens. The village was exempt from taxes and thus became a haven for smugglers. Some of the smugglers' mansions can still be seen today. A delightful place to stop is the **Hôtel-restaurant du Martinet**, furnished with country furniture and run by a charming family. They gather, cook and serve delicious oysters, and their menu offers some of the best food you can

taste in the region. Telephone for details of opening times. (Place du Général-Charette. ☎ 02 51 49 08 94) Just outside the village the **Ferme-auberge du Jaunay** specialises in duck, eel and 'marsh lamb' (*agneau de présalé*). It features oak beams and a piano accompaniment. (☎ 02 51 49 12 11; all year round; booking required; also B&B).

Night excursions and champagne at the abbey

The **Benedictine abbey on the Île Chauvet**, at Bois-de-Céné, was founded on an islet in the 12th C. Its roofless ruins are surrounded by marshland (☎ 02 51 68 13 19, July-August, daily except Sat., 2-7pm). The nearby Pinta farm is the headquarters of **Pistes Nouvelles et Traces**

Anciennes (☎ 02 51 49 22
17), which offers night-time
canoe trips to the abbey with
dinner and champagne. This
would be a lovely way to
celebrate a special occasion.

Buying oysters in the port

The ports nestling in the
mouth of the drainage canals
look very similar. You'll find
mazes of pickets and wooden
pontoons on the mudflats,
beached rowing boats and
the special aroma of salt
and shellfish. Oyster-farmers
raise the famous Vendée-
Atlantique hollow oysters
here, and you can buy them
straight from the producer.
Bouin has four harbours: La
Louippe, Port des Brochets,

Port des Champs and **Port
du Bec** of Epoids. The last is
the most attractive, with a
forest of stakes, brightly
painted boats and a little café
near to the lock.

The Passage du Gois

The Passage du Gois is a
sea road to the island of
Noirmoutier, and is usable
only at low tide. A system of
refuge buoys, protecting
travellers taken unawares by
the rising tide, dates back to
the late 18th C. The road was
not paved until just before
World War II. Timetables for
the crossing are signposted
at each end of the island and
at Beauvoir. A running race,
the **Foulées du Gois**, is held
every year. The 'off' is given
at the last minute from
Noirmoutier as soon as the
water is ankle-deep. Runners
must cover the 2.6 miles
(4.2 km) in the water,
and beat the rising tide!
Exhausting even to watch!

Donkey rides

Visit the **Maison de l'Âne** at
Beauvoir-sur-Mer to meet the
Cadichon donkey, an animal
which is reared in this area.
You can go donkey trekking

through the marshes for a
day or more. Children, in
particular, love these patient
animals, with their gentle
eyes, hairy noses and large
ears. The donkey stud and
trekking centre is on the road
towards Gois (☎ 02 51 93 85
70, closed Tues. and Wed.).
See also p. 20, the Poitou
mule.

Spotcheck
A 1 - A 2

Things to do
• Rambling in the marshes
• Crossing the Passage
du Gois
• Buying oysters from the
port

Things to do with children
• Donkey rides at Beauvoir

Within easy reach
Noirmoutier (p. 110)
Saint-Jean-de-Monts
(p. 114)
Challans (p. 116)

Tourist Office
Beauvoir-sur-Mer:
☎ 02 51 68 71 13

WALKING ON THE MARSHES
Ask for the brochure entitled **Promenades du
Marais Insolite** (walking alone in the marshes)
from the Tourist Office in Beauvoir-sur-Mer.
You can choose between seven signposted routes
with commentary, ranging in length from 4-9
miles (7-14 km). Wear tough waterproof
footwear and bring binoculars. Routes 5 and 6
pass by the **Votive
Chapel of Bourdevert**,
a miniature chapel built
in gratitude by two ship-
wrecked sailors. Inside,
the moving display
includes a model of a
ship and a pair of
children's shoes left in
the chapel as votive
offerings.

Île de Noirmoutier
mimosa, roses and oyster beds

Despite the action of the sea, Noirmoutier has preserved its island character and old-world charm. The best time to visit the island, known for its mimosa and rambling roses, salt marshes and fishing boats, is out of season and by bicycle, when you can take your time discovering its secrets. Other attractions include shopping at Noirmoutier-en-l'Île, the farms of Le Vieil, fishing at L'Herbaudière, salt at Épine and oysters at La Guérinière.

Quays, boatyards and mudflats

Noirmoutier-en-l'Île is the 'capital' of the island. It has a **château** and pedestrianised streets. Walk down the quays on the south side. You can admire the skills of the ship-builders as they work in the boatyards. Visit the **maritime museum** which is housed in an old salt-boat to discover how boats are built. Then wander over to the mudflats and the boat cemetery. On the north shore, the Jacobsen jetty running out towards Fort Larron will take you to the salt marsh and **bird sanctuary**. The Banzeau district, facing the mudflats, is one of the oldest and most interesting parts of the town. Explore its narrow streets and little chapel; look out for an alley called the Venelle des Trois Ivrognes (three drunkards' passageway).

Bistro food

Just behind the château you'll find the self-service bistro **Iode**, which serves delicious local dishes in a

very friendly atmosphere. The landlord has also opened a shop that sells local foods and pretty pieces of bric-à-brac. (Rue du Vieil Hôpital ☎ 02 51 39 55 49; open Easter to 1 Nov.; closed on Mon. except July-Aug.)

La Chaize woods

The island's famous **mimosa** grows abundantly in this evergreen oak forest. Plan your visit in February when the trees are in flower and wander along the dirt roads lined with old rococo villas. The **Plage des Dames** still has wooden bathing huts from the early 20th C. where the ladies changed their clothes safe from prying eyes. In early August, for the past 200 years, the **Régates du Bois de la Chaize** has taken place featuring three days of tall ship racing and displays.

Under full sail

If you yearn for the days of wooden hulls, ropes of natural fibre, lovingly coiled, and heavy canvas sails, then climb aboard the tall ship *O'Abandonado*, built in 1916. There are trips along the coast, 2-day cruises to the

The Atelier des Fleurs at Le Vieil

Spotcheck
A 1

Île d'Yeu and 4-day cruises to Belle-Île, all of which offer you the opportunity to hoist the sails and man the tiller. For more information and reservations contact the **Association Le Galeao**, Noirmoutier-en-l'Île, ☎ 02 51 39 89 57.

A CRAZE FOR CURTAINS

Isabelle Gallois-Morin has two jobs. She not only works in the salt marshes, but is also a weaver. She makes little blue-and-white curtains to fit the windows of the island's houses. Next to the attic where she sells salt is her workshop and loom, and from here she sells beautiful woven cloth and lace items, including curtains and peasant head-dresses. **Le Nez à la Fenêtre**, Rue du Four-Commun, Le Vieil, ☎ 02 51 39 33 83.

A village film location

This is where the well-known French film, *César et Rosalie*, was shot. **Le Vieil** is incredibly quaint, with flower-decked streets and low houses with outside staircases, water pumps in the yards and low drystone walls. This is the village of the *patatous*, the famous potatoes of Noirmoutier. You'll find some delicious dishes in the village square at **Tantine Berthe** (☎ 02 51 35 83 96; open from Apr. to late Sept.).
As you leave the village, stop at the **Atelier des Fleurs**, where a young couple make up original bouquets of fresh and dried flowers, as well as arrangements of driftwood, shells and pebbles, and small items of furniture. (☎ 02 51 35 87 10; daily July-Aug.; telephone first out of season.)

Meeting the salt marsh workers

Noirmoutier salt has experienced a revival, thanks to the popularity of natural foods.

For centuries the silhouette of the salt marsh worker has been a familiar sight in the landscape of the Vendée coast

Things to do
- Take a trip on a sailing ship
- Visit a salt marsh and meet the salt marsh workers

Within easy reach
Bouin, Beauvoir (p. 108)
Saint-Jean-de-Monts (p. 114)
Île d'Yeu (p. 112)

Tourist Office
Noirmoutier:
☎ 02 51 39 80 71

Noirmoutier potatoes are unequalled in flavour

A quarter of the island is covered in salt marshes and a new generation of salt marsh workers has started harvesting the salt. From May to September, **Michel Gallois** (Route de L'Épine), organises visits daily at 6pm, except on Sundays (☎ 02 51 39 52 72).

Île d'Yeu
a hint of Greece and Brittany

When you arrive in the white painted village, you might almost think you had been transported to Greece, while the rocky coast and the gorse bushes will remind you of Brittany. The island, 6 miles (10 km) long and 2½ miles (4 km) wide, is like a different world from the mainland, with its semicircular harbour full of brightly coloured fishing-boats. But be warned – during the summer, it gets packed.

Walking on the quay

Port-Joinville is a very busy fishing port. Go and watch the morning fish auction, then pay a visit to the blue-and-white fishmongers **Chez Gaston**. The deep channels around the island form natural fishponds and more lobster is sold here than anywhere else in the Vendée. Wander along the harbour to look at the wonderful assortment of sailing ships and old rowing boats. The market sells local produce, water-colour paintings and weather vanes (a local speciality) in the shape of fish, mermaids and dolphins (daily mid-June to mid-Sept.; Sat. out of season). The village streets have pretty names, such as Rue des Fées (Fairy Street) Rue du Paradis (Paradise Street) and Rue Coin-du-Chat (Cat's Corner Street). In the Rue des Mariés note the little square lighthouse. Finally, you'll be ready to take a rest at one of the port's many cafés, such as **L'Abri** or **Chez Jeannette**.

The prison island

The **Fort de Pierre-Levée** in the upper town was built in the 19th C. to defend the island against the British, and it was used as a prison for Marshal Pétain. He is buried in the cemetery of Port-Joinville, his grave facing the mainland, unlike those of the

islanders. Pétain's wife stayed at the **Hôtel des Voyageurs**, and the owner has created a little memorial museum to the couple.

Cycling round the island

You could rent a bicycle at Port-Joinville and ride right round the island in 5½ hours. The seaward-facing coast is the most bracing, with paths running parallel to the sea. If it's windy it is best to go on foot. Adventurous people can

SOUVENIRS TO TAKE HOME

In the village of **Saint-Sauveur** the typical low houses are often decorated with unusual weather vanes. Visit Pierre Cadou's shop, **La Madrounia** (☎ 02 51 58 55 13). This former boat-builder makes all kinds of wooden objects, models, letter-boxes and decorative chests etc. These wooden souvenirs make great gifts to take home.

Spotcheck
A 2

Things to do

• Touring the island by bicycle
• Visiting the fish-market at Port-Joinville
• Souvenir shopping at Saint-Sauveur

Things to do with children

• The cave at the Anse des Soux

Within easy reach

Saint-Jean-de-Monts (p. 114)
Saint-Gilles (p. 118)
Brem-sur-Mer (p. 120)

Tourist Office

Île d'Yeu: ☎ 02 51 58 32 58

climb the 198 steps of the **Grand Phare** (lighthouse), 183 ft (56 m) high, which dominates the island. Its beams of light can be seen for nearly 95 miles (150 km). Visit the **Vieux Château**, a ghostly 11th-14th C. ruin, over which the English and French fought for centuries. The nearby **Plage des Sabias** makes a pleasant place to stop for a picnic.

Good sunbathing

You have a fine choice of coves along the south coast.

The **Anse des Soux** is sheltered and has a huge cave that is accessible at low tide. You'll find safe beaches wth clear shallow water at the **Grande Conche**, the **Ovaires** and **Ker Châlon**, near the camping ground.

A break at Port de la Meule

Port de la Meule is particularly beautiful. The white chapel on the cliff looks like one you might see on a Greek island. Little huts, painted with the

names of ships, line the harbour. One of the best and most enjoyable ways of staying in the vicinity is to take a room in a *chambre d'hôte*, where delicious meals made from local produce are often also provided.

All aboard!

There are three routes to the island, depending on the season. An adult return costs about €24. Whichever way you choose, you must book in summer. The easiest journey is from **Fromentine**. There are 2-6 sailings a day, all year round, depending on the tides. The crossing takes 35 minutes (fast motorboat) or 80 minutes (standard ferry). (☎ 02 51 49 59 69). From **Saint-Gilles-Croix-de-Vie**, in season, the crossing takes 90 minutes. **Compagnie des îles** (☎ 02 51 55 45 42) or **Vedettes Inter-îles Vendéennes** (☎ 02 51 54 15 15). From **Noirmoutier (Barbâtre)** in season (☎ 02 51 39 00 00).

Saint-Jean-de-Monts
marshes and sandy beaches

The Pays de Monts consists of more than 12½ miles (20 km) of fine sand and a pine forest planted on the dunes. Although the hinterland has suffered the effects of excessive urbanisation, the area of the Breton-Vendée marshes still offers scope for pleasant excursions. The beaches are very safe and provide all the activities that families enjoy.

Sand karting

Sand-karting is a relatively new sport, which is becoming increasingly popular. It requires huge stretches of flat sand, exactly like those found in the Monts district. This is really like windsurfing except that it takes place on land not

water, and the pilot lies almost horizontal to the ground, with the sail stretched above. The sensation is exhilarating. Adventurous children will love it. **Centre Nautique**, Avenue de L'Estacade, Saint-Jean-de-Monts. ☎ 02 51 58 00 75. Closed Dec. and Jan.

Notre-Dame-de-Monts
4 miles (7 km) NW of Saint-Jean-de-Monts
A walk in the forest
Maison de la Dune et de la Forêt, Avenue de l'Abbé Thibaud. ☎ 02 51 58 83 02

Daily 11am-1pm 8.30-10pm
Free admission.
The forest of the Monts covers 5600 acres (2280 ha) of sand dunes, though not all of the area is wooded. The ecosystem is fragile, and planting has been carried out to stop the movement of sand. The area is divided into three zones: the white dunes next to the beaches, the grey dunes that are covered with marram and couch grasses, and the forest. Signposted paths for walks and rambles or mountain-bike trails lead you through an environment that is both tranquil and wild.

Sea-kayaking
Les Alligators montois 20 Boulevard des Dunes, Notre-Dame-de-Monts
☎ **02 51 58 05 66**
All year round.

There is nothing like being out at sea to get a different perspective. After a short initiation course, you can spend the day sea-kayaking. Explore places of interest, such as Bourgneuf Bay, or sail around the island of Noirmoutier.

Fishing for shellfish
The **Pont d'Yeu**, south of Notre-Dame-de-Monts, is not a bridge but a rocky causeway leading into the sea. It is exposed for almost 2 miles (3 km) at low tide and is a great place for collecting shellfish, such as whelks, cockles and clams. Beware of getting caught by the tide, which comes in quickly here, leaving just a small sandbank surrounded by water.

Sea-kayaking is an exhilarating experience, especially for a beginner

La Barre-de-Monts
*7 miles (11 km) N
of Saint-Jean-de-Monts*
**An old-fashioned
farm**
Le Daviaud
☎ 02 51 68 57 03
1 May-30 Sept. 10am-
7pm, Sun. 2-7pm.
1 Feb.-15 Nov. 2-6pm
except Mon.
*Admission charge. For
reductions ask for* the
'passeport patrimoine'.

A KITE-FLYING
FESTIVAL
**If you're interested in
the world of kites
(***cerf-volants*** in French),
both kite-flying and
kite-making lessons
are offered at Saint-
Jean (L'Ouragan, 25
Esplanade de la Mer,
near the casino,
☎ 02 51 59 88 45).
The Festival Passion
Cerf-volant takes
place every year on
the weekend following
Ascension Day. For
two days there are
displays, team events,
workshops, and
competitions for the
most beautiful kite.
At Notre-Dame-de-
Monts, the Excès
d'z'ailes Association,
teaches all levels of
skill as well as showing
you how to build and
repair a kite (Michel
Boucard,** ☎ 02 51 58
21 72).

Le Daviaud is part of the
Écomusée de la Vendée. It is
typical of the old-fashioned

farms once common all over
the Breton marshes. In
addition to harvesting, salt-
collecting and building
bourrines (wattle-and-daub
buildings), there are special
events throughout the season,
including, dancing, music,
bread-baking and donkey rides.

**A swinging
summer**
Saint-Jean-de-Monts and
Notre-Dame-de-Monts have

Spotcheck
A 2

Things to do
• Sea-kayaking
• Fishing for shellfish on the
Pont d'Yeu
• Walking in the forest

Things to do
with children
• Learning to sand-kart
• Learning to fly a kite

Within easy reach
*Bouin, Beauvoir (p. 108)
Saint-Gilles (p. 118)
La Roche-sur-Yon (p. 124)*

Tourist Offices
Saint-Jean-de-Monts:
☎ 02 51 59 60 61
Notre-Dame-de-Monts:
☎ 02 51 58 84 97 or
02 51 68 51 83

joined up with Barbâtre,
Saint-Hilaire-de-Riez, Les
Sables-d'Olonne and La
Tranche-sur-Mer to create
the **Festival de la Déferlante**
(festival of the wave), which
features concerts, street
theatre and a variety of
unusual events. (Details
of the programmes at the
Tourist Offices of Saint-
Jean-de-Monts ☎ 02 51 59
60 61. Notre-Dame-de-Monts
☎ 02 51 58 84 97 or
68 51 83.)

Feeding time for the pigs at the Daviaud Écomusée

Challans
a market town

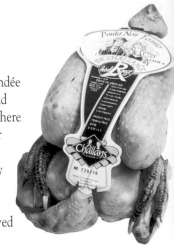

Challans, the capital of the Breton-Vendée marshes, is famous for its chickens and ducks. It is a market and fair town, where local producers and farmers come to sell their wares. On market days, the town is full of activity and noise, the cackling of the poultry and the crash of tools being unloaded. Clothing and shoes are also sold here. The proximity of so many seaside resorts has revived trade and industry in Challans.

An old-fashioned fair

The **Challans market**, held every Tuesday is a real treat, while the **Foire des Quatre Jeudis** (Four Thursdays' Fair) held in July and August, will take you back to the early days of the last century. All the locals attend and dress up in old-fashioned clothes. You'll find horse fairs, butter fairs, poultry fairs, the local hops and general festivities. You can end the day with dinner and trip to a funfair (information at the Tourist Office ☎ 02 51 93 19 75).

Sallertaine

5 miles (8 km) W of Challans
The spell of the chapel

The village of **Sallertaine**, with its narrow lanes and low houses, is typical of the marshes. Visit the 12th C. Romanesque church of Saint-Martin, which has an unusual ribbed cupola. The author, René Bazin, discovered the chapel while researching material for his novel *La Terre qui Meurt* (The Dying Earth), a story about the sufferings of a family thrown off their land) and did much to have it preserved. From June to September the chapel holds ethnographic exhibitions.

Visit a mill

The **Rairé Windmill**, near Sallertaine, was built in 1560, and has been a working mill ever since. The miller can tell you all about flour and wheat, and don't miss the wonderful view over the marshes from the top floor (☎ 02 51 35 51 82. Daily in summer. In the afternoon from April to Sept. Admission charge). If you want, you can approach it in an extremely unusual manner, by canoe. Take a 3½-hour trip with a guide, along canals and marsh ditches, right up to the mill. Reservations from Pinta, near the old church at Sallertaine. ☎ 02 51 68 27 84. Departures 9.30am and 2.30pm.

Soullans

4 miles (6 km) S of Challans
Jean Yole, a local painter from the Vendée

Le Bois-Durand, Soullans ☎ 02 51 35 03 84 Daily except Mon. July-Aug. 10am-12.30pm; 2.30-7pm. Apr.-Sept. 10am-noon and 2-6pm. Out of season telephone in advance. *Admission charge.*

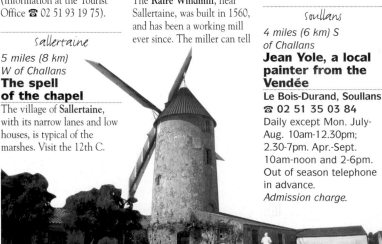

The little roads that lead to **Soullans**, south of Challans, wind through delightful countryside and are at their best in morning and evening. The **Musée Milcendeau-Jean Yole** is dedicated to this painter and writer who made Soullans famous. Two *bourrines* (wattle-and-daub cottages) house some of his paintings – the Moorish room decorated by the painter and photos of Jean Yole – in a beautiful setting.

Canoeing up the Vie

The Vie is a long, peaceful river that runs past pretty villages. An unusual way to see the countryside is by canoeing up the river. Meet at the Place de l'Église in Soullans for a 7-hour trip that takes you to the foot of the

Château d'Apremont along the shady banks. A picnic is provided. Wear hardwearing clothing and gloves to prevent blisters! Reservations from Pinta, ☎ 02 51 68 27 84.

Le Perrier
6 miles (10 km) SW of Challans
Boating on the marsh

From the village of Le Perrier, you can take a *yole*, the long, flat-bottomed boat of the marshes, the French version of a punt. The *yole* was once

the only way to get around this flatland, criss-crossed with canals. (Booking information ☎ 02 51 68 09 05. July-Aug., daily except on Sun.) On the second Sunday of August, if you attend the **Grands Jeux**

Spotcheck
B 2

Things to do
• Canoeing on the Vie
• Visit a mill
• Shopping for crafts at Sallertaine

Things to do with children
• Boating in a *yole* on the marshes

Within easy reach
Bouin-Beauvoir (p. 120)
Saint Jean de Monts (p. 114)
Saint-Gilles (p. 118)
La Roche-sur-Yon (p. 124)

Tourist Offices
Challans: ☎ 02 51 93 19 75
Soullans: ☎ 02 51 35 28 68

Maraichins (the Marsh Games) you will be able to see some unique skills being practised, such as throwing wooden sticks, *yole* races and many other watery sports that can only be played in the marshes.

THE CRAFTSMEN OF SALLERTAINE

The village of Sallertaine offers further proof that the art of the craftsman is being preserved in towns and villages all over France. The Île aux Artisans, covering the village and its surroundings, is open to visitors all summer. Local delicacies on offer include *confit de canard* and traditional pastries. Crafts include flower-arranging, marquetry, and weaving. You can also buy painted lampshades and goods made of leather, wood and glass.

Saint-Gilles-Croix-de-Vie
on the banks of the river

S aint-Gilles, situated on either side of the river Vie, combines sea-faring and farming traditions. It is the premier sardine fishing port in the Vendée and has become an important sailing centre, because it is the headquarters of the yacht-builder Bénéteau. You can explore the hinterland of the Breton marshland which is still a wilderness, and visit the nearby historic villages of Apremont and Commequiers.

Fishing the traditional way
Maison du Pêcheur,
22 Rue du Maroc,
Saint-Gilles
☎ **02 51 54 08 09**
July-Aug., daily except
Tues. and Sun. 2.30-
6.30pm. Out of season,
open by appointment.
Admission charge.
This fisherman's cottage dates from the 1920s and the period furniture and clothing show how tough life was for the

fishermen. To get an even better idea, take a trip to sea on a tall ship, *The Hope*, an old sardine boat built at Saint-Gilles, like so many others of the sardine fleet.

Walking along the clifftop
The **Corniche Vendéenne** runs along the cliffs from the Pointe de Grosse-Terre to Sion-sur-l'Océan, the only cliffs on this coast. The sea has carved caves and coves into the rocks, which have been given such evocative names as *Trou du Diable* (Devil's Hole) and *Chaos* etc. On windy days, the waves smash spectacularly against the rocks. Visit the **Forêt Domaniale de Sion** for a

beautiful forest walk. The French writer Julien Gracq spent a lot of time here and recalls it in his book *Les Carnets du grand chemin*.

Jazz and blues
Every Whit Sunday, the **Festival Saint-Jazz-sur-Vie** makes the port resound to the sounds of swing and gospel.

Jazz concerts take place in the bars, especially **Les Alizés** (at the port de plaisance ☎ 02 51 55 58 49), and there is live music every day during the festival. The **Festival de la Déferlante** is held at nearby coastal resorts. (For information ☎ 02 51 59 94 03).

Le Fenouiller

2½ miles (4 km) N of Saint-Gilles-Croix-de-Vie

A traditional rustic soirée

Enjoy a traditional evening of lively entertainment in the Vendée style combining a feast of local dishes with plenty to drink, and traditional music and dancing. You'll need lots of energy to keep up with the *rondes* and *bourrées* dances, a healthy appetite and a strong head for alcohol! **Le Pouct'on**, Le Pas-Opton, Le Fenouiller (for information ☎ 02 51 54 00 42).

Le Pissot

1¼ miles (2 km) N of Saint-Gilles

In the countryside

Visit the **Bourrine du Bois-Juquaud,** part of the Ecomusée du Marais Breton. This long, wattle-and-daub, thatched cottage is typical of the region. Its traditional

layout gives you an idea of how the marsh-dwellers lived. Reeds and mud were used to build the houses and thatch the roofs, whilst dung provided fuel, and the vegetable garden food. In the village of **Commequiers**, a little further inland, you'll find a handsome 15th C. château surrounded by a moat. At the village station, take the **vélo-rail**, a peculiar pedal-powered vehicle, along the railway track to Coëx (☎ 02 51 54 79 99, daily, July-Sept. 10am-7pm; admission charge). Finish your day with a visit to **Apremont**, with its handsome twin-towered Renaissance château standing beside the river Vie. A dip in the village lake should make a very pleasant end to the day.

Givrand

2 miles (3 km) S of Saint-Gilles

Where to eat

Ferme-auberge du Rocher, Chemin des Landes
All year round, except Mon. out of season
☎ 02 51 54 59 04
The Vendée is well known for its poultry. At the **Ferme-Auberge du Rocher** a husband and wife team, René and Marie-Claude Audéon, cook delicious local food including farmhouse specialities. *Confit de canard*, foie gras, *magrets* and other dishes can be eaten on the spot or bought to take away.

Spotcheck
A 2

Things to do

• Sea trip on an old fishing boat
• Walking along the cliffs
• A traditional soirée

Within easy reach

Saint-Jean-de-Monts (p. 114)
Ile d'Yeu (p. 112)
Brem-sur-Mer (p. 120)
La Roche-sur-Yon (p. 124)

Tourist Office

Saint-Gilles-Croix-de-Vie:
☎ **02 51 55 03 66**

A SOUVENIR OF THE SEA
Coëx
8 miles (13 km) E of Saint-Gilles
Gilles Corson is a distinguished local painter and craftsman. In his little workshop/studio he makes what he poetically calls *petits théâtres*. These are bas-relief pictures, mostly seascapes, featuring rolling surf, massive waves, lighthouses, storm-tossed yachts and so on. Corson enjoys showing his work to visitors, who can also purchase one of his pieces. La Boucherie, Coëx. ☎ 02 51 55 02 56. By appointment only.

Brem-sur-Mer
pottery and vineyards

The second largest vineyard of the Fiefs Vendéens, as the Vendée vineyards are called, is at Brem-sur-Mer. Brem also has other attractions. Situated between the forest and the Olonne marshes in the south and the surf beaches of Brétignolles in the north, you'll find many things to do here – wine tastings, walks in the forest, and visits to a potter's workshop and a garden of fragrances.

Wine tasting

The vineyard extends beyond Brem, to Brétignolles, the isle of Olonne, Olonne-sur-Mer, Landevieille and Vairé. Although Brem was once famous for white wine, two-thirds of the vines now produce red and rosé wines. At Brem **Jean-Pierre Richard** (5 Impasse Richelieu, ☎ 02 51 90 56 84) will welcome you to his ancient cellar. You can sit among the casks and sample his whites and rosés. On the island of Olonne, **Michon Père et Fils, Domaine Saint-Nicolas** should be visited for its light reds and rosés. (Tastings all year round, 11 Rue des Vallées, Brem, *chai* (wine cellar) open in summer, by appointment. La Croix Bégaud, ☎ 02 51 33 13 04.)

Visit to a pottery workshop
Atelier de Poterie-céramique La Corde, Brem-sur-Mer
☎ **02 51 90 50 77**
Daily in season, 9am-8pm; out of season, phone for opening hours. On leaving Brem for Les Sables-d'Olonne, take the road to the island of Olonne. This pottery, inspired by Japanese and Korean tech-

niques, is completely unlike anything you will see else-where. You can help to fire *raku* pottery and examine the Korean kiln. You'll get a good explanation of how pottery is made and there are pieces on sale to suit every purse.

Brétignolles-sur-Mer
Riding the waves
This is one of the favourite spots for experienced surfers in western France. **La Sauzaie**, at Brétignolles-sur-Mer, sees some awe-inspiring waves breaking onto the shore, easily reaching between 13 and 16 ft (4 and 5 m) in height. However as there are underwater rocks, it's not

recommended unless you're an expert surfer or body-boarder. Try the beaches of **Sauveterre** and **Aubraie**. The latter is safer at mid-tide, but beware of the mussel rocks.

Olonne-sur-Mer

Rambling and pony-trekking in the forest

The **Forest of Olonne** has a variety of trees and covers 6 miles (9 km) of dunes. Its paths are well signposted and if you're lucky you might see some deer, wild boar, red squirrels and many types of birds. The GR364 crosses the forest and marsh. The Tourist Office of Olonne (☎ 02 51 90 75 45, all year round) can suggest a range of hiking routes. The **Centre Équestre de Sauveterre** (Route de la Mer, Olonne-sur-Mer, ☎ 02 51 90 76 96) organises pony-trekking in the forest and on the beach.

Birdwatching in the marshes

Against the superb backdrop of the Olonne marshes, the volunteer guides of the **Observatoire des Oiseaux** (bird sanctuary) will lend you binoculars and help you to identify birds. You will also find a good range of souvenirs in the shop. (L'Ileau, L'Ile d'Olonne (D38) ☎ 02 51 33 12 97. July-Aug. 9.30am-noon 3-7pm. Free admission.) On the island of Olonne the **Rivoleau salt marsh**

(☎ 02 51 33 13 85) is the last from which salt is still extracted. If asked, André Raffin, a local salt-marsh worker and celebrity, will give you a guided tour.

The canals by rowing boat

For a 3-hour trip in a rowing boat through the canals of the marsh, accompanied by a guide who knows the area like the back of his hand, visit the **Ferme du Puy-Babin**, at Saint-Mathurin (information on the excursion plan, ☎ 02 51 22 74 11). It's great fun and you'll learn a lot about the local wildlife.

Spotcheck
B 2

Things to do
• Surfing at la Sauzaie
• Rambling in the forest

Things to do with children
• Pony-trekking through the forest

Within easy reach
Ile d'Yeu (p. 112)
Saint-Gilles (p. 118)
Les Sables-d'Olonne (p. 122)
La Roche-sur-Yon (p. 124)

Tourist Offices
Brem-sur-Mer:
☎ 02 51 90 92 33
Brétignolles-sur-Mer:
☎ 02 51 90 12 78
Olonne-sur-Mer:
☎ 02 51 90 75 45

LED BY THE NOSE

The **Olfactorium de Coëx** (8 miles (13 km) E of Saint-Gilles-Croix-de-Vie), is a new type of garden. The plants are classified by scent, so you're guided by your nose. As you walk around the garden see how many different scents you can identify. (☎ 02 51 55 53 41; June-Oct. daily. 10am-7pm. Admission charge.) At **Saint-Révérend** (between Coëx and Saint-Gilles), the **Roseraie de Vendée** has 8,000 rose bushes featuring more than 700 varieties in the most amazing colours. Amateur rose-growers can pick up useful tips, and anyone with a sweet tooth will love the rose petal jam, rose petal syrup and rose-flavoured liqueur. (☎ 02 51 55 24 03; 15 May-15 Oct., 9.30am-7pm. Admission charge but children free.)

Les Sables-d'Olonne
the largest seaside resort in the Vendée

Les Sables-d'Olonne is one the leading seaside resorts in the Vendée and has been fashionable since the 19th C. It boasts every kind of facility – beaches, shops, casinos and a zoo, to name but a few. It has important fishing and sailing connections – the four-yearly *Vendée Globe* race takes places every leap year – and the salt pans contain many interesting things to discover.

You will never look at the sea in the same way once you have seen the treasures it yields. This museum contains specimens from every ocean, from the smallest to largest. You'll discover a whole new universe of fabulous shells, corals and crustaceans.

A wealth of salt
Jardin des Salines
L'Aubraie-La-Chaume
☎ **02 51 90 87 74**
Mid-June to late Aug.
10am-noon 2.30-7pm.
Admission charge.
Salt was once the wealth of the Vendée and made the area prosperous long before the arrival of tourism. There is a display of traditional salt-working implements and reconstructions showing how the salt pans have been worked since the time of the Romans. You can rent a canoe to explore the Olonne salt marsh in deatail and spend the day paddling around the chequerboard of salt pans.

In the harbour
The **fishing port** is located in the old quarter. Wander along the quays and watch the fish auction, held when the trawlers return with their catch. Then take the Passeur shuttle to **La Chaume,** an area dominated by the **Arundel Tower,** a monument that has great symbolic importance for Les Sables d'Olonne. In this part of the port, you'll find the liveliest drinking dens, frequented by local fishermen.

Recognising shells
Muséum du Coquillage,
8 Rue du Mal-Leclerc
☎ **02 51 23 50 00**
The whole year round, except Sat., Sun. 9.30-noon, 2-7pm.
Admission charge.

Discovering contemporary art

**Musée de l'Abbaye
Sainte-Croix,
Rue de Verdun**
☎ 02 51 32 01 16
Daily except Mon. and
feast days. Oct.-mid-June
2.30-5.30pm. Mid-June
to Sept. 10am-noon
2.30-6.30pm. *Admission
charge (free on Sundays).*
This collection of contemporary art is one of the best
in France. **Gaston Chaissac,**
a champion of using recycled
materials, and **Victor
Brauner,** with his strange
imaginary compositions, are
the stars of the show, but
there are plenty of others.
The museum also has a
collection of local and maritime ethnography.

Local produce

If you like markets try the
halles centrales, a pretty
covered market selling food.
It has a very bright and
bustling atmosphere. (Daily
8am-1pm mid-June to mid-
Sept. Closed on Mon. out of
season). On the other hand,
if you are interested in more

unusual plants try **Potager
Extraordinaire** (literally –
'extraordinary kitchen garden')
situated on a headland of the
Route de La Roche. There
you can taste an assortment of
strange fruits and vegetables
(Les Mares, La Mothe
Achard, ☎ 02 51 46 67 83).
At Katiska not far away, they
rear goats which produce
milk, cheese and even angora

wool! Nothing is wasted.
(Katsika, Élevage de Chèvres,
Moulin du Puy-Gaudin, Le
Girouard, ☎ 02 51 46 61 79).

Vintage cars

**Musée de l'Automobile,
Route de Talmont
(5 miles/8 km from
Les Sables)**
☎ 02 51 22 05 81
Daily, 1 June-15 Sept,
9.30am-9pm; April-June

9.30am-noon, 2-6.30pm
Admission charge.
Many early models are
exhibited, including
prototypes; there are also
mopeds, bicycles and horse-
drawn carriages on display.

**Spotcheck
B 3**

Things to do

• Fishing at sea
• Visit to the vintage car
museum

Within easy reach

*Brem-sur-Mer (p. 120)
La Roche-sur-Yon
(p. 124)
Luçon (p.154)
The bay of Aiguillon
(p. 156)*

Tourist Office

Les Sables-d'Olonne:
☎ 02 51 96 85 85

GOING SEA FISHING

To be a real sea-fisherman for a day, take a trip
on the trawler *Kifanlo* (mid-March to mid-Oct.
Assoc. **Océam,** ☎ 02 51 32 03 28) or try casting
your line on board the *L'Aigue-marine* (Tues. Thurs.
Sat. 11 Apr.-30 June, 1-19 Sept. Daily, July-Aug.
7-11am, equipment provided. ☎ 02 51 21 31 43).
Fans of shellfish collecting and sea-angling should
try Eco Pêche (☎ 02 51 32 67 14) for **casting
lessons**. The same school offers **beachcombing
walks** along the Côte Sauvage. You'll learn to
identifiy seaweed, shellfish and crustaceans –
invaluable information for a successful catch! The
Association Sablaise des Pêcheurs du Bord de Mer
also offers courses for novices (Apr.-Nov. ASPBM
☎ 02 51 95 48 44).

La Roche-sur-Yon
would-be capital of the Vendée

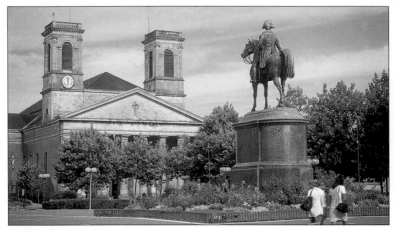

D ue to an accident of history, La Roche-sur-Yon never became the capital of the Vendée. Yet as the headquarters of the Republican army, it was ideally placed to keep a watchful eye on the rebel province. In 1804 Napoleon made it a *préfecture* and developed its neo-Classical, imperial style.

Strolling around town

The equestrian statue of Napoleon in the town centre sets the tone. The grid pattern layout and buildings in the minimalist style of the early 19th C. create an angular, modern city. Look out for the **church of Saint-Louis** and the conservatory of music facing each other across the main square. The old town clusters around the **Place de la Vieille-Horloge**; you may wish to stop at the **Maison des Métiers**, which exhibits

and sells local crafts (☎ 02 51 62 51 33. Tues.-Sat. 9.15am-noon, 2.15-6.30pm). Throughout the summer there are open-air concerts, as well as poetry readings, dancing and comedy, in the gardens of the town hall. **Les Cafés de l'Été**, information at the Tourist Office ☎ 02 51 36 00 85.

Horse riding at la Roche
Haras National, Boulevard des États-Unis
☎ **02 51 46 14 47**

July-Aug. daily 10.30am-noon 2-6pm except Sun. and holidays.
Admission charge.
Horses of every breed are reared here at this centre of national repute – Arab, Anglo-Arab, Connemara, etc. and you can even find the *Baudet de Poitou* (*see p. 20*). You can also visit the tackroom, farrier, forge and stables, all set in lovely grounds.

Shopping for crafts

If you're interested in model ships, visit Cristelle Picaud while you're in La Roche. She makes exquisite models of ships of every kind, including the *Pen Duick*, a tall ship and the Vendée tuna-boats. (☎ 02 51 37 60 14). **Monique Biron**, at **Poiré-sur-Vie**, is a weaver who will happily explain to you the source of her inspiration and how she works. The Vendée

Spotcheck
B 2

Things to do

• Shopping for crafts
• Taking a stroll around town

Things to do with children

• Horse-riding at la Roche
• Discover the transport museum

Within easy reach

Les Sables-d'Olonne (p. 122)
Pouzauges (p. 126)
Legacy of the Vendée wars (p. 128)
Luçon (p. 154)

Tourist Offices

La Mothe-Achard:
☎ 02 51 05 90 49
La Roche-sur-Yon:
☎ 02 51 36 00 85

was once famous for its weaving and you should be able to find some examples to take home as souvenirs. (**La Micherie**, 3 miles (5 km) W of Poiré, ☎ 02 51 31 85 68; all year round by appointment.) Pottery-making in the village of Nesmy dates back to the 13th C. This tradition continues to be maintained in a pleasantly cluttered work-

shop, producing **hand-painted pottery** in the old-fashioned way. **Poterie de Nesmy**, Rue Georges-Clemenceau, Nesmy; ☎ 02 51 07 62 57. Workshop: Mon.-Fri. 8.30am-noon, 1.30-5pm. Shop: Mon.-Sat. 10am-noon, 2-6.30pm, Sun. 2.30-6.30pm.

La Chaize-le-Vicomte
5 miles (8 km) E of La Roche-sur-Yon
Romanesque church

La Chaize-le-Vicomte has an interesting Romanesque church, the largest in the Vendée, with very imposing granite fortifications. Note in particular the dramatic examples of Romanesque art, with imaginative depictions of unusual creatures. Then visit the **Ferme Équestre de la Batardraie** at Fougeré (☎ 02 51 05 72 41) to spend a day pony-trekking in the forest.

Landeronde
7½ miles (12 km) W of La Roche-sur-Yon
Angels at your table

From the road to Les Sables-d'Olonne, take the left fork to Beaulieu-sous-la-Roche and

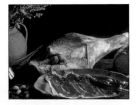

TRANSPORT MUSEUM

Musée La Roue Tourne
13 Rue de la Gare
La Mothe-Achard
11 miles (18 km) SW of La Roche-sur-Yon
☎ 02 51 94 79 16
Easter to 1 Nov., Sun. afternoon; July-Aug., daily, 2-7pm
Admission charge.
Every type of wheeled vehicle, from landaus to baby carriages, in wicker, leather and plastic, as well as an assortment of bicycles, can be found here. This unusual collection borders on a jumble sale in parts, but is delightfully original and idiosyncratic.

stop at Landeronde. The little **chapel** in the village contains a very charming and colourful painted altar screen. Beribboned angels encircle the Virgin as she rises heavenward, her veil flowing out behind her. The chapel is near **Beaulieu-sous-la-Roche**, where simple, inexpensive and delicious local dishes can be found at the **Café des Arts**. (Rue de la Poste, ☎ 02 51 98 24 80, daily except on Wed. evening and Thurs. evenings; menu from €8.)

Pouzauges

gypsy caravans and country lanes

Unlike the vast flatlands of the marshes, the hilly farmland of the interior, known as the *bocage*, is a patchwork of little fields and narrow country lanes. The roads rise and fall, and local customs and pastimes match the landscape. It was here, in this land of windmills and secluded châteaux, that opposition to the Revolution in the Vendée persisted the longest.

By gypsy caravan

A lovely way to explore the Poitou hinterland is by renting a gypsy caravan (for 5 or 6 people) and travelling at the pace of a horse. Ideal for the stressed-out townie! (**Les Roulottes du Sud Vendée**, La Réorthe, 85 210 Sainte-Hermine, ☎ 02 51 46 83 49.) Take a detour around Pouzauges, one of the castles of the legendary Bluebeard. Catherine de Thouars, his wife, lived in the château. However, today the town is famous for less a gruesome reason as it is the headquarters of Fleury-Michon, a major manufacturer of delicatessen products. When you are in Pouzauges-le-Vieux, visit the church of Notre-Dame, decorated with magnificent 13th C. frescoes, illustrating the childhood and youth of the Virgin.

Le Puy Crapaud
1½ miles (2.5 km)
E of Pouzauges
Dizzying heights
Not quite Everest, le **Puy Crapaud** is a mere 935 ft (285 m) high. As well as the wonderful view from the top, the place is remembered for the struggles that took place in the bitter Vendée wars. Take one of the signposted paths to the top, especially the abbey path, a 2½-hour hike. To choose one of the

43 listed walks in the area, buy a guide to the Pays de Pouzauges (€4 at the Tourist Office), and ask for the *Pass touristique du haut bocage*, which entitles you to a discount on admission charges.

La Flocellière
4 miles (7 km) N
of Pouzauges
Discovering country life
Maison de la Vie Rurale, Ferme de la Bernardière
☎ **02 51 57 77 14**
16 June-15 Sept.
10.30am-6.30pm; out of season 2.30-6.30pm
Admission charge (Tourist pass).
This little museum features artefacts from daily life and local traditions, as well as having farm produce on sale. The **Village de la Flocellière** has beautiful old houses and a château converted into a

Frescoes in the church of Notre-Dame

guest house. The castle keep and a tower is all that remains of the 12th C. building (rooms can be booked, ☎ 02 51 57 22 03). The rest was burned down by the Revolutionary armies who also massacred many of the villagers.

Saint-Michel-du-Mont-Mercure

4 miles (7 km) NW of Pouzauges
Visit a mill
Moulin des Justices
☎ 02 51 57 79 09
15 June-15 Sept. daily 10am-noon, 2-7pm. 15th March-15th Oct., weekends. Holidays 3-7pm. *Admission charge (Tourist pass).*

Visit the mill which harkens back to the traditions of the past, producing organic flour in the old-fashioned way. They also sell local produce and crêpes. The village of **Saint-Michel-du-Mont-Mercure** owes its name to the gilded archangel that tops the bell tower. Many sanctures dedicated to St Michael are built in high places and this one is right on the summit of the Vendée.

Spotcheck
C 2

Things to do
• Factory outlet shopping
• Climb the Puy Crapaud

Things to do with children
• Hand-made chocolate
• Gypsy caravan tours

Within easy reach
La Roche-sur-Yon (p. 124)
Legacy of the Vendée wars (p. 128)
Le Puy-du-Fou (p. 130)
Bressuire (p. 132)

Tourist Office
Les Herbiers:
☎ 02 51 92 92 92
Pouzauges:
☎ 02 51 91 82 46

Les Herbiers

12 miles (19 km) NW of Pouzauges
From windmills to chocolate
Les Herbiers is at the economic heart of the Vendée. There are a number of interesting places to visit, such as the windmills of **Mont des Alouettes,** to the north of the town and the **abbey of La Grainetière** to the south. Whilst in the town itself, plan a visit to the **Vendée Chocolat** (113 Rue Nationale, ☎ 02 51 66 94 34; tours in summer; admission charge) where you can see the chocolate being made and taste it of course.

SMART SHOPPING

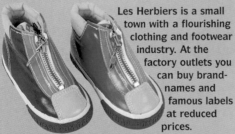

Les Herbiers is a small town with a flourishing clothing and footwear industry. At the factory outlets you can buy brand-names and famous labels at reduced prices.

• *Vecopri*, Z.I. de La Buzenière, Route de La Roche, Les Herbiers ☎ 02 51 66 91 00. Clothing for kids aged 3-16, including Naf Naf Enfant, Chevignon Kid, DKNY, Kenzo Jungle, Timberland.
• *Alain Manoukian*, Z.I. de La Buzenière, Route de La Roche, Les Herbiers ☎ 02 51 64 92 39. Daily except Sun. 10am-7pm. Alain Manoukian men's and women's clothing.
• *L'Entrepôt*, La Gaubretière ☎ 02 51 66 36 65 Daily 10am-noon, 2-7pm, except Sun. Children's and adults' shoes, including Pom d'Api, Free Lance, No Name, Spring Court, JB Rautereau.
• *France Mode*, Rue de l'Industrie, Les Epesses ☎ 02 51 57 45 88. Tues. to Fri. 2-6pm, Sat. 10am-12.30pm, 2-7pm. Women's shoes.

Legacy of the Vendée wars

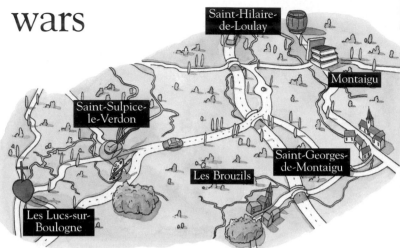

Saint-Hilaire-de-Loulay

Montaigu

Saint-Sulpice-le-Verdon

Saint-Georges-de-Montaigu

Les Brouzils

Les Lucs-sur-Boulogne

The civil wars have left their mark on the collective memory of Vendée, even after two centuries. The north of the province was the domain of the leader Charette, who was opposed to the Revolution, and the area has many memorials to this bitter period. Châteaux, churches and villages all have their painful history and reminders of this time.

Les Lucs-sur-Boulogne

In the footsteps of a massacre

Les Lucs-sur-Boulogne serves as a permanent reminder of Vendéen martyrdom.

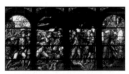

On 28 February 1794, 563 women, children and old men were locked in the church and massacred by Republican soldiers who were looking for Charette and his followers. The brightly coloured stained glass windows of the village church tell the story of this terrible chapter of Vendéen and French history, while the site of the massacre itself is marked by a chapel built in the 19th C.

Memorial to the dead

**Mémorial de Vendée,
Les Lucs-sur-Boulogne
☎ 02 51 42 81 00**
All year round, except
Jan.; daily, 9.30am-6pm
Free admission.
This austere, grey cube was built to commemorate the Vendéen massacres. It helps to trace the course of the uprising, its utterly ruthless suppression and what happened in the aftermath. The abstract forms and displays are quietly thought-provoking.

Saint-Sulpice-le-Verdon

9 miles (14.5 km)
SW of Montaigu

Charette, hero of the Vendée

**Logis de La Chabotterie
☎ 02 51 42 81 00**
All year round, except
Jan.; daily, 9.30am-6pm.
*Admission charge
(Tourist pass).*
This 15th-C. manor house is typical of the homes of the minor aristocracy. The interior has been furnished to look exactly as it did in

Charette's time. Everyday objects provide poignant reminders of another age. This is where he was arrested, and his jacket and hat have been left as a reminder. There is also a lovely formal garden.

A detour to Montaigu

Try to visit Montaigu in May when the **Printemps du Livre** is held. This literary festival is attended by local authors and fans of literature about the Vendée (information ☎ 02 51 46 45 45). Afterwards, treat yourself to a delicious butter brioche and eat it in the **Parc Rochette** a 27-acre (11 ha) which has a wonderful collection of exotic trees. While you are here, visit the **Musée du Nord Vendée**. (☎ 02 51 06 39 17; open 1 July-15 Sept., Sat., Sun. 10am-12.30pm, 2.30-6.30pm Wed, Fri. 2.30-6.30pm. Free admission.) A lovely pavillion near a medieval château contains exhibits about life in the northern Vendée.

Saint-Hilaire-de-Loulay
2 miles (3 km)
N of Montaigu
A local winery
Château de La Preuille
☎ 02 51 46 32 32
15 June-15 Sept.
9.30am-12.30pm, 2-6pm; 16 Sept.-14 June, closed Sun. and Mon.
Free admission.

Christian Dumortier welcomes visitors to the Château de La Preuille.

A glass of wine will help to restore any spirits saddened after learning about the wars of the Vendée. In the heart of a region with a long wine-making tradition, this feudal château has ancient cellars and a wine museum. It offers tastings and sells local wines.

Les Brouzils
7 miles (11 km)
S of Montaigu
Visit the refuges in the forest
Refuge de Grasla, Les Brouzils
☎ 02 51 42 95 67
16 June-15 Sept. 11am-1pm, 2-6pm Mid-Apr. to mid-June, 16-30 Sept, 2-6pm.
Admission charge (Tourist pass).

Whole families fled from the Revolutionary armies and took refuge in the woods, living in crude huts made of branches and mud. The Grasla forest concealed an entire community, with its own church and shops. A footpath leads through the forest to the Grasla refuge and to the Chevreulz oak, a rallying point for the rebel army.

LEARNING DECORATIVE CRAFTS

La Chabotterie, near Saint-Sulpice (11 miles (17.5 km) SW of Montaigu), is a craft centre where you can learn unusual skills, such as painting on china, manuscript illumination, tapestry making, French polishing, furniture decoration and making pot-pourri. You can also learn the secrets of traditional decoration techniques. In July and August youngsters can spend Wednesdays at the **Mercredis de La Chabotterie**, learning clay modelling, oil painting and marquetry, among other things. They take home what they have made. Information and booking ☎ 02 51 42 81 00.

Le Puy-du-Fou
bring history to life

I n the heart of the countryside, near Les Épesses, you will find one of the biggest theme parks in France. The whole history of the Vendée is explained in a brilliant *son et lumière* display. There are gigantic reconstructions, daytime events and a whole host of willing local participants whose aim it is to make this the greatest show in France.

Son et lumière show

Cinéscénie du Puy-du-Fou, Les Épesses
☎ 02 51 64 11 11
Early June to early Sept. Fri. and Sat. evening. *Admission charge (book in advance).*
This show lasts 1 hour 40 minutes and attracts 10,000 spectators each night. There are 800 actors, 50 knights, fountains, light displays and fireworks – it's all on a gigantic scale. The theme is everyday life for the peasant in the days of the Chouans, set against the background of an illuminated château. It's Hollywood-in-Vendée and an incredible sight. The seats are not under cover so you'll need to take a sweater and a waterproof.

18th-C. village

Le Grand Parcours, Le Puy-du-Fou
May: Sun. and public holidays 10am-7pm. 1 June to 13 Sept., daily 10am-7pm. *Admission charge.*

This themed museum features a fortress from the year 1000, an 18th-C. village and scenes from the time of the civil war. Volunteers dress in period costume and re-enact the ambushes. A complete village has been re-created, with people practising ancient occupations, including craftsmen, falconers, and musicians. There are even performances in the restaurants! Allow a whole day for your visit. Picnicking is not allowed, but you can leave the area to eat and be re-admitted later.

Vendée museum
Écomusée de Vendée,
Château du Puy-du-Fou
☎ 02 51 57 60 60
Daily except Mon.
1 Feb.-30 Apr. and
1 Oct-30 Dec.10am-
noon, 2-6pm; 1 May-
30 Sept. 10am-7pm
*Admission charge
(Tourist pass).*
This museum is solely
devoted to the history of
the Vendée, covering everything from prehistory to the
present day. It explains the
legacy of the Romans, the
Wars of Religion and the
civil war of the Vendée,
describing the effect that
these two conflicts have had
on the local character.

STORY-TELLING
IN THE WOODS

Promenades Contées,
APAHB, La
Chemillardière 85700
Saint-Mesmin (Booking
before 20 July
☎ 02 51 91 96 88,
reception at 7pm)
**Every year during the
last weekend in July, a
group of local people
organise an evening of
traditional entertain-
ment. It starts at the
farm with an apéritif
and a meal of local
food. As soon as
night falls, everyone
ventures out into the
woods where story-
tellers and actors
perform their tales.
On your return, you'll
be offered a reviving
snack of local brioche.**

Saint-Mars-la-Réorthe
*3 miles (5 km)
S of Les Épesses*
History depicted
in stained glass
windows
South of Les Epesses, the
little town of Saint-Mars-la
Réorthe has a church whose
stained-glass windows tell
its sad story. The town was a
stronghold of Catholicism

and so the Revolutionary
persecutions left their share
of martyrs. 20th-C. craftsmen
have depicted the tragic
episodes in the life of the
village in the stained glass
windows of the **church of
Saint-Mars**. After witnessing
the re-enactments at the *son
et lumière* show, you'll find
that these are more poignant
images of the Vendée's
suffering.

Chambretaud
*5 miles (7.5 km)
NW of Les Epesses*
The joys of
the countryside
**Ferme des Coûts,
Chantal and
Joseph Hérault**
☎02 51 91 51 44
Daily.
Free admission.
This husband and wife
team raise deer for
organic venison, their

Spotcheck
C 2

Things to do
• Attend the *son et lumière*
show
• Listen to stories in the
woods.

**Things to do
with children**
• Visit the 18th-C. village

Within easy reach
*La Roche-sur-Yon (p. 124)
Pouzauges (p. 126)
Tiffauges (p. 132)
Legacy of the Vendée wars
(p. 128)*

Tourist Office
Le Puy-du-Fou:
☎ 02 51 57 39 08

animals roaming freely
about the countryside.
You can also buy filling
local snacks here which are
enough to satisfy even the
heartiest appetite. The
village is celebrated in a local
folksong, *La mariée de
Chambretaud* (the bride of
Chambretaud), and there's
a small house containing a
simple but evocative display
of country wedding acces-
sories, such as wreaths,
starched coifs, bridal dresses
and tableware. (**Maison de
la Mariée**, Chambretaud,
June-Aug., open daily except
Mon. 9am-noon, 4-8pm.
Free admission.)

Around Tiffauges
little Switzerland

A fortress, an ogre and an underground river – the scene is set. Gilles de Rais was a fearsome slayer of the English and companion at arms to the heroine Joan of Arc, but he was also cruelly murdered hundreds of children. This now peaceful area has seen its share of blood-thirsty activities...

Haunted by terrible memories: the Château de Gilles de Rais

Bluebeard's castle
Château de Gilles de Rais, Tiffauges
☎ 02 51 65 70 51
July-Aug., daily, 11am-7pm; call out of season.
Admission charge (Tourist pass).
In this foreboding castle, once owned by the notorious Gilles de Rais, you'll find a display of medieval war machines and weaponry, and you can even try the cross-bows or the giant catapult for yourself. There are guided tours which tell the story of the hero-turned-villain Bluebeard, as well as an alchemists laboratory, where medieval sorcerers tried to turn base metal into gold.

Visit a model village
Village Vendéen Miniature, Rue du Moulin-Vieux, Tiffauges
☎ 02 41 30 22 25
July-Aug., daily 10am-noon and 2-7pm; telephone out of season.
Admission charge (Tourist pass).
15,000 working hours were devoted to creating this faithful miniature reconstruction of a village, using real stones and tiles. Even the tiny figures wear authentic costumes.

The amount of detail and artistry in this homage to Lilliput is quite outstanding.

Les Landes-Génusson
4 miles (6.5 km)
S of Tiffauges
Birds of passage
Cité des Oiseaux-étangs des Boucheries
☎ 02 51 91 72 25
1 May-15 Sept., daily 10am-noon and 2-7pm
Admission charge for the discovery centre (Tourist pass); free admission to the reserve and the observatories.
This bird reserve is on a migration route, and in autumn and winter is visited by 2,000 birds a day. The centre offers video shows and presentations. Free visits to the hides can be arranged by the curator on request.

FACTORY OUTLETS

Mortagne is only 6 miles (10 km) from Cholet, home to many clothing manufacturers and also factory outlets. On arrival, you will find the Club des Marques (Z. I. du Cormier) for Cacharel shoes and Lacoste and New Man clothing. To get to the centre, take the bypass towards Nantes and follow La Séguinière. You'll find many well-known designer labels, such as Catimini, IKKS, Jean Bourget, Levis, Wrangler, Diesel, Quicksilver – all styles for all ages. With over 10 shops to choose from you can buy a whole new wardrobe.

Mortagne-sur-Sèvre
11½ miles (18.5 km) SE of Tiffauges

The *Bocage* Express

**Train à Vapeur de Vendée, Gare de Mortagne-sur-Sèvre
☎ 02 51 63 02 01**
June, Sept. on Sun.; July-Aug., Wed. Fri. Sat.
Sun. departure 3.30pm return 5.30pm
Admission charge (Tourist pass).
This steam train travels 14 miles (22 km) crossing three valleys and many viaducts, stopping at Les Épesses to visit the station-museum. Obviously, this is not a trip across frontiers,

but romantics should book lunch or dinner in the buffet car to capture the true spirit of the Pullman trains and the mythical *Orient-Express*.

Exploring little Switzerland

The valley of the Sèvre Nantaise has given itself the name of Vendéen Switzerland. It's not a well-known area, even to the French. A succession of villages along wooded banks, make it a delightful place for walks or canoeing trips, including **Mortagne-sur-Sèvre** with its ancient streets, and **Saint-Laurent-sur-Sèvre,** a holy city with 36,000 churches and the Parc de La Barbinière. There's plenty of opportunity to explore the countryside around **Mallièvre**. You can get advice on rambling from the local tourist offices.

The River Sèvre

If you follow the Sèvre inland, you reach **La Vallée de Poupet** leisure centre. You can simply relax in the countryside, rent a kayak, go rock-climbing or pony-trekking (☎ 02 51 67 86 24). There's a camp site (☎ 02 51 92 31 45) and a

Spotcheck
C 1

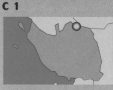

Things to do

- Shopping at factory outlets
- Taking the *Bocage* Express steam train
- Hiking in little Switzerland

Things to do with children

- Visit a model village.

Within easy reach

Pouzauges (p. 132)
Le Puy-du-Fou (p. 130)
Legacy of the Vendée wars (p. 128)

Tourist Office

Mortagne-sur-Sèvre:
☎ 02 51 65 11 32

gîte (☎ 02 51 92 38 29) for hikers. In July and August **Les Arts à la Campagne** festival offers live performances, including comedy (every Sun. 3.30-8pm; free for under-14s). In **Mallièvre**, at the **Maison de l'Eau** you can learn all about the river (☎ 02 51 65 33 99; 15 June-15 Sept; 10am-noon, 2-7pm daily; telephone out of season; admission charge, tourist pass). Spend some time afterwards in this pretty village and stop to visit a local weaver and see the numerous fountains.

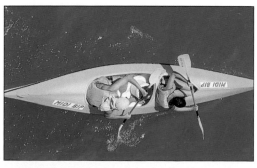

Bressuire
good grazing land

The Deux-Sèvres region, which suffered so badly in the wars of the Vendée, is famous for its beef cattle. They graze on the pastures of Bressuire, crossed by the Argent, Madoire and Argenton rivers. The river valleys are steep and rocky enough to attract rock-climbers and canoe enthusiasts.

Quality beef and the cattle market

The Bressuire grazing land is famous for the quality of its beef and the cattle-farmers win national prizes. The Bressuire fairground is the best place to see the Charolais and Maine-Anjou breeds of cattle, as well as red breeds of sheep from the western Vendée. Every Tuesday morning, at 7am, thousands of cattle are bought and sold here in a fascinating auction. Later in the day, the traditional market takes place in the town centre. The same cattle are resold, but this time they fetch retail prices.

Nueil-sur-Argent
8 miles (13 km)
NW of Bressuire
Parc de Tournelay
9250 Nueil-sur-Argent
☎ **05 49 65 61 13**

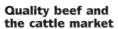

Open daily, 1 July-24 Aug., 2-6pm; out of season by appointment
Admission charge.
This 74-acre (30 ha) park, which dominates the surrounding countryside has many beauty spots and pleasant walks. It was first planted in 1860, with more than 20,000 trees enclosed by a wall 3 miles (5 km) long. You can walk beside banks of boxwood and lilac, through plantations of pine, poplar and oak, and stroll in the gardens which are laid out very formally in the French style.

Mauléon
12½ miles (20 km)
N of Bressuire
Musée de la Vie des Jouets
6 Rue du Château,
79700 Mauléon
☎ **05 49 81 64 12**
Open July-Aug., daily 10am-1pm and 2-7pm; Sept.-June, Wed.-Sat., 2-6pm and Sun., 2.30-7pm
Admission charge.
This unusual museum contains 5,000 toys from every period from 1830 to the present day. You will soon realise that the simplest of toys were once enough to keep children amused.

Jean-Luc Beau in the Musée de la Vie des Jouets (toy museum)

LAC D'HAUTIBUS

Argenton-Château
*10½ miles (17 km)
W of Thouars*
☎ 05 49 65 70 22
Open permanently.
Free admission.
This artificial lake was created out of the river Argenton, in a deep, wooded valley. The lake is a great place for a day out with the family.

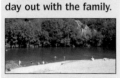

If you want to do something active, you can always rent a canoe, kayak, pedalo, or even a bobsleigh. It's an ideal spot for children. The beach has been converted into a play area with a paddling pool, as swimming is not permitted in the lake. There are also tennis courts and miniature golf links for the more sporty.

There are many traditional toys, including a tricycle, a hobby horse dating from 1830, fragile porcelain dolls, very different from modern Barbie dolls, a big wheel and a model of a big dipper (over 10 ft (3 m) by 7 ft (2.1 m) from the 1930s, complete with lifesize wooden figures.

Saint-Mesmin-la-Ville
12½ miles (20 km) W of Bressuire
Château de Saint-Mesmin-la-Ville
☎ 02 51 91 24 61
or 02 51 91 97 30

The 100 ft (30 m) castle keep of this 14th C. fortress is still well-preserved. The original complex consisted of seven towers of which only two now survive. They stand on either side of a gateway, protected by a portcullis and drawbridge, like any self-respecting medieval fortress. The castle keep, parapet walk, guard-room and kitchens are all open to visitors. There's an exhibition about the history of the castle which will transport you back to the time of gallant knights and their ladies.

Montravers
*9 miles (14 km)
W of Bressuire*
Château du Deffend
☎ 05 49 80 53 63
Open daily, 15 Aug.-30 Sept., 2-6.30pm.
Admission charge.
This castle was only built in 1869, making it much newer than the other châteaux in the region. As a result it is very well preserved. Standing

Spotcheck
D 2

Things to do

• Attend the cattle auction
• Take a walk in the Parc de Tournelay

Things to do with children

• Visit the Musée de la Vie de Jouets
• Canoeing, kayaking and pedalos on the Hautibus lake

Within easy reach

*Thouars (p. 136)
East Gâtine (p. 142)
Parthenay (p. 140)
Pouzauges (p. 126)*

Tourist Offices

Argenton-Château:
☎ 05 49 65 96 56
Bressuire:
☎ 05 49 65 10 27
Mauléon:
☎ 05 49 81 95 22

in 72 acres (30 ha) of beautiful grounds, it is built of granite, white Chauvigny stone, brick and slate. Inside, there are some impressive paintings illustrating some of La Fontaine's fables in the reception rooms, which have beautiful painted ceilings and fine panelling.

Thouars
proud of its military past

T houars, which stands on a promontory overlooking the river Touet, is an ancient medieval fortress, a handsome reminder of the area's military past. Wander through the picturesque lanes of old Thouars, taking in its Romanesque bridges and half-timbered houses, and stroll along the ramparts to the towers of the old fortifications.

A hilltop château

You can't miss this 17th C. château perched on a rocky spur. The façade is over 360 ft (110 m) long and the courtyard is surrounded by a porticoed gallery each side of which is 230 ft (70 m) in length. The home of the Dukes of La Trémoille, this is the largest and most handsome of the châteaux in the Deux-Sèvres département. The combination of white stone and slate is the work of Jacques Lemercier, one of the architects of the Louvre. Only students of the château's school are allowed inside, but the magnificent courtyard and orangery are open to visitors.

The 'iron maidens' in the Prince of Wales tower

Rue du Président-Tyndo
☎ 05 49 67 93 79
Open daily, except Tues., July-15 Sept., 10am-noon and 3-7pm; weekends in June, 3-7pm; out of season (Sept.-May) 3-7pm. *Free admission.*

This circular tower forms part of the ancient fortifications of the town, and was used to defend the gateway. In the 17th C. the tower was used as a prison for salt smugglers who refused to pay the *gabelle* (salt tax). They were kept in cages called *fillettes* (iron maidens), which you can see on the second floor. In 1880 they were used as accommodation for teachers!

A walk along the river

3 miles (5 km), lasting 1½ hours

If you walk along the left bank of the Thouet, you will get a wonderful view of the old city and the ramparts. From the Hôtel des Postes, the way down to Le Crevant leads to the river Thouet, which you can cross by a footbridge. Follow the shady path on the left along the river, before turning into a little road that runs up to **Saint-Jacques-de-Thouars**. A bridge takes you back over the Thouet. From here, the road leads you to the gardens and **fields of the Ursulines**.

LOCAL PRODUCE AND CRAFTS

Maison des Produits du Terroir
21 Avenue Victor-Hugo
☎ 05 49 66 68 68.
The skills of the craftsmen of Thouars and neighbouring district are on display here. Pride of place goes to **local foods**: foie gras, terrines and tasty dishes of every kind, vins de pays and A.O.C. wines – a treat for the tastebuds. There's also a wide range of pottery and wooden items. Don't be surprised if you end up with a shopping-basket full of souvenirs take home.

An imposing gateway

La Porte au Prévost
The town was vulnerable from the north and west, so the viscounts of Thouars built a massive wall with a deep moat in front of it. The Prévost gate-tower was the main entrance to the town and, in time of war, its best defence. It was built in the 12th and 13th C. and is flanked by two huge turrets

130 ft (40 m) high. Note the three openings in the vault over the gateway, from where defenders could throw down anything that came to hand – rocks, burning pitch, or melted lead – to ward off the attackers.

A museum for every taste

Musée Henri-Barré
7 Rue Marie-de-la-Tour-d'Auvergne
☎ 05 49 66 36 97

Open daily, July-Sept., except Tues., 3-7pm; May-June and Oct., at weekends, public holidays, 3-7pm; out of season by appointment (information at the museum or at the Tourist Office ☎ 05 49 66 17 65).
Admission charge.
This museum is located in a neo-Gothic house that once belonged to Henri Barré, a physician and avid collector. Everyone will find something to interest them here: French and foreign ceramics, paintings, Directoire and French Empire furniture, as well as peasant head-dresses and clothing from the time of the French Revolution.

Spotcheck
D 1

Things to do

• Buying local foods
• A walk beside the river Thouët

Within easy reach

Bressuire (p. 134)
Pouzauges (p. 126)
The Thouars district (p. 138)
East Gâtine (p. 142)

Tourist Office

Thouars.
☎ 05 49 66 17 65

Reliving life in old Thouars

La Cité Libre du Vieux Thouars is an organisation dedicated to reviving the traditions and folklore of this ancient city. It organises festivals and special events in which the participants take on various roles, such as *garde champêtre* (policeman), fireman etc. Every November the association holds a grand ball which is very 'belle époque' in spirit. Marriages are celebrated in 19th C. style, and in the autumn there are festivities to mark the grape harvest.

Medieval festivals organised by the Cité Libre du Vieux Thouars

Around Thouars
in Anjou and Poitou, châteaux, churches and regional wines

The Thouars district falls partly in the old province of Poitou and partly in Anjou, but it has refused to choose between the two different traditions. Here, red tiles combine with slate, and medieval fortresses with Renaissance châteaux. The wines are those of Anjou, the food is that of Poitou. A road that winds along the valley of the river Thouet leads to the plain and to charming little hilltop villages.

Oiron

**6 miles (10 km)
E of Thouars**
The château
☎ 05 49 96 51 25
Open daily, 15 April-30 Sept., 10.30am-6.30pm; 1 Oct.-14 April, 9.30am-12.30pm, 1.30-5.30pm. Closed on Mon. 1 Sept-31 May.
Admission charge.
The Château d'Oiron was started in the 16th C. and finished by the Marquise de Montespan, a favourite of Louis XIV. It has a long terrace overlooking vast formal gardens. The magnificent gallery, which is 180 ft (55 m) long, is decorated with 1,600 painted wooden panels and 14 paintings of country scenes. The more exotic Cabinet des Muses is decorated with frescoes of elephants, leopards, camels and fruit trees.

Contemporary art at the Château d'Oiron
Since June 1993 the Château d'Oiron has housed a collection of contemporary art inspired by the 16th and 17th C. 'cabinet of curiosities'. In the dining-room, you'll find dozens of plates, the work of Raoul Marek, depicting the profiles of famous people. Don't miss the brightly coloured geometric figures of Sol Le Witt or the portrait gallery, which houses many interesting photographs of generations of Oiron schoolchildren.

Bouillé-Loretz

**9 miles (15 km)
W of Thouars**
Quality wines
Vignoble des Coteaux du Thouet et de l'Argenton
This vineyard, covering the communes of Bouillé-Loretz, Bouillé-Saint-Paul, Cersay and Argenton-l'Église, produces Anjou

appellation wines. Wine-makers have joined forces at the **Maison des Vins de Bouillé-Loretz** to sell their products to the general public. Be sure to stop and sample a few of these mouth-watering local wines. The **Anjou Blanc Demi-sec**

MUSEUM
OF WINE-MAKING

**Maison des Vins
79290 Bouillé-Loretz
☎ 05 49 67 08 59**
Open daily,
except Monday,
10am-1pm and
2-7pm. Closed in Jan.
Admission charge.
The Ecomuseum of
Wine-making is well
worth a visit. There
are film shows which
explain the traditional
methods of making
corks such as those
made by Sabaté, as
well as glass bottles,
like the ones from
the factories at Arques
and Hartzviller.
All the steps that go
into wine-making are
covered –
working
in the
vineyards,
pruning,
harvest-
ing, dis-
tilling,
and stor-
ing in
barrels
to allow
the wine
to age.
Among
the equip-
ment on
display is a tractor
fitted with a cater-
pillar track dating
from the 1930s.
After your tour, you
can sample some of
the wines and buy
your favourites to take
home with you.

and **Anjou Rouge Gamay**
are highly recommended, as
is **Anjou Villages**, a superior
quality wine that can be
stored for up to 15 years –
if you have the patience!

*Saint-Jouin-de-
Marnes*

*10 miles (16 km)
SE of Thouars*
Abbey church
The abbey church of Saint-
Jouin-de-Marnes, perched on
a rock, dominates the plain
below. This ancient abbey
church is built in typical
Poitou Romanesque style.
It was founded in the 4th C,
then rebuilt in the 11th C.,
and is remarkable for the

richness of its Renaissance
façade. The stone vaulting
of the portal is carved with
plants, shells and masks in
scenes depicting the months
of the year. Look out for the
unusual ambulatory and its
connecting side-chapels.

Tourtenay

*6 miles (10 km) NE
of Thouars*
Underground
pigeon loft
☎ 05 49 67 77 09
Open 1 May-30 Sept.
*Admission charge, by
arrangement with
M. Pichot.*

Spotcheck
D 1

Things to do

• Taste the local wines at
the museum of wine making
• Visit an underground
pigeon loft

Within easy reach

*Bressuire (p. 134)
Thouars (p. 136)
Parthenay (p. 140)
East Gâtine (p. 142)*

Tourist Office

Thouars:
☎ 05 49 66 17 65

This pigeon loft is more than
1,000 years old and is unique
in France. It is part of a
gigantic underground city
complex carved out of the
rock, which served as a
shelter in times of trouble.
Instead of building a fortress
to protect their city, the local
people of Tourtenay dug
galleries, homes, stables and
sheep-pens out of the ground.
As many as 1,875 holes have
been cut into the tufa stone
(*boulins*) to house pigeons,
so pigeon fanciers should be
prepared to be impressed by
this very unusual loft.

*The extraordinary pigeon-loft
at Tourtenay*

Parthenay
a medieval, rural town

Parthenay is another fortified town on the banks of the Thouet. It benefited from being on the route to the shrine of St James of Compostela, and the wealth contributed to its coffers by the pilgrims. The Vau-Saint-Jacques district, with its half-timbered houses and streets so narrow that you can hardly see the sky, remains much as it did in medieval times.

A walk through the medieval town

The **bridge** and the **Saint-Jacques gate** are part of the triple ramparts that extend for nearly 2 miles (3 km). Flanked by 30 towers and numerous fortified gates, these massive ramparts made Parthenay completely impregnable in the 13th C. Access to the medieval citadel is through the **Porte de l'Horloge** (clock gate), a 15th-C. Gothic structure. Inside the enclosure, explore the churches of **Sainte-Croix** and **Notre-Dame-de-la-Couldre.** Continue to the esplanade, where the castle once stood,

although only two of its towers are left. From here there's a wonderful view of the Vau-Saint-Jacques district and the river Thouet.

In the footsteps of the pilgrims
Rue de la Vau-Saint-Jacques

This street is situated between the **Saint-Jacques gate** and the **citadel gate**. It consists of a remarkable row of half-timbered houses with corbels dating from the 14th and 15th C. These houses once contained shops, inns and workshops, and it's here that pilgrims on their way to the shrine of St James of Compostela stopped to rest

and refresh themselves. Amazingly, craftsmen still work here, practising traditional medieval crafts. There's a sculptor at no. 62 and an enameller at nos. 52 and 8. The 15th-C. Maison-Dieu, decorated with a black statue of the Virgin, is now the Tourist Office.

Georges-Turpin Municipal Museum

1 Rue de la Vau-Saint-Jacques
☎ **05 49 64 53 73**
Open daily, June-Sept., 10am-noon and 2.30-6.30pm except Tues. and Sat.-Sun. morning. Out of season, open daily, 10am-noon and 2-6pm, except Tues. and weekends.
Free admission.

The Saint-Jacques gate

A model of the town in the Musée Georges-Turpin

This museum traces the development and history of Parthenay since the late Middle Ages, explaining the importance of pilgrims on their way to the shrine of St James of Compostela for the economic development of the town. If history is not your thing, take a look at the delicate Parthenay ceramics produced in the late 19th C. The best known makes are Jouneau and Amirault.

The Parthenay festival of games
☎ 05 49 94 24 20.

In the first two weeks of July Parthenay becomes a huge playground and everyone is invited to take part in the festivities. All the streets are decorated with items associated with games of all sorts, from gambling and casino games to board games. Giant dice and playing cards adorn the streets and shop windows. Traditional games (including normal size building blocks) are available, as well as video games such as Tetris and Play Station. Hundreds of other games are also on offer, all of them free. For budding chess masters, Parthenay organises an international chess open tournament. Good luck!

Auvergne cooking
La Truffade,
14 Pl. du 11-Novembre.
☎ **05 49 64 02 26**
Open daily; out of season, closed Tues. evening and Wed.
Menus at €11, €17, €21 and €26.
La Truffade lovingly cultivates the Auvergne culinary tradition. This restaurant, with its plain decor and checked tablecloths, has some wonderful treats in store, such as *truffade*, a house speciality, made from potatoes and fresh Cantal cheese served with a choice of Auvergnat sausages, *tripou* (mutton tripe), preserved duck or the fine red meat of Parthenay. Traditional French cooking at its best.

THE CATTLE MARKET

Foirail de Bellevue
19 Rue Salvador-Allende
Guided tour of the market, Wed. morning at 7.30am.
☎ 05 49 94 30 61

For two centuries Parthenay and its surrounding district has been reputed for the quality of its local beef and mutton. Since the 18th C., the town has held one of the most important livestock markets in France, which is one of the 16 markets whose prices are used as national references. Hundreds of calves, cows, bulls, heifers, sheep and goats change hands – often in heated negotiations! In this market, a tap on the hand to seal a promise of sale is worth more than an official legal contract.

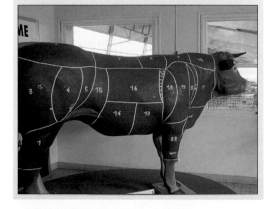

Spotcheck
D 2

Things to do
• Attending the cattle market
• Taking part in the Parthenay festival of games

Within easy reach
Bressuire (p. 134)
East Gâtine (p. 142)
West Gâtine (p. 144)
Saint-Maixent-l'École (p. 168)

Tourist Office
Parthenay:
☎ 05 49 64 24 24

East Gâtine
Voltaire's birthplace

Three rivers run through the Gâtine valley to the east of Parthenay – the Thouet, the Cébron and the Vonne – their courses lined with willows and poplars. Sheep grazing in the pastures are vital to the local economy. In fact, the town of Vasles is dedicated to sheep.

Lhoumois

9 miles (15 km) NE of Parthenay

Château de La Roche-Faton

Tour of the exterior, daily, 22 Aug.-30 Sept. and weekends Apr., May, June.
Free admission.

The Château de La Roche-Faton, standing on the right bank of the Thouet, dates back to the 12th C. It was burned down in 1417 and largely rebuilt in the 15th and 16th C. No expense was spared to make it one of the most pleasant and comfortable places to live. Open grounds replaced the fortified walls, and a formal garden was created. The château has eight impressive pepperpot towers, which are topped with conical roofs. It is one of the best preserved châteaux you'll see and is typical of the region.

Vasles

12 miles (19 km) SE of Parthenay

Wolves in the sheepfold

Mouton-Village
Rue de la Buté, 79340 Vasles
☎ 05 49 69 12 12
Open daily, 1 June-14 Sept., except Mon. morning, 10am-7pm; Apr.-31 May and 14 Sept.-30 Nov., 10am-6pm, Tue., Sat.-Sun. and holidays.
Admission charge.

Mouton-Village is a park combined with an open-air museum dedicated to teaching the history of sheep-rearing in France. The Jardin du Mouton contains 23 different breeds as well as wolves and goats. You can listen to a story about the origin of sheep accompanied by traditional music. The Maison du Mouton has an audio-visual presentation about farm life in the Gâtine valley and an exhibition about shearing, carding, combing and weaving. On the Sentier du Bélier (ram path) you'll find many examples of animals typical of this area.

Saint-Loup-Lamairé

9 miles (15 km) N of Parthenay

Château de Saint-Loup-sur-Thouet
☎ 05 49 64 81 73
Open 1 May-30 Sept., 2-7pm, Sat. Sun. and public holidays.
Admission charge.

This château was built in 1610 on the former site of a feudal fortress, of which only the castle keep remains. It consists of two short wings and a central building.

FESTIVAL OF WORLD MUSIC

Centre Socio-culturel, Airvault
13 miles (21 km) SE of Thouars
☎ **05 49 64 73 10** *Admission charge.*
Since 1992 Airvault has organised a festival of singing and dancing from all over the world. The performances, commencing at 9pm, are held in the open air at Airvault and elsewhere (look out for posters). Every continent is represented with displays of dance as well as instrumental and vocal concerts.

Unfortunately, the château is not open to visitors, but you can go as far as the courtyard to admire the façade. The formal gardens, parks and orangery were recently restored according to original 18th C. plans, and these are open to the public.

Swimming in lake Cébron

☎ **05 49 64 60 21**
This lake is part of the river Cébron, a tributary of the Thouet, and is the largest in the region. A visit to Cébron makes a great day out for the whole family. Watersport enthusiasts can try wind-

surfing, take out a pedalo, or simply go for a relaxing swim. The lake is surrounded by willows and poplars. Other facilities include a tennis court and miniature golf course. Angling is also permitted on the lake, so you could try your luck at catching something for the evening meal.

Airvault

13 miles (21 km) SE of Thouars
Voltaire's birthplace

This little village was the birthplace of the author Jean-Baptiste Arouet, better

Spotcheck
D 2 - E 2

Things to do

• Walking through Airvault, Voltaire's birthplace

Things to do with children

• Visit the wolves at the Mouton-Village park
• Swimming, windsurfing and pedalo on lake Cébron

Within easy reach

Parthenay (p. 140)
Bressuire (p. 134)
Thouars (p. 136)

Tourist Offices

Airvault: ☎ 05 49 70 84 03
Parthenay: ☎ 05 49 64 24 24
Saint-Loup-sur-Thouet:
☎ 05 49 64 82 45

known as Voltaire; his pen-name is based on a reversal of the two syllables of Airvault. This village is well worth a visit. An underground stream, the Ruisseau Saint-Pierre, runs beneath the Place du Minage and crosses the lower town. Narrow steps lead down from the Place to a vaulted chamber containing the well that once supplied all the commune's water. Look out for the church of Saint-Pierre with its half-buried porch. The **Musée des Arts et Traditions du Poitou** is housed in one of the abbey buildings. Visit the prison and see the huge basin in which the washing was done, the underground cells and the little chapel with a sculpted font. (☎ 05 49 70 84 07; open daily, 1 July-10 Sept., 2.30-6pm out of season, Sun.; and public holidays, 2-6pm.)

West Gâtine
from Niort to Parthenay, apple-growing country

Apple trees have grown wild in this part of the Gâtine, west of Parthenay, since the Middle Ages. The growing of apples, especially the Clocharde variety, ensured the economic development and reputation of west Gâtine. The Gâtine valley has three rivers – the Cébron, the Autize and the Thouet. Its damp climate is a foretaste of the nearby Poitou marshes.

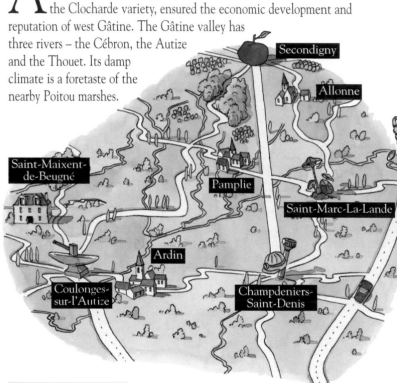

Secondigny

Allonne

Saint-Maixent-de-Beugné

Pamplie

Saint-Marc-La-Lande

Ardin

Coulonges-sur-l'Autize

Champdeniers-Saint-Denis

Champdeniers-Saint-Denis

13 miles (21 km) N of Niort
Following an underground river
La Grande Fontaine, ask for the keys at the Café du Paradis
☎ **05 49 25 68 99**
(booking advisable)
Free admission.
Borrow helmets from the Café du Paradis (€5 deposit), and make sure that you wear old clothes that you won't mind

getting wet or dirty. Take a torch and wear old shoes (not boots, which will be too heavy in the mud). To access the underground river, which was first discovered by children, follow the path behind the church, which leads to a cave with a ladder down to the water. The start of the walk is difficult for the first 45 yds (40 m) – you will have to walk hunched over and through the water, so you definitely risk getting wet feet – but the rest of this unguided mystery tour is perfectly safe.

Saint-Marc-la-Lande

16 miles (26 km) N of Niort
Hallucinogenic mushrooms
La Commanderie des Antonins
☎ **05 49 63 31 13**
Open Thurs.-Sun.
12 July-30 Sept. 2-7pm.
Out of season, by appointment
The chapel of Saint-Antoine, situated on the pilgrimage route to the shrine of St James of Compostela, is an ancient command post of the

order of the Knights of St John of Jerusalem. The knights treated pilgrims suffering from St Anthony's fire, a disease caused by a fungus called ergot, which grows on mouldy rye. The fungus caused hallucinations and even gangrene. The chapel has a lovely 16th C. façade. The other buildings of the *Commanderie* date from the 17th C.

Coulonges-sur-l'Autize

14 miles (22 km) NW of Niort
Traditional regional crafts
Musée de la Tonnellerie,
Rue du Minage
☎ 05 49 06 10 72
This cooperage museum displays the tools of the craft and shows the various stages in making the oak barrels for wine and cognac, as well as wheels for the drays, which were once horse drawn.
A reconstructed forge demonstrates how horseshoes and agricultural implements were made, and how iron bands were added to wheels.

Jazz beside the waters of the Gâtine
Information and booking at the Parthenay Tourist Office
☎ 05 49 64 24 24.
Each year, in the second week of July, the greatest names in jazz meet up in the Gâtine. Concerts take place at the Palais des Congrès in Parthenay or along the riverbanks in the other communes of the region. The festival is becoming increasingly successful thanks to the stars who turn up to perform, including Louis Sclavis, Aldo Romano and the American saxophonist Dave Liman. An inclusive ticket will give you unrestricted access to this jazz festival.

Saint-Maixent-de-Beugné

15 miles (24 km) NW of Niort
Château de la Roussière
☎ 05 49 06 12 11
Open daily by appointment, for groups of 10 people.
Admission charge.

Nothing remains of the original building, which was burned down in 1567, except the handsome gatehouse. The château was rebuilt in the 18th C. on the original foundations and has two storeys on the courtyard side and three facing the garden. The upper floor features triangular dormer windows, that look disproportionately large. It also boasts a lovely formal garden and a maze.

Spotcheck
D 2 - D 3

Things to do
• Eating apples at Secondigny
• The Gâtine jazz festival

Things to do with children
• Explore an underground river

Within easy reach
Parthenay (p. 140)
Saint-Maixent-l'École (p. 168)
Niort (p.158)

Tourist Offices
Parthenay:
☎ 05 49 64 24 24
Secondigny:
☎ 05 49 63 70 15
Coulonges:
☎ 05 49 06 10 72
Niort: ☎ 05 49 24 18 79

KING OF THE APPLE
E.A.R.L. Desnous, La Marchandière
9 miles (14 km) W of Parthenay Access by the D748 between Secondigny and Champdeniers
☎ 05 49 63 72 32

Open daily, Sept.-June, except Sun., 10am-6pm.
It's hard to say how many varieties of apple grow here. You'll find the famous Clocharde, the Gâtine's special apple, which costs 50-90 cents for 2¼ lb (1 kg), along with the acid green Granny Smith, the Idared and Elstar, sweet red apples and the classic Golden Delicious, Royal and Mondial Gala, which are also very sweet, plus many others. Monsieur Desnous will be happy to let you in on the secrets of growing beautiful apples.

The Poitou marshes
a well-preserved wetland landscape

The marsh is divided into two distinct areas. Begin your trip in the so-called 'drained' part, with its wide open spaces and golden light. Take a walk beside the canals and see the spectacular flights of migrating birds. The 'wet' part or flood plain is more lush and is best viewed from the water. You will discover villages full of character and a way of life that still remains very close to nature.

Chaillé-les-Marais

12½ miles (20 km) SW of Fontenay-le-Comte

An island in the marsh

The site of Chaillé-les-Marais was originally a limestone cliff. To the east you can look out over some of the

An eel trap

marshland which has been drained. Make sure you visit the canal des Cinq-Abbés, whose name commemorates the hard labours of the monks. A visit to the **Maison du Petit Poitou** will help you get to grips with the local way of life, costumes and occupations. You'll see farm animals here, including the strange breed of long-haired donkey known as *baudet du Poitou* (Chaillé-les-Marais, ☎ 02 51 56 77 30; April-Sept. 10am-6pm, except Sun. morning).

Roger Mercier in his vineyard on the family estate

Vix

7 miles (11 km) SW of Fontenay-le-Comte

Exploring a vineyard

Vix is the fourth of the vineyards known as Les Fiefs Vendéens. Although not very well known, the vineyard is of long standing and was mainly planted around the abbeys, since vine-growing was traditionally linked to the monastic life. Rabelais, the most famous of the wine-growing monks, spent time at nearby Maillezais. Today, the Mercier brothers run their family estate **La Chaignée**.

Sampling some of their reds and rosés will certainly add extra sunshine to your summer (in season ☎ 02 51 00 65 14; open 9am-noon, 1.30-8pm). After your visit take the D25 to the river Sèvre, crossing it and continuing along the opposite bank for a pleasant walk.

La Ronde
15½ miles (25 km) S of Fontenay-le-Comte

Camping in the marsh

If you are an adventurous type, rent a canoe for two days or more at La Ronde, and take a circular canoeing tour of the marsh. You will need to take camping gear and maps (**Bateaux Jacques Renaud**, ☎ 05 46 27 87 60; a canoe with camping gear can be rented for several days). This is the best way to enjoy sunset and sunrise over the canals and to view the wildlife, which is often disturbed during the day by groups of visitors making too much noise. If you scrape the bottom of the marsh with a barge pole you may see bubbles of gas caused by the rotting vegetation rising to the surface.

Regional specialities from the Maillezais honey farm: try the spring honey, the sunflower honey and the mixed flower honey

Maillezais
8 miles (13 km) SE of Fontenay-le-Comte

In the footsteps of the monks

Maillezais is the historic capital of the wet marsh. The **Romanesque abbey of Saint-Pierre**, beside the Jeune Autise river, was founded in the 10th C. by Guillaume Fier-à-Bras of Poitou. It is now in ruins, but it's clear that the monks knew how to live well. In the little port of **Maillezais**, nearby, eat at **La Grange aux Roseaux** and hire a rowing boat to admire the abbey from the river. The town has many beautiful houses, some of them built of carved stones pillaged from the abbey after the Revolution.

A basket of goodies

There are so many local food specialities that you will be spoiled for choice. Try the **farmhouse goat's cheese** and those with a sweet tooth will want to visit the **Miellerie de Maillezais** (☎ 02 51 87 26 25) to taste the honey. In addition to honey,

Spotcheck
C 3

Things to do

• Biking through the marshes
• Camping in the marsh
• Shopping for food and crafts in Coulon

Things to do with children

• Listen to a storytelling session
• Pony-trekking or caravanning on the marsh

Within easy reach

Fontenay-le-Comte (p. 150)
Niort (p. 158)
The Niort district (p. 162)
Luçon (p. 154)

Tourist Offices

Arçais: ☎ 05 49 35 43 44
Chaillé-les-Marais: ☎ 02 51 56 71 17
Fontenay-le-Comte: ☎ 02 51 69 44 99
Maillezais: (☎ 02 51 87 23 01

you can buy mead and hand-made beeswax candles. Try the brandy at the **Distillerie de la Venise Verte** (☎ 02 51 00 72 02) in the village of the same name. At nearby Liez, stop at **L'Arche aux Fruits** (☎ 02 51 00 76 82) where you can buy delicious jams, fruit preserves, syrups and herb jellies. In the summer, a craft fair and **folk market** is held at Liez on the second and fourth Saturdays of July and August.

THE ROLLS ROYCE OF THE MARSHES

The *platte* (which is pronounced 'piatte') is the Rolls Royce of the marshes, and enables the marsh-dweller to travel along the network of waterways. The 'big head', the widest part, is at the front and the oarsman stands at the back in the 'little head'. The *platte* can be used like a punt (the punting pole is known as a *pigouille*) or manned with a *palle* (a paddle). It takes a while to learn how to handle both these implements, and it can be difficult to keep the boat straight at first.

Horseback or gypsy caravan

Those who prefer dry land can choose pony-trekking through the marsh. The equestrian centre **L'Ecurie du Marais** at Sainte-Christine is a great place for horse-lovers. Accommodation is available at the camp site or a gîte, so there is something for every budget. The centre will help you choose treks and trails. On the farm itself you can fish and take boating trips (booking on ☎ 02 51 52 98 38). If you have always wanted to find out what it was like to ride

Poitevin, information at the Mairie de Damvix, ☎ 02 51 87 14 20.

in a **gypsy caravan**, this is your chance. This is an ecologically friendly way to see the country. The caravans sleep four or five. **Roulottes du Marais**

Angling in the marshes

With so much water around, it's hard to resist the call of the fishing-rod. The locals have some ingenious systems for getting rid of pondweed. Like them, enjoy sitting under a sunshade and watching for that tug on your line. Carp, bream and pike can be caught by the seasoned angler, but it's not easy for children. Eels can also be caught if you use a traditional wicker trap. You can buy tackle and the compulsory fishing licence at **La Pêcherie de Damvix** (M. Damour, ☎ 02 51 87 11 69) and **L'Aquarium** (8 Place de l'Église, Coulon, ☎ 05 49 35 90 31).

Cycling by the water

The **Damvix** and **Arçais** region is particularly suitable for biking. The route between the two villages runs beside the canal lined with anglers and marsh cottages. The best routes are those on this side of the marsh. Buy an IGN map for hiking, rambling or cycling at the local Tourist Office. For bicycle rental, try **Garage Dugué**, at Damvix (☎ 02 51 87 13 09) or **La Bicyclette Verte** at Arçais (☎ 05 49 35 42 56). Open all year round.

Picturesque marshland villages

Arçais is a good example of a typical marsh village. It has picturesque cottages and a little port. Stroll along the lanes and visit the craftsmen, then take the **towpath**, close to the château, and visit the old district of **La Garenne**. From the top of the slope you will get a view of the wild marshland. Follow the road to **Le Vanneau**, a pretty village with lush greenery, and cross the iron footbridge

préfou (garlic bread), grilled eels as well as wicker baskets and eel traps. Don't miss the craft shops, especially **La Grange à Camille** where local handiwork is displayed.

Life in the marshlands

Eight houses in various parts of the region contain displays of various aspects of marsh life. The **Maison des Marais Mouillés** (Wet Marshes House) at Coulon illustrates the history, landscapes and traditions of the marsh. All the activities are explained, including fishing and angling techniques, livestock management and the cultivation of

to the allotments. Finally, visit **La Garette**, a picturesque hamlet with crooked cottages situated beside the banks of the Vieille Sèvre.

poplar trees (daily except Mon., Feb.-Nov., ☎ 05 49 35 81 04). If you take the towpath along the Sèvre to Irleau, you'll pass the **Embarcadère aux Volets Bleus** (embarkation point with the blue shutters), one of the picture postcard views of the marsh. This may well tempt you to hire a rowing-boat and go for a trip on the water (☎ 05 49 35 93 66).

Coulon
7 miles (11 km) W of Niort

At the market

Coulon, beside the Sèvre, is the busiest and most central of the villages. In summer you may even find some traffic jams. Set aside a Friday or Sunday morning to visit the market. Wares include goat's cheese cheesecake, jams, angelica liqueur, herb jellies,

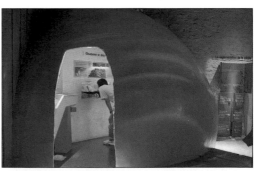

The eel room in the Maison des Marais Mouillés

Fontenay-le-Comte
gateway to the Poitou marshes

Fontenay-le-Comte lies midway between the Poitou marshes and the forest of Mervent. Its hour of glory was during the Renaissance, when the city was favoured by intellectuals such as Rabelais, the mathematician Viète and others. The city has retained its beautiful architecture, with houses of golden stone, and a particularly relaxed pace of life.

Strolling in the old town

Visit the town on Saturday – market day. You'll find signposts to the most attractive houses and you can look out for the sculpted balconies, windows and half-timbering in the Place Belliard, Rue des Loges and in the old lanes. The church of Notre-Dame is worth a visit for its Romanesque crypt and for the fine view of the town from the top of its tower. Make sure you see the Fontaine des Quatre-Tias (fountain) and the Parc Baron. In June there is a festival of nomadic, mainly gypsy, music called **Nuits Gitanes et d'Ailleurs**. Throughout the summer **Les Ricochets** has street theatre, and in the Parc Baron the **Festival des Histoires d'Été**, holds evenings of storytelling. (Information at the Tourist Office ☎ 02 51 69 44 99.)

Learning about the Vendée
Musée Vendéen, next to the church.
☎ 02 51 69 31 31
In season Tues.-Sun. 10am-noon, 2-6pm. Out of season Wed.-Sun. 2-6pm.
Admission charge.
The museum houses a collection of ancient artefacts discovered during local archaeological digs. Furniture, clothing, and jewellery can often tell us more about how our ancestors lived than any book. The best painters of the Vendée are also well represented here, and a display shows what the town was like during the Renaissance.

Antique glass at the Musée Vendéen

Renaissance château
Château de Terre-Neuve
☎ 02 51 69 17 75 or 02 51 69 99 41
Daily 1 May-30 Sept.
Admission charge.

This elegant Renaissance château lies on the edge of the town. It was built by the poet Nicolas Rapin and gives you some idea of how the intelligentsia lived during this period. It contains beautiful furniture, carved ceilings, doors bearing the coat of arms

FIEF VENDÉEN WINES

Pissotte

(4 km) N of Fontenay-le-Comte

To the north of Fontenay you'll find the so-called Fiefs Vendéens vineyards that make Pissotte wine. Visit Xavier Coirier in the village: you can sample and buy wine from his delightful garden (25 Rue des Gélinières, Pissotte; ☎ 02 51 69 34 19). Further up the street is the Crêperie Le Pommier, owned by Xavier's brother. The generously sized crêpes have imaginative fillings and can be washed down with the family wines (9 Rue des Gélinières, ☎ 02 51 69 08 06; closed Sun. afternoon and Mon.). To end the day take a look at the painted furniture at the Atelier du Pommier (☎ 02 51 69 08 06; open in the afternoon).

of François I and collections of artefacts that bring to life the great minds who stayed here, including Sully, Agrippa d'Aubigné, Viète, Simenon and Queneau.

Learning to play croquet

Croquet is a civilised and sedate game played on a smooth lawn. Extremely popular in the late 19th C., it is played by knocking balls through a series of hoops, using a mallet. All the family can play and the equipment is on sale at many shops. The game is very popular at Fontenay-le-Comte, where the world croquet championship is held. **Fédération Française de Croquet**, events and instruction ☎ 02 51 69 70 58.

Nieul-sur-l'Autise

7 miles (11 km) SE of Fontenay-le-Comte

The abbey church

This village is worth a visit to look at the **Royal Abbey of Saint-Vincent**. (☎ 02 51 52 49 03; daily 9am-noon, 2-6pm; July-Aug. 9.30am-7.30pm; admission charge). Look out for the Romanesque façade of the church, its sloping pillars and in particular the four-galleried cloister surrounding a little garden. In summer the church holds **Les Rencontres Imaginaires**, a night-time performance based on the story of Eleanor of Aquitaine. In the village pay a visit to the **Maison de la Meunerie**, a water-mill that still produces flour and the **Atelier du Sabotier**, a clog-maker. (☎ 02 51 52 47 43; 1 June-30 Sept., daily 10am-noon, 2-7pm; Easter holidays; Wednesdays and weekends, 1 May-15 Oct, 2-6pm;

Things to do

- Visit the Pissotte wine cellars
- Stroll through the old town

Things to do with children

- Play a game of croquet

Within easy reach

Marais Poitevin (p. 146)
West Gâtine (p. 144)
The Forest of Mervent (p. 152)
Luçon (p. 154)

Tourist Office

Fontenay-le-Comte:
☎ 02 51 69 44 99

admission charge). You can also learn how to make wickerwork and buy some wicker souvenirs at **Atelier du Vannier** (7 Rue Aliénor-d'Aquitaine. ☎ 02 51 52 49 56).

Crafts at Nieul-sur-l'Autise

The forest of Mervent
a nature lover's paradise

This is a land of story-telling and fairytales. This vast, mixed forest covers 12,360 acres (5000 ha) near Fontenay-le-Comte, and is a nature-lover's paradise. You'll find cliffs, escarpments, lakes and rivers to explore in this area.

Fun in the forest
Mervent is your starting point for visiting the forest. Make sure you get a map of the forest paths from the Tourist Office. All the footpaths are marked and signposted. From the château, head for the viewing site at the lake. Then stop at the **Maison des Amis de la Forêt** (Rte La Bironnière, Mervent ☎ 02 51 00 00 87; daily 1 Apr.-30 Oct., except Sat. and Sun.

morning; admission charge) to watch videos about the animals, wild mushrooms and crafts of the forest. There's a play area for children and access to fishing. Not far away, the **Parc de Pierre Brune** offers attractions for children of all ages, with more than 60 games and roundabouts, bumper boats, mini-golf and tennis (☎ 02 51 00 20 18; daily from Easter to 1 Nov., 10am-7pm; admission charge)

The Mervent water-sports centre

Sporting activities
Active visitors can enjoy exploring the forest on a mountain-bike. (**Centre VTT La Girouette**, Vouvant, rental and routes, ☎ 02 51 50 10 60). Bruno Ripaud, at **La Ferme Equestre de La Garrelière**, offers excursions on mountain-bike or horse-back as well as riding lessons on the farm (Saint-Maurice-des-Noues, north of the forest, ☎ 02 51 00 81 55). A popular rock-climbing site is the escarpment at the **Pierre Blanche** (Mervent, ☎ 06 08 71 87 64, levels 4 to 7). All the lakes in the forest are suitable for water-sports, from swimming to angling from a boat. You can also hire pedalos and canoes to cruise along the wooded banks (**Base Nautique de**

Mervent, ☎ 02 51 00 22 13, dinghy, canoe and kayak rental; teaching for individuals and groups).

Watching forest animals

There are several places to visit to watch animals. The **Parc Zoologique de Mervent**

in the heart of the forest contains more than 350 species from all over the world, including monkeys, deer and large mammals. The neighbouring **Centre Équestre** offers pony-trekking. The **Parc Animalier de Pagnolle** (Saint-Michel-le-Cloucq ☎ 02 51 69 02 55; daily 1 Apr.-30 Oct., 9am-dusk; admission charge) has more than 180 species of birds and many animals, some of which are quite tame.

A MEDIEVAL VILLAGE
Vouvant
5 miles (8 km) N of Mervent

Vouvant has all the ingredients of a picture postcard village: medieval ramparts, the Mélusine Tower, cobbled lanes, pretty houses, and several craft shops. The church is a classic example of Poitou Romanesque, with an impressive sculpted portal. At the **Maison de Mélusine** hear the story of the forest fairy who seduced the lord of the manor (Place du Bail, 02 51 00 86 80, daily 15 June-15 Sept., 10am-noon, 3-6pm, out of season from Mon. to Sat., 2-5pm). At the end of July and early August, the **Festival des Contes et Légendes d'Europe** is held: a festival of folk stories and legends, with street theatre and evening performances.

Foussais-Payré
3 miles (5 km) E of Mervent
An historic inn

Foussais-Payré, a village east of the forest, has a covered market and half-timbered Renaissance houses, one of which was the home of the mathematician François Viète. This 14th C. posthouse is now the Auberge Sainte-Catherine (☎ 02 51 51 43 13; closed on Tues., from €12). The church portal is rather like a medieval cartoon strip carved in wood, part horror story, part Gospel. In the forest, visit the

Château de la Citardière, (Les Ouillères de Mervent, ☎ 02 51 00 27 04; daily except Wed., June-Sept., out of season, weekends only; free admission). Try the crêperie in the courtyard.

Spotcheck
C-D-3

Things to do

- Mountain-biking in the forest
- Sporting activities: rock-climbing at La Pierre Blanche, swimming and watersports

Things to do with children

- Visiting the Mervent zoo
- Pony-trekking in the forest

Within easy reach

Fontenay-le-Comte (p. 150)
West Gâtine (p. 144)
Poitou marshes (p. 146)
Luçon (p. 154)

Tourist Offices

Mervent:
☎ 02 51 00 20 97
Vouvant:
☎ 02 51 00 86 80

Saint-Michel-le-Cloucq
3½ miles (5.5 km) S of Mervent
Local dishes

Many of the farms in the area serve local cuisine. At Saint-Michel-le-Cloucq, the **Ferme-auberge de Mélusine** (☎ 02 51 51 07 61) serves traditional dishes: lamb, *mojettes* (white beans), *préfou* (garlic bread), eels, and Poitou ham; book in advance. If you fancy an unusual weekend, you could try your hand at learning how to cook duck at the **Logis de la Cornelière**. The owner will initiate you into the secrets of his recipes in this picturesque old house. (At Mervent, except July and August. Loisirs Accueil Vendée, ☎ 02 51 62 76 82.)

Luçon
links with Cardinal Richelieu

L uçon is a quiet little town near the plain and the marsh, a bishopric whose most famous incumbent was Cardinal Richelieu. It is the spiritual capital of the southern Vendée and a former inland port. The town has a beautiful cathedral, lively streets, delicious food and summer concerts. It's a great place to use as a base for visits to the local vineyards, the Fiefs Vendéens, and for exploring the nearby villages.

Richelieu's preaching

The **Cathedral of Notre-Dame** has a strange façade, because it was built in three different styles. Part of the cathedral's interior is where Richelieu preached. It holds the great Cavaillé-Coll organ and a cloister whose pilasters are interspersed with rose windows.

A stroll in the garden

The charming **Jardin Dumaine** has an air of 19th C. Second Empire romanticism, and the park benches are favourites with lovers. It has an orangery, a bandstand, an artificial lake with an island planted with bamboo and willow, statues, an avenue of yew trees, magnolias, orange trees, and brightly coloured flowers. Children will love the topiary work of the boxwood shrubs, which represent animals from the fables of La Fontaine.

Classical music

The **Festival des Nocturnes Océanes** (information at the Tourist Office, E.-Henriot Square, ☎ 02 51 56 36 52) takes place every July. Concerts of light classical music in the

The cathedral of Notre-Dame, from the cloister

Ursuline chapel at Luçon

evenings in the Cour Richelieu of the great seminary. Leading orchestras play compositions by Tchaikovsky, Saint-Saëns, Ravel, Schumann, Debussy and Rachmaninov.

La Communauté de Sainte-Ursule

In addition to the cathedral, Luçon's religious past is represented by the **Community of Sainte-Ursule**. The brightly coloured chapel of this convent has a coloured marble altar screen and a panelled ceiling 110 ft (33 m) long, decorated with floral patterns and paintings based around the theme of Christ's Passion,

(information at the Tourist Office, ☎ 02 51 56 36 52). Close by you'll notice a strange edifice in the Champ de Foire, a sort of empty square tower. It was, in fact, the first concrete water-tower, built in 1914.

Mareuil-sur-Lay-Dissais
6 miles (10 km) N of Luçon
Wine tasting

From Luçon take the road to Mareuil-sur-Lay, the first and most important of the vineyards of the Fiefs Vendéens. The appellation was granted a VDQS (*Vin Délimité de Qualité Supérieure*) in 1984. You are now in the heart of a grape-growing region with an ancient tradition. This is a good excuse to taste wine and buy it from an estate whose wines are hard to find, even in other parts of France. Light reds, rosés and whites, as well as *Trousse-pinette*, a Vendéen apéritif, are sold at **Maison Mourat**, Rte de la Roche, Mareuil-

Spotcheck
C 3

Things to do
• Tasting local liqueurs
• Strolling in the Dumaine garden
• Listening to classical music at the Nocturnes Océanes

Things to do with children
• Picnic and games at the à la Court-d'Aron

Within easy reach
Fontenay-le-Comte (p. 150)
The Poitou marshes (p. 146)
The bay of Aiguillon (p. 156)
La Roche-sur-Yon (p. 124)

Tourist Offices
Luçon: ☎ 02 51 56 36 52
Mareuil-sur-Lay: ☎ 02 51 30 51 05
Saint-Cyr-en-Talmondais: ☎ 02 51 30 82 82

sur-Lay (☎ 02 51 97 20 10, daily, except Sundays.)

Saint-Cyr-en-Talmondais
6 miles (10 km) W of Luçon
Parc floral de la Court-d'Aron
☎ 02 51 30 86 74
Early May to late Sept., 10am-6pm
Admission charge.
This lovely park has a picnic area and children's playground by the water. There's also a waterside restaurant, bamboo and banana trees, a lotus-covered pond and ancient trees. The park, the grounds of a Renaissance château, was created by Mathysse, a Dutchman, who brought the cultivation and passion for tulips to France.

L'Aiguillon and the Flower Coast
'la côte des fleurs'

The Bay of Aiguillon is the outlet for the drained part of the Poitou marshes and a natural bird sanctuary for migratory birds, attracted by the mudflats. The bay is also used for cultivating mussels. Further up the coast, in an area known as the Côte des Fleurs (Flower Coast), the resorts of La Faute-sur-Mer and La Tranche-sur-Mer have large, sandy beaches, perfect for family holidays.

Walking around L'Aiguillon-sur-Mer

This little fishing port, with its houses built on stilts, is an important centre for mussel cultivation. The countryside is delightful. If you walk from the dyke to the cape, especially at low tide, you'll be able to see the birds on the mudflats and the wooden fishing-huts. The Tourist Office sells a brochure (€1.50) containing suggestions for 24 walks in the vicinity. **La Pergola,** a restaurant overlooking the bay (320 Route de la Pointe de l'Aiguillon, ☎ 02 51 56 41 08; Feb.-March at weekends, 1 April-30 Sept., daily except Wed., July-Aug., daily; from €11), specialises in all the local seafood.

Saint-Denis-du-Payré
8 miles (13 km) NE of L'Aiguillon-sur-Mer
Birdwatching
Réserve Ornithologique from Saint-Denis-du-Payré on the D 25, towards Triaize,
☎ **02 51 27 23 92**
Daily in July-Aug., 10am-noon, 3-7pm; first Sun. of the month out of season, 2-6pm.
Admission charge.
This bird sanctuary has been created and is maintained by enthusiasts. It has hides for watching birds that stop over in the mudflats. You can hire binoculars and there are guides who will explain the fragile balance of the eco-system and identify the various species, which include barnacle geese, avocets, herons, ducks and even storks.

Charron

19 miles (30.5 km)
SE of L'Aiguillon-sur-Mer

A trip to the mussel-beds

**Association du Vieux Tape-cul, 17230 Charron
☎ 05 46 01 30 29**
Daily 15 June–30 Sept.
Admission charge.

This association is made up of retired fishermen who take visitors out to the mussel-beds on an old sailing yacht. You'll have the chance to take the tiller, under the watchful eyes of these old sea-dogs. The trip to sea takes around

6 hours – plenty of time to imagine yourself as a real mussel-farmer – and explore the bay and its wildlife. If you want to know more, visit **La Maison de la Mytiliculture** at Esnandes, which explains mussel cultivation since the Middle Ages, the cycle of the tides, types of boat and related occupations. (Rue de l'Océan, ☎ 05 46 01 34 64. Apr.-June, daily, except Tues., 2-7pm. July-Aug., daily, 10am-12.30pm, 2-7.30pm. Out of season, telephone in advance. Admission charge).

La Tranche-sur-Mer

Sailing into the wind

The south coast of the Vendée is also known as 'Little California', because of its exceptionally mild micro-climate. Families love the vast, sandy beaches, which are particularly safe and backed by wooded dunes. At **La Faute-sur-Mer** and at **La Tranche-sur-Mer**, the wind is bracing enough for sand-karting, surfing and fun-boarding. Courses and lessons are available from local sailing schools. The resorts also have naturist beaches.

Spotcheck
B 3 - C 3

Things to do
• Sand-karting and fun-boarding
• Learning surfing, fun-boarding and body-boarding

Things to do with children
• Birdwatching
• Parc des Floralies and the forest
• Bathing in the beaches of La Tranche

Within easy reach
Luçon (p. 154)
Île de Ré (p. 218)
La Rochelle (p. 212)
Les Sables-d'Olonne (p 122)

Tourist Offices
L'Aiguillon-sur-Mer:
☎ 02 51 56 43 87
La Tranche-sur-Mer:
☎ 02 51 30 33 96

From the Parc des Floralies to the forest

In 1953 a Dutchman fell in love with the climate at La Tranche and decided to grow bulbs here. The resort holds a colourful **Fête des Fleurs** (flower festival) in April, and has inherited a popular flower park. (Parc des Floralies, ☎ 02 51 30 33 96. 10am-6pm, Mar., Apr., end of June to early Sept., admission charge.) From the flower park and the municipal camping grounds you can walk to the **Forêt Domaniale de Longeville** in the north. There's a path leading to two hiking trails: 1²⁄₃ miles (2.7 km) and 3 miles (5 km). The latter goes past the Dune de Paris, the highest of the dunes. and takes you to **La Terrière**, a wild beach popular with surfers.

CALIFORNIA FUN

Wave School-Fanatic Center
Grande Plage, La Tranche-sur-Mer
☎ 04 76 94 12 32
Surfing, fun-boarding and body-boarding fans meet up at La Tranche. The spot facing the light-house at the Pointe de Grouin, left of the pier, is ideal for beginners. The more experienced surfers prefer Bud Bud, located north of the resort. The surfing crowd get together to shoot the breeze at the **Café Bud House** (☎ 02 51 33 30 10), in the village of Les Conches, in the commune of Longeville.

Niort, from the banks of the Sèvre to the gateway to the marshes

N iort is right in the valley of the river Sèvre at the gateway to the Poitou marshes. It is known as the capital of angelica – and also of mutual insurance societies! The city stands on twin hills and has a rich historic heritage, including a magnificent 12th C. castle keep. The river, with its wooded banks, winds through the city, making visitors feel they are in the country, rather than in the middle of a city.

A bird's eye view of Niort
Le Donjon,
Rue Du Guesclin.
The castle originally had two keeps, topped by a crenellated parapet. They were linked by pavilions that housed a paved

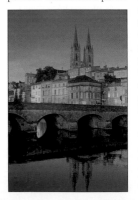

courtyard. Inside the keep the doors have heavy locks, a reminder that the French word for keep, *donjon*, also means a dungeon. From the terrace, the view of the town is unique, but climbing the stone steps that lead to it is a risky exercise. The steps are no wider than 4 in (10 cm)! You'll find a small **museum** in the keep. One room is devoted entirely to the history and techniques of chamois leather making and glove-making, which have been industries here since the 13th C. On the next floor, there's a reconstruction of an early 19th C. Poitou interior with furniture. (**Musée du Donjon**, ☎ 05 49 28 14 28; open daily, except Tues.,

May-15 Sept., 9am-noon and 2-6pm (5pm out of season. Admission charge).

Walking through the town
Discover Niort's many charms by roaming through the old streets. From the Pilori, the 16th-C. former town hall, walk to the present town hall, a Renaissance building, then to the Prefecture, whose frontage is adorned with the figures of two women,

symbolising the two rivers called the Sèvre. Take one of the little bridges over the Sèvre at the foot of

the castle keep, to examine the complex system of canals and locks. This is where the first port of Niort was built in the 13th C. At the Vieux-Pont (old bridge), take the Rue du Pont, where you can admire the attractive half-timbered houses. They include the 16th-C. Hôtel Chabot, and no. 5, the house in which Françoise d'Aubigné, the future Madame de Maintenon and second wife of Louis XIV, was born.

The land of angels

Angelica has been a speciality of this region since the Middle Ages. The plant, which takes its name from its supposedly heavenly origins, can grow to over 7 ft (2.1 m) in height. The green stems can be dried and candied or are used to make liqueurs. They can also be eaten in an omelette, with trout or in ice-cream.

Towards 'green Venice'

From the botanical garden to the Sèvre

From the church of Saint-André, walk to the Place Chanzy. The garden's entrance is to the left of the Centre Du Guesclin. This garden may be in the centre of town, but you'll feel as if you're in the country. From the top of the hill, the castle keep and the church of Saint-André can be glimpsed through the trees. Follow the steep winding paths through the hills to reach the Quai de la Régatterie beside the Sèvre. The ash trees and the typically green water of this part of the Sèvre will give you a foretaste of the 'green Venice' of the Poitou marshland.

Spotcheck
D 3

Things to do
- Shopping in the Marché des Halles
- Picnicking in the Parc de la Coulée Verte

Things to do with children
- Buying sweets at Angéli-Cado

Within easy reach
The Niort district (p. 162)
The Poitou marshes (p. 146)
West Gâtine (p. 144)
The Melle district (p. 166)

Tourist Office
Niort:
☎ 05 49 24 18 79

SHOPPING IN THE MARKET
The **Marché des Halles**, Quai Cronstadt. The cast iron arches and the expanse of glass make these market halls a favourite place to shop for the inhabitants of Niort. The market is held daily, but try to visit on Saturday, when there are more traders and the market is much busier. You can buy the goat's milk cheeses, such as **chabichou** and the **mothais-sur-feuille,** which are the specialities of the Deux-Sèvres. You will also find organic **Pineau** (see p. 80), **brioche Vendéenne,** honey and blackcurrant syrup. Don't forget to buy an **angelica plant** – all the nursery stalls in the market sell them (about €5 each).

The **Angéli-Cado** confiserie (6 bis, Rue Sainte-Marthe, ☎ 05 49 24 10 23, sells candied angelica shapes of animals native to the marshes, such as tortoises, snails and frogs (€9 each).

Le Pilori, the old town hall
Rue Mathurin Berthomé.
The former town hall, called Le Pilori, stands on the site of the medieval pillory, where condemned men and women were displayed to the public. Strangely, the building has retained the name of this unpleasant form of punishment. It has circular, crenellated towers on each corner, a belfry dating from the 17th C. and a bell-tower from the 19th C. It's worth looking inside to see the beautifully painted parlour.

Knights of the Round Table
Le Logis de l'Hercule, 16 Rue Cloche-Perce
☎ 05 49 05 18 33
Open daily, 10am-1pm and 3-7pm, 15 June-15 Sept. Out of season, only by appointment at the Tourist Office.
(fax: 05 49 05 18 38).
Admission charge.
Le Logis de l'Hercule is a strange place where ancient chivalry still prevails. In the 16th C. plague victims were treated here with angelica, which was believed to have miraculous powers. A guided tour retraces the main events in the history of Niort, its importance as a river port and the famous plague epidemic of 1603. A permanent exhibition in the handsome vaulted cellar features a collection of artefacts from the Middle Ages. Taste the angelica or be tempted by rather unusual medieval drinks – they're on the house.

Capital of the 'mutuelles'
Niort would not be what it is today without the numerous *mutuelles*, 'friendly' or mutual insurance societies. They were started in 1936, when the MAIF was founded by teachers who insured each other for a small membership fee. The idea grew, and today the CAMIF, the MAAF and the MACIF, provide a great deal of the town's employment and prosperity. The MAIF now has more than 2 million members and is one of the largest mutual societies in France. It is the Niort's largest employer.

In praise of local artists
Musée Bernard-d'Agesci, 28 Avenue de Limoges
☎ 05 49 77 16 70
Open daily, except Tues., May-15 Sept., 9am-noon and 2-6pm (5pm, out of season).
Free admission Wed.
Niort's fine art museum is housed in a former school. You actually reach the exhibition halls through the playground. The first room contains several beautiful bronze sculptures by Pierre-Marie Poisson, an early 20th-C. artist from Niort, who was fascinated by Algeria. Bernard d'Agesci, an 18th-C. painter whose *The Abduction of Europa* is renowned, is one of the other featured local artists.

Saint Liguaire

4 miles (6 km) W of Niort

A place to eat outside the town

Auberge de la Rousille

☎ 05 49 06 98 38

Open 9.30am-midnight. Closed Sun. evening and Mon.

It's easy to see why the Auberge de la Rousille is such a favourite with the people of Niort. It occupies the former lock-keeper's house, built in 1803, and offers typical specialities of the marshes, such as eels and frogs etc. The inn also serves ice-cream and crêpes. (Menu from €14). You can eat on the large, shady terrace or in a fire-lit room overlooking the Sèvre. After the meal, you could explore the Coulée Verte, using the little boats that the inn provides for customers. As you row along the river, you'll encounter swans, wild duck, herons, plovers, kingfishers and many other wild birds.

Échiré

5 miles (8 km) N of Niort

Buttering up

Laiterie Coopérative

☎ 05 49 25 70 01

Open by appointment only; telephone in advance

This cooperative dairy is where the famous Échiré butter is made using the most traditional methods possible. The butter is churned with a paddle in a teak wooden churn; teak does not rot and contains no tannin. You can buy 'the best butter in the world' in the shop; a 2¼ lb (1 kg) portion of butter costs €8. This may seem like a lot of butter, but because it's so delicious, you'll find it doesn't last long.

LA COULÉE VERTE

The Coulée Verte, meaning 'the green flow', is what local people call the banks of the Sèvre. The river is surrounded by greenery but earns its name from its green appearance. This is a wonderful area for rambling and picnics. The

Bigotine, Ombragée and Passante footbridges make it possible to cross from one bank to the other and to reach the central part of the park, which is planted with the same types of trees as found on the Poitou marshes. The Coulée Verte is extremely popular with residents of Niort.

Around Niort
the heart of the marshlands

To the west of Niort, the network of canals of the wet marsh of Poitou begins. This lush green countryside is dotted with poplar trees and brightly painted houses. You'll have the chance to 'mess about in boats' and discover the traditions and cooking of the Poitou marsh-dwellers.

Arçais
12½ miles (20 km)
W of Niort
The Venice of the marshes
This is the only village in the Poitou marshes to have 25 miles (40 km) of navigable canals and an area of 2,471 acres (1000 ha) of wet marsh. It has a small port with wooden cranes which were used for lifting tree-trunks that had been sent down the canals. The main street is the Rue de la Garenne; its typical marsh-dwellers' cottages face the street on one side and the marsh on the other. A large wharf, the **Logis**, dominates the port, where salt, wood and wine were once stored. In late July or early August, a *son et lumière* show about the life of the marsh-dwellers lights up the Conches d'Arçais (the Arçais salt pans). Information: ☎ 05 49 35 37 12.

Coulon
6 miles (10 km)
SW of Niort
Musée des Marais mouillés
Place de la Coutume, 79510 Coulon
☎ **05 49 35 81 04**
Open daily, July-Aug., 10am-8pm, out of season, 10am-noon and 2-7pm; closed on Mon., except Dec.-Jan.
Admission charge.

This museum of the marshes provides an introduction to the history and traditions of the Poitou wetlands. You'll be surprised to learn that the thousands of poplars grown in the marshes were imported from the United States. One of the exhibits is a gigantic model of an eel's egg, which you walk through to learn about the eels' journey every year from the Sargasso Sea into the Sèvre estuary at Niort, right through to the salt pans. A huge model of the wet marsh with special lighting explains what life was like in the marshes in the 19th C.

Vouillé
4 miles (7 km)
SE of Niort
Agricultural Machinery
Musée Jardins des Ruralies, Vouillé
Access by the A10 or by the D948
☎ **05 49 75 68 27**
Open daily, 10am-6pm (7pm in summer)
Admission charge.
Les Ruralies is dedicated to agricultural machinery and traditional gardens. You can take a pleasant walk in the kitchen garden and enjoy the 500 species of roses.

You can also learn about the development of agricultural machinery, and see the wonderful collection of early 20th C. posters, extolling the merits of a particular seed merchant or fertiliser. To keep children entertained, there's a variety of farmyard animals, including the elegant Poitou goose.

Échiré
6 miles (10 km)
N of Niort
Château de Coudray-Salbart
☎ 05 49 25 25 08
Open daily, Apr.-Oct., 9am-7pm, Nov.-March, 9am-noon and 2-5pm
Admission charge.
If you're fascinated by old ruins, the Fortress of Coudray-Salbart won't disappoint you. The ruins are among the most interesting in western Europe. The fortress overlooks the Sèvre and consists of six large towers of unequal sizes, which were once linked by a rampart walk. Don't miss the tunnel dug into the ramparts, which made it possible to move troops quickly from one part of the fortress to another.

Spotchock
D 3

Things to do
• Walk along the canals
• Taste the regional cooking

Things to do with children
• Visit the farm animals at Vouillé

Within easy reach
Niort (p. 158)
The Poitou marshes (p. 146)
Fontenay-le-Comte (p. 150)
West Gâtine (p. 144)

Tourist Offices
Arçais:
☎ 05 49 35 43 44
Coulon:
☎ 05 49 35 99 29
Niort:
☎ 05 49 24 18 79

The flavour market
Les Ruralies,
Vouillé. Via the A10 or the D948
☎ 05 49 75 67 30
Open daily, March-Oct., 9am-7pm, Nov.-Feb., 9.30am-6.30pm
The market is in a motorway lay-by, believe it or not, so it's an unusual setting to discover the regional food of the area. You'll find a host of delicious local specialities, such as *broyé du Poitou* (a butter biscuit), *goulibeur* (a sponge cake at around €3), authentic **Charentais** stuffing (of pork and courgettes (zucchini); €8 per 2¼ lb (1 kg), or sea-salt from the Île de Ré, *pain d'épice* (spice cake), **brioche** and **goose rillettes** (€6 for a terrine), all of which can be washed down with an Haut-Poitou wine.

Magné
6 miles (10 km)
W of Niort
Festival of painting
☎ 05 49 73 41 31
Magné stands on an island at the gateway to the 'green Venice'. It is linked to terra firma by five bridges, including a drawbridge built in 1855. Participants in the painting festival, held on the third weekend of July, find their inspiration in this landscape of salt pans dotted with poplar trees. Budding artists have a whole day to produce their work, which is on a subject of their own choice. The paintings are then exhibited in the gardens of the town hall, where they are judged by a jury. Who knows, you may even be a winner.

Melle
the gateway to Poitou

Melle was the site of a mint in the Gallo-Roman period and was a necessary stop for pilgrims on their way to the shrine of St James of Compostela in the Middle Ages. In the 19th C. it was a breeding centre for the *baudet de Poitou*, the local long-haired donkey.

Sacred music at the church of Saint-Hilaire

The church of Saint-Hilaire is without doubt the most beautiful of the three churches in Melle. You can't fail to admire the north façade, with its portal topped with vaulting and sculptures illustrating the changes of the seasons and signs of the zodiac. Above the door is a niche containing an equestrian statue, believed to depict Emperor Constantine, represented by a seated figure, defeating paganism. Make sure that you see the apses and admire the red tiles on the roof, then take a look at the ambulatory and the choir.

There's a sort of 'ecclesiastical juke-box' in the church, which plays hymns and chants from all over the world.

Wash-houses and fountains

The wash-houses and fountains of Melle are worth a visit. About 440 yds (400 m) from the church of Saint-Pierre, you'll find a small octagonal building surrounded by an arcade. It contains a fountain which spouts from the rock and an oval basin, around which the washer-women would gather. In the meadow, known as the Pré de la Maladrerie, the medieval fountain and its round basin were reserved for lepers. Near the caves of Loubeau and the silver mines you'll find the old wash-house of Loubeau.

A prison rededicated to culture

The church of Saint-Savinien

The church was built in the 11th and 13th C., and for a long time served as a prison. The entrance is framed by two blind arches and topped with a lintel on which Christ is depicted between two lions. Stop to admire the ancient sculptures under the cornice, showing a knight, birds, a hind, fish and wrestlers. In August, the **Festival of Melle** is held in the church (exhibitions, fireworks etc).

Silver mines of the Frankish kings

☎ 05 49 29 19 54
Open daily, June-Sept., 10am-noon and 2.30-7.30pm, Oct.-15 Nov., March-May, weekends

and public holidays, 2.30-6.30pm These are the oldest silver mines in Europe that are still open to the public. They supplied lead and silver to the mint at Melle, which struck royal coins. The mine is a 12½-mile (20 km) labyrinth of tunnels of which 1,150 ft (350 m) can be visited. You can see the fascinating silver-bearing tungsten formations as well as two reconstructed furnaces in which the metals were melted to separate the lead from the silver.

This is a group of local artists and craftsmen who have banded together to promote local products and crafts. You can buy honey, *rillettes* (chitterlings) and butter biscuits, as well as pottery and other craft items that will make ideal gifts to take home.

Local crafts
Singulier Pluriel:
Art et Terroir
3 Rue Émilien-Traver
☎ 05 49 29 10 30
Open Tues.-Sat., 9am-noon and 2.30-6pm.

A collection of trees
Arboretum,
Chemin de la
Découverte. Information
at the Tourist
Office, Place
de la
Poste
☎ 05 49 29
15 10
Explore the old town by following this 4-mile (6 km) route, part of which is overgrown. You will pass more than 1,000 species of trees and shrubs from all the temperate climates of the world, and see a beautiful collection of old roses (around 100 varieties). Don't miss the fascinating **bosquet d'écorces** (bark grove) where you can feel the bark of 50 different species of tree.

Spotcheck
D 3

Things to do
• Learning to recognise trees in the Melle arboretum
• Shopping for local crafts
• Visiting wash-houses and fountains

Things to do with children
• Visiting the Guignol puppets

Within easy reach
The Melle district (p. 166)
Niort (p. 158)
Saint-Maixent-l'École (p. 168)

Tourist Office
Melle:
☎ 05 49 29 15 10

GUIGNOL IN THE DEUX-SÈVRES
Maison des Marionnettes
and **Théâtre du Gros Bonhomme**
6 miles (10 km) SW of Melle, 79360 Lusseray
☎ 05 49 07 26 09
Open by appointment from 1 June to 30 Sept. *Admission charge.*
No fewer than 300 marionnettes, stick puppets and glove puppets have been gathered together to form this extraordinary museum (guided tours available). Africa, Asia and Europe are all represented in this unusual collection, with giant carnival heads completing the display. There's also a workshop where you can see the traditional Grand Guignol puppets being made. Every Sunday at 6pm there is a puppet show for children. The annual country Marionnette Festival (first two weeks of August) includes special performances at Lusseray, with shows, conferences, exhibitions and lots of puppets and puppeteers.

Around Melle
historic châteaux and art treasures

The area around Melle, including Celle-sur-Belle, Chef-Boutonne and Lezay, is full of Romanesque châteaux and art treasures. Mills, fountains and wash-houses are dotted along the courses of the Sèvre, the Boutonne and the Belle. There are forests of chestnut, walnut and parasol pines. This is also an important gastronomic region, specialising in *fouace* (hearth-baked bread), goat's cheese and, above all, one of the few traditional French cheesecakes, the *tourteau fromager*.

Celle-sur-Belle
4¼ miles (7 km)
NW of Melle
The royal abbey
Information at the
Tourist Office:
☎ 05 49 32 92 28
Open daily, visits
at 11am and 3pm
Free admission.
A magnificent and imposing building, the abbey is very richly decorated inside. It was built between 1676 and 1682, in the Classical style and is 272 ft (83 m) long by 56 ft (17 m) high. Inside the abbey look out for the monumental wrought iron staircase and the remains of the ancient monastery. Take a detour to the abbey church, where the 12th-C. Romanesque portal inside the church makes a surprising contrast to the rest of the 15th-C. Gothic interior.

Villiers-en-Bois
15 miles (24 km)
SW of Melle
Zoorama in the Forest of Chizé
79360 Villiers-en-Bois
☎ 05 49 77 17 17
Open daily 9am-8pm, closed on Tuesday except May-August.
Admission charge.
The Chizé Zoorama covers 62 acres (25 ha) and is in the heart of the Chizé forest, close to Beauvoir-sur-Niort, at a place called Virollet. Along with the Zoo de la Palmyre (see p. 234) this is one of the finest zoos in France. You can watch the 600 animals in their vast enclosures, from observation ditches or hides. Many of the animals are quite rare in northern Europe, for example, bisons, aurochs (gigantic cattle, which are the ancestors of our cattle)

LAMBON LAKE
Prailles-Vitré
16 miles (10 km)
NW of Melle
☎ 05 49 32 85 11
Open daily in season, 10am-7pm.
Admission charge.

This leisure centre should be able to cater for the needs of every member of the family. Water-sports enthusiasts can learn to row or sailboard. If that doesn't tempt you, then you could simply go for a swim or hire a horse and go for a ride around the 120 acres (50 ha) of the site. Fishing is permitted in the lake (with a licence for category two waterways), and there are tennis courts and a playground for the children.

and *tarpans* (European wild horses). There are also rather better known but equally interesting animals, such as wolves, lynxes, snakes and huge lizards, which are best viewed in safety from behind glass.

Chef-Boutonne
10 miles (16 km)
SE of Melle
Château of Javarzay
Syndicat d'Initiatives:
☎ 05 49 29 86 31

Open daily, July-August, 10am-noon and 3-6pm, out of season, 3-6pm except on Mon. *Admission charge.*
This handsome château was built in the early 16th C. and is one of the earliest examples of a Renaissance château in Poitou. Of special interest is the large, round tower topped by a gallery and you can visit the chapel and the walk along the top of the walls. The square tower, with its little watchtowers in each corner, could easily be the fairytale castle in which Sleeping Beauty lived. Inside there's an interesting exhibition of 19th-C. head-dresses and of the old mills of the region.

The best cheesecakes in town

The *tourteau fromager* is a cheesecake which is the particular speciality of the Melle district. It's a savoury dish based on a combination of shortcrust pastry, fresh goat's cheese and eggs. The top crust is almost black, but the filling is a soft, fluffy mixture with a delicate flavour. The cake should be eaten cold accompanied by a glass of red wine or a cup of coffee. The best places to buy *tourteau fromager* are either **M. Gaston Baubeau** (Lartigault, commune de

Spotcheck
D 3

Things to do
• Tasting the best cheesecakes

Things to do with children
• Visiting the animals at the Zoorama of Chizé
• Bathing in the Lambon lake

Within easy reach
Niort (p. 158)
Melle (p. 164)
Saint-Maixent-l'École (p. 168)

Tourist Offices
Celle-sur-Belle:
☎ 05 49 32 92 28
Chef-Boutonne:
☎ 05 49 29 86 31
Melle:
☎ 05 49 29 15 10

Lezay, 6 miles (10 km) NE of Melle, ☎ 05 49 29 32 30) or the cooperative bakery in Lezay (6 Rue de Melle, ☎ 05 49 29 40 58). This is one of the few cheesecakes that is traditionally French.

The tourteau fromager *is derived from a very basic cake that was eaten to celebrate country weddings*

Around Saint-Maixent-l'École

local culinary specialities

S aint-Maixent-l'École, which was famous for its military academy, is also well known for delicious varieties of goat's cheese, such as Mothais-sur-Feuille, La Bûche and Chabichou. The river Sèvre runs through the town centre and beside the Parc Chaigneau, then divides into little canals. The region is full of ancient remains and there is a prehistoric site at Bougon.

A walk through Saint-Maixent

Enter via the Porte Chalon, an 18th C. white stone gateway, and follow the Rue Chalon to the Rue Garran-de-Balzan where you will find the romantic ruins of the church of Saint-Léger. Then skirt around the 12th C. abbey to see the Canclaux cloister, which once housed the military academy. Walk down the Rue Anatole-France in which there is a 15th C. half-timbered apothecary's house. Note the inscription on the façade which reads: *Hic Valetudo* (Latin, 'here is health'). Then cross the Charrault bridge and wander along the Sèvre past the Quai des Tanneries. Continue on to the Parc Chaigneau, where you'll get an excellent view of the town and its ancient ramparts.

Bougon
11 miles (18 km) SE of Saint-Maixent

Return to the stone age

Bougon prehistoric site
☎ 05 49 05 12 13
Open daily in season 10am-7pm, 6pm out of season, except Wed. morning, Sat.-Sun., 10am-8pm
Admission charge.

This vast park contains a cemetery from a bygone age, a necropolis created some 4500 years ago. The tumuli contain huge funerary chambers; for example, Tumulus C measures 190 ft (57 m) in diameter and is 13 ft (4 m) high. You can also attend archaeological workshops (Weds. and Sat. in summer). Adults can learn to make flint axes, children will find out how to make fire without matches, and gourmets can take lessons in prehistoric cookery!

Spotcheck
D 3

Things to do
• Take the goat's cheese route
• Taste real *fouace mothaise*

Within easy reach
Niort (p. 158)
Melle (p. 164)
The Melle district (p. 166)
Parthenay (p. 140)

Tourist Office
Saint-Maixent-l'École:
☎ **05 49 05 54 05**

La Mothe-Saint-Héray

7 miles (11 km) SE of Saint-Maixent

Goat's cheese

If you're interested in how goat's cheese is made, you can follow a circular route that starts from Saint-Maixent and goes in the direction of Chef-Boutonne. Local breeders and cheese-makers will be delighted to welcome you during this gastronomic tour. To stock up on goat's cheese in its various shapes – logs, cylinders and pyramids – visit La Fromagerie Poitou-Chèvre at La Mothe-Saint-Héray (☎ 05 49 05 13 02). For the Mothais-sur-Feuille, M. Georgelet à Villemain (☎ 05 49 07 88 72) is a real specialist. He will also offer you a free tasting.

The orangery
Allée de l'Orangerie

The orangery was built near a medieval château, of which all that remains are the out-houses. The lower gallery's walls are rough-plastered in a brick red colour, in contrast to the white stones of the corners and window frames. It's a long building with enormous round upper windows and neo-Classical doors. Plenty of light was always needed in orangeries, which were used during winter to protect delicate citrus trees from frost. Orange and lemon trees from the formal gardens here are still brought inside for the winter. The orangery is surrounded by beautiful grounds.

MASTER BAKER OF *FOUACE MOTHAISE*

15 Rue du Maréchal-Joffre
La Mothe-Saint-Héray
☎ **05 49 05 01 53.**
This pâtisserie has been making the rich yeast cake called *fouace mothaise* for about a century. The cake itself has been manufactured in the region since at least 1610, as is evident from the marriage deed of a master fouace-baker in Niort, but it was probably made long before, as Rabelais mentions it as a traditional delicacy. **Monsieu Favreau** is the only pâtissier to make it in the classic way, although pale imitations can be found elsewhere. The recipe is kept secret by

the bakers and each shop has its own version. This is a good opportunity to taste the real thing at a low price (€2 for a six-portion cake).

Angoulême
and the cartoon strip

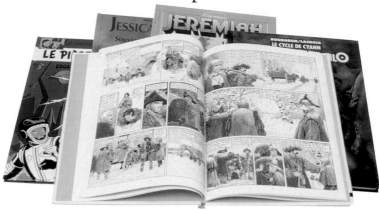

S tanding on a rock overlooking the river Charentes, Angoulême is an ancient city and the capital of Angoumois, the district named after it. Once famous for its pottery and paper mills, it is now best known for its international comic strip festival, which generates a great deal of excitement in this city of red roofs.

The cathedral of Saint-Pierre

Rempart Desaix
Free admission.
The early 12th C. cathedral has a richly carved façade depicting 75 figures, making it one of the most impressive in western France. Paul Abadie, who designed the basilica of the Sacré-Cœur in Paris, made significant alterations to the cathedral in the 19th C., including the gable end and two towers. The cathedral has a beautiful Romanesque bell-tower, and when the bells are rung the noise resounds through the whole city.

Walking round the ramparts

The best way to discover Angoulême is by walking around the ramparts of this old fortified city. From the end of the Place de New York, follow the Desaix rampart, leading you to the

foot of the cathedral of Saint-Pierre, which faces the Rempart du Midi that leads up to the **Place Beaulieu**. The extension of this part of the wall offers the best view over Angoulême and district and of the **Tour Ladent** below.

Comic strip capital

Centre National de la Bande Dessinée et de l'Image
121 Route de Bordeaux
☎ **05 45 38 65 65**

Open Tues.-Fri., 10am-6pm (7pm in season), Sat.-Sun., 2-6pm (7pm in season). Open daily during school holidays (10am-7pm)
Admission charge.
The CNBDI is housed in a futurist building on a hill-side. This massive collection and museum devoted to the art of the comic strip and caricature is a wonderful place to spend the day. The museum takes you through the story of French cartoon

Spotcheck
E 5

Things to do

• Walking round the ramparts
• Visit the comic strip museum
• Cruising on the Charente

Within easy reach

Angoulême district (p. 174)
Forest of Horte (p.184)
La Rochefoucauld (p. 176)
Ruffec district (p. 186)

Tourist Office

Angoulême:
☎ 05 45 95 16 84

characters, including those that are famous worldwide such as Tintin and Asterix, as well as less well known examples, including Spirou, Blueberry, Corto Maltese, Blake and Mortimer and Jack Palmer. You will learn how the cartoon bubble was invented in 1925 and there's a well-stocked library on the upper floor.

Toilet paper or cigarette paper?
Le Nil Paper Museum
134 rue de Bordeaux
☎ 05 45 92 73 43
Open daily, except Mon. and public holidays, 2-6pm.
Free admission.
This museum is housed in a former paper mill which straddles the river Charente.

The ground floor rooms trace the history of paper-making. You will learn, for example, that the first cigarette papers were sold under the name of *papier hygénique*, which is what lavatory paper is now called in French! Upstairs, old machinery and documents show the history of the cigarette paper. You can buy luxurious vellum and laid paper in the shop (from around €3 for 50 sheets).

Cruising on the Charente
Tourist Office of the Pays d'Angoulême,
Place des Halles
☎ 05 45 95 16 84
The river Charente is navigable and will lead you to some of the best tourist

attractions in the Angoulême district. There's a 'paper cruise', specially designed for families (€30 for 4 people), which takes you through the locks to Fleurac, where you can visit a paper mill (p. 17). For conoisseurs, there are cruises with special themes; for example, a trip to the *chais* – the cognac vaults (**The Bacchus Cruise**), or **La Croisière Gourmande,** which will take you to the Letuffe chocolate factory at Trois-Palis.

Shop till you drop
Le Marché Victor-Hugo
Place Victor-Hugo
Every morning Tues.-Sun.
Best on Sunday.
The Victor-Hugo market is located just outside the town and is where all the locals meet up on Sunday mornings. The atmosphere is warm and lively, and your mouth will water at the lovely displays of dried and candied fruits (taste the candied pineapple and peaches and the dried pears) and spices. There are also many stalls selling flowers and plants suitable for a kitchen garden.

Musée Lhomme
Musée des Beaux-Arts
1 Rue Friedland
☎ **05 45 95 07 69**
Open daily, noon-6pm,
2-6pm at weekends.
Closed on public holidays.

*Admission charge
(free from Mon. to Fri.,
noon-2pm).*
This museum is housed in a former bishop's palace and contains a rich collection of 12th C. sculpted capitals representing humans and mythical beasts. The third room contains examples of the finest Charentes pottery produced by artists such as Sazerac and Renoleau. The museum also has the fourth largest collection of African art in France. All the exhibits were assembled by a local collector, Dr Lhomme, who donated them to the town to create a museum. It's hard to believe, but he had amassed a collection of almost 3000 items without ever travelling; his health being too delicate to allow it. Most of the African items were brought back by his friends.

Place de New York and the theatre
You may not be aware of it but one of the early names of New York was Nouvelle-Angoulême. An Italian working for François I, duke of Angoulême, gave it the name in honour of his sovereign. So what could be more natural than that in return, Angoulême gave this large square the name of the American city. The 19th C. theatre is worth a look. Its façade is topped with musical angels, and the side windows are glazed with modern stained glass. In summer the theatre bars are pleasant meeting places.

Vintage cars
Hôtel de Ville (town hall)
☎ **05 45 94 95 67**
Free admission.
In mid-September every year, Angoulême hosts one of the most important events for vintage and classic car enthusiasts from all over France and abroad. The highlight is the **Circuit des Remparts**, a classic and vintage car race around the city walls. The festival lasts for three days and includes rallies and a *concours d'élégance*. The race around

the ramparts takes place on the Sunday, the last day of the event.

Les Halles d'Angoulême

These were built in 1886 by the architect Édouard Warin, to replace the Châtelet (the castle of the Taillefer family), whose ruins can still be seen. The halles, a good example of 19th C. metal construction, is a covered market hall and the surrounding district has recently been renovated. A covered market is held in the building, which sells speciality foods of the region.

Craft pottery

Atelier Roux Majoliques
198 Rue Montmoreau
☎ **05 45 61 06 35**
Visit Mon.-Fri. 8.30am-noon and 2-6.30pm. Closed public holidays. *Free admission.*
Simone and Claude Roux, two enthusiastic potters, will welcome you into their studio at the top of the Rue Montmoreau. Everything is hand-made, from the

A DREAM OF A SWEET SHOP
Chocolaterie Letuffe
10 Place Francis-Louvel
☎ **05 45 95 00 54**
The caramels, nougat and marrons glacés of this chocolate factory have a reputation well beyond the borders of the département. You can't leave Angoulême without tasting some of these succulent specialities, which include *guinettes* (cherries in cognac), *duchesses* (nougatines) and *marguerites d'Angoulême* (orange-flavoured chocolate). About €6 for 10½ oz (300 g).

modelling to the decoration. The shop has a wide choice of items for sale – many of them unique – including lamp bases (between €80 and €305).

A meal break in Angoulême

The **Chez Paul** brasserie is the ideal place for a family lunch. The portions are large and the choice of desserts is extensive, including *Cannelé de Bordeaux*, a local pastry flavoured with rum and cinnamon (8 Place Francis-Louvel, ☎ 05 45 90 04 61, menus €15, excluding wine. Open daily). A stone's throw

away you'll find **Le Tire-Bouchon**, a wine bar and restaurant. This is the perfect chance to sample some of the local wines. Le Tire-Bouchon has a *plat du jour* (served from Tues. to Fri.) with green salad and coffee for around €9 (18 Rue Cloche-Verte, ☎ 05 45 95 00 12. Open Tues.-Fri. from 2pm. Closed on Sun. except in winter).

Around Angoulême
on the banks of the river Charente

The banks of the river Charente a few miles from Angoulême are full of pleasant surprises. You will find opportunities to learn how paper is made, visit a chocolate factory and to stroll in the shade beside the river. And don't forget to bring your fishing rod!

Saint-Michel-d'Entraigues

Exit SW of Angoulême
The church of Saint-Michel-d'Entraigues

This is the only church in the region to be built in the shape of an octagon. Construction work started in 1137 and the church consists of eight small apses with blind arcades. The portal decoration is a wonderful example of Hispano-Moorish influence. The tympanum depicts St Michael slaying a dragon.

Trois-Palis

4 miles (6 km) W of Angoulême
The Letuffe chocolate factory
Le Bourg, 16730 Trois-Palis ☎ 05 45 91 05 21
Open Mon.-Fri. 8am-noon and 2-5.30pm, weekends and public holidays 2-5pm.

The Chocolaterie Letuffe has a reputation that extends far beyond the frontiers of Charentes. Since 1873 the **Marguerite d'Angoulême**, a dark, orange-flavoured chocolate and the **Duchesse**, nougatine stuffed with praline, have been specialities of the house. A visit to the factory is a must for any chocaholics who can not only get their fix, but also learn the tricks of the trade. In the kitchen, copper pans of chocolate, caramel and toffee simmer on the stove. If you want to impress your friends, take a chocolate-making course and learn, for example, how to make Easter eggs. (Information at the Angoulême Tourist Office ☎ 05 45 95 16 84.)

Nersac
6 miles (10 km)
SW of Angoulême
Fleurac paper mill
☎ 05 45 91 50 69
Open daily, except Tues.,
from 1 Apr.-31 Oct.
10am-noon, 2-7pm during the week, weekends
and public holidays
11am-noon, 3-7pm;
out of season: 2-6pm.
Weekends and public
holidays 3-6pm.
Admission charge.

This mill, specialising in
hand-made paper, stands
near the Charente and is
accessible by barge or launch.
You will find out all there is
to know about paper-making
here. François Mitterrand's
personal writing paper was
made in this mill, and the
owner still has a few samples
left, but don't expect him to
sell them. If you hold the
paper up to the light, you can
see the impressive watermark
representing the presidential
emblem of an oak and an
olive tree. The paper used for
restoring the archives of the
Bibliothèque Nationale de
France is also made here.
When you have finished your
tour of the mill, don't forget
to visit the shop which sells
poems and songs printed on
vellum or laid paper (around
€9), as well as writing paper,
engravings and special art
papers for painting and
drawing.

A walk beside the Charente

Take your time to wander
along the banks of the river
behind the Fleurac mill.
Footbridges lead to little
islands almost hidden in
thick foliage. Anglers should
not forget to bring a rod
because fish are plentiful in
the waters around the islands,
attracted by the protection
afforded by the islands and
the strong current.

Puymoyen
4 miles (6.5 km)
SE of Angoulême
**Verger paper
mill**
☎ 05 45 61 10 38
Open daily, 9am-noon
and 2-6pm, and at
weekends 3-6pm
Free admission.
The Moulin du Verger,
which stands on a mill-race
on the little tributary of
Eaux-Claires, is classified as
a historic site. The paper mill
was founded in 1539, and
paper is still made in the
same way as it always has
been. Water is used to power
the machinery, in the form
of a turbine and the owner
makes

paper and prints engravings
while you watch.
At the end of the visit, you
can buy some luxury hand-made paper, and all types of
art paper are also on sale.

Champagne-Vigny
12 miles (19.5 km)
SW of Angoulême
Visiting a vineyard
**Rumeau et Fils,
Domaine Les Quillets**
☎ 05 45 64 02 92
Open daily, visits by
appointment.
A few miles south of
Angoulême, M. Rumeau
will offer you a warm
welcome at his magnificent
19th-C. estate. Here you
can visit the presses and the
vats, as well as the storage
building. The shop
sells Pineau at an
affordable price
(€7 a bottle) as
well as coffee-
and passion-
fruit flavoured
cognac.

Spotcheck
E 5

Things to do
• Visit a paper mill
• Visit a vineyard and taste
Pineau and cognac

Things to do
with children

• Visit the Letuffe chocolate
factory

Within easy reach

Angoulême (p. 174)
*Champagne Charentaise
(p.194)*
Barbezieux (p. 196)
[Blanzac]

Tourist Office

Angoulême:
☎ 05 45 95 16 84

La Rochefoucauld
historic château and convent

This little town on the banks of the river Tardoire is dominated by a magnificent château, equal in beauty to the châteaux of the Loire. As you wander through La Rochefoucauld admire its ancient streets, convent and collegiate church.

The Château de La Rochefoucauld
☎ 05 45 62 07 42
Open daily, from Easter-1 Nov., 10am-7pm; out of season Sun. and public holidays, 2-7pm.
Admission charge.
The château was founded in 980, then rebuilt between the 11th and 18th C.

It was the home of the La Rochefoucauld family, including the famous writer, François, Duke of La Rouchefoucauld (1613-80). The château stands on a rock overlooking the whole town and the banks of the Tardoire. With its square Romanesque castle keep and four entrance towers, monumental spiral staircase and Gothic chapel, it well deserves to be called 'the pearl of the Angoulême district'.

Visiting a convent
Cloister of the former Carmelite convent Grande-Rue
The Carmelite convent was founded in the 14th C. by a member of the La Rochefoucauld family. Only the Gothic cloister remains, but it is still worth seeing. Admire the delicate architecture of the galleries of the ambulatory. The Carmelite nuns must have found the peace and quiet of this place ideal for contemplation.

Relics of the distant past
Musée de la Préhistoire, Grande-Rue
☎ 05 45 63 12 26
Open daily July-Aug. 3-7pm except Tues.; out of season on request at the Tourist Office
☎ 05 45 63 07 45
Free admission.
The Museum of Prehistory is immediately next door to the ruins of the Carmelite

---

THE CHARENTAISE SLIPPER
Rondinaud
43 Rue des Halles
☎ 05 45 63 01 09
Open 9am-noon and 2.30-7pm daily except Sun. and Mon.
With more than 500 styles, this shop is a paradise for those who love comfortable slippers. You will pay around €6 for a basic slipper with a black felt sole, or €8 for one with a rubber sole. The Jéva brand, the finest quality, in tartan wool, will cost around €10. These are the most comfortable and will keep you warm on many a long winter night.

convent. This region is one of the richest in France in terms of prehistoric sites. There are flintstones and objects made of bone and antler, all carved and engraved by people in the Palaeolithic Age.

A walk through the old town

Take the 17th-C. humpback bridge on the way to the château, and note the crescent-shaped alcoves that allowed pedestrians to take refuge when carts or carriages rolled past. Nowadays, horse-drawn carts are rare, but take in the view from here of the château and the Tardoire. The **Jardin Saint-Florent** (1 Rue Florent, daily except Mon. from May to Oct. 2.30-6.30pm), by the bridge, grows lovely plants, some of which can be bought in the shop. Don't miss the corbelled, half-timbered houses in the Rue des Bans, Grande-Rue and the Rue du Bourg-Pailler.

Ruficaldiens or Pichotiers?

Ruficaldiens and Pichotiers, – the inhabitants of La Rochefoucauld are called by both names. A *Pichotte* is a migratory bird and also a local chocolate speciality, but the name Pichotier may well

derive from the word for a maker of pitchers. The *pichotte*, a chocolate-coated marzipan sweet was created in the 1940s. You won't be given the secret of the recipe, but you can buy and taste delicious *pichottes* at the **Chocolaterie Brun** (39 Grande-Rue, ☎ 05 45 63 00 26; open 9am-12.30pm and 3-7.30pm, closed Sun. afternoon and Mon.).

Musée de l'Hôpital

Place du Champ-de-Foire. Information at the hospital admissions desk
☎ 05 45 67 54 00
Open daily, 10am-noon and 2-5pm.
Free admission.

The hospital was founded in 1685 and houses a medical museum. The exhibits include old apothecary jars and lovely 16th and 17th C. pottery. There's also a

surgical kit belonging to a doctor in Napoleon's army. When you look at the instruments, and remember that anaesthetics had not been invented, you'll realise that in those days it was wise to avoid surgery at all costs!

Confolens
folklore and tradition

Confolens, which stands at the confluence of the rivers Vienne and Goire, is a delightful medieval town with a castle keep and natural spring. Every year the whole world meets in its streets to celebrate folklore and traditional music from all over the world. The beds of the local rivers contain minute deposits of gold and garnet, for which you can prospect.

A walk in the town

The best way to see the town is on foot. The Pont-Vieux, the main bridge, once had three towers and a draw-bridge, but it is now more modest although still an excellent place from which to get a general view of the old town. On the left bank at one end of the bridge is the **Fontaine du Fontorse**, a natural spring at least five centuries old, where water wells up out of the ground. The lanes of the old town contain lovely houses with wooden eaves, especially in the Rue du Soleil, and 18th-C. mansions, the most handsome of which is the town hall. Unfortunately, all that remains of the château is a 12th–13th-C. square granite tower.

International festival of folklore

☎ 05 45 84 00 77
Mid-Aug.

Every year troupes of perform-ers, folk singers, musicians and dancers from 20 or more countries descend on Confolens and turn it into a huge festival. Intercultural communication is encouraged, Mexicans dance with Koreans, Turks with Peruvians and Ukranians with Brazilians –

anything goes! The folklore groups parade in the streets in their colourful national costumes. If you're going to be in Confolens for the occasion, brush up on your dance steps before leaving home, and be prepared to party!

Kroumirs and *éphémères*

Chocolaterie Fabrice Fort
1 Rue Émile-Fort,
16500 Confolens.
☎ 05 45 84 03 89

The *kroumir* and the *éphémère* have been made here for more than a century. *Kroumir*

is a sweet made of almond paste and cracknel (around €5 for 3½ oz/100 g). *Éphémères*, whose name derives from the speed with which they melt in the mouth, is a light combination of chocolate and fresh cream, covered with a dark chocolate coating.

A restaurant to remember

**L'Auberge de la Tour
Le Bourg, 16500
Saint Germain.
☎ 05 45 84 15 27**
Menu at €23.
Specialities in this delightful restaurant include Limousin beef with shallots, *salade de gésiers* with raspberry vinaigrette, and veal in a blue cheese sauce. If you would prefer something a little lighter, try the local speciality of omelette with ceps. Enjoy a glass of wine with your meal, sit back and relax. It's well worth the trip.

Saint-Germain-de-Confolens

*4 miles (7 km)
N of Confolens*

The domaine de Longeville

☎ 05 45 85 36 17
Open daily, July-Aug., 10am-8pm, from Easter to 1 Nov., Sun. afternoon.
Admission charge.
The owners of this vast estate breed some rather unusual animals. They have 200 roe deer, 50 wild boar and about a 100 fallow deer. Depending on your beliefs and feelings, you can either simply admire

**Spotcheck
F 4**

Things to do

• Eating and shopping on the Longeville estate
• Eating in L'Auberge de la Tour

Things to do with children

• Prospecting for gold

Within easy reach

*Ruffec district (p. 186)
Charente-Limousine
(p. 180)
La Rochefoucauld
(p. 176)*

Tourist Office

Confolens:
☎ 05 45 84 22 22

these magnificent creatures, or you can enjoy venison they produce in many guises at local restaurants. Terrines made of wild boar and venison pâté – €5 for 7 oz (200 g) – will delight any gourmet, unless, of course, they prefer the jugged venison or roast wild boar (€13 for a 3-portion pack). The estate has a restaurant and crêperie, where all these delicacies can be sampled.

PROSPECTING FOR GOLD

**La Tulette, 16 500 Confolens, southern exit.
Service de la Jeunesse et des Sports,
Eté Actif à Confolens
☎ 05 45 84 02 84**
Open daily except Sun. from 2 July to 22 August, 9am-noon and 2-6pm.
Like all the rivers that rise in the Massif Central, the Vienne carries minute deposits of gold and garnet. The Sports and Youth Service offers trips to teach **panning for gold**. Don't think you'll make your fortune here, the bits of gold are minute. However, the garnets, which are deep red semi-precious stones, are found here in quite reasonable quantities.

Charente-Limousine
and a tiny Scottish enclave

T his southern part of the Charentes has soil that is a mixture of granite and clay which produces a very characteristic vegetation. It is interesting to note that the Limousin and Périgourdin dialects are still spoken here. Charentes-Limousine is also well-known cattle-rearing country. Its valleys are criss-crossed with rivers, perfect for angling and canoeing, and you could also explore the area by mountain-bike.

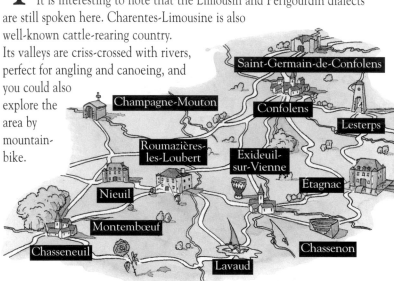

Saint-Germain-de-Confolens

Champagne-Mouton

Confolens

Lesterps

Roumazières-les-Loubert

Exideuil-sur-Vienne

Étagnac

Nieuil

Montembœuf

Chasseneuil

Lavaud

Chassenon

Saint-Germain-de-Confolens

4 miles (7 km)
N of Confolens
A historic village
The ruins of the fortress of Saint-Germain-de-Confolens, built in the 12th and 15th C., dominate the valleys of the Issoire and the Vienne. Its inner courtyard is flanked by

four towers. For several years a group of young volunteers has been working to preserve and restore the site, and it is largely thanks to their efforts that you can now admire the arrow-slits, loopholes and vaulted rooms of the basement. Saint-Germain is also a pleasant village to explore, with its weaver's house, medieval bridge and 12th C. church.

Lesterps

5 miles (8.5 km) E
of Confolens
An ancient abbey church
The abbey church of Lesterps was destroyed in 1040, then restored in the late 12th C. It belonged to a monastery founded in AD 980 by Augustinian monks. The granite belfry is 140 ft

(43 m) high. Admire the capitals on the columns inside the church, for which it is noted, and then explore the abbey ruins and old houses of the village.

Champagne-Mouton

16 miles (25 km)
W of Confolens
A Scottish tomb
The church of Champagne-Mouton is interesting because it contains the tomb of Chambers, a high constable of Scottish origin, whose arms feature on one of the

keystones of the vaults.
In the 15th C. a group of
Scottish families came and
settled in the town. The lamb
above the main door of the
church gave its name to the
town (*mouton* means sheep).

Étagnac
4 miles (6.5 km)
NE of Chabanais

Château de Rochebrune
☎ 05 45 89 08 29
Open daily, July-Aug.,
10am-noon and 2-6pm;
June-Sept., 2-6pm,
except Tues. Guided tour
Admission charge.
The four round towers of the
château, were inhabited by
the lords of Chabanais in the
11th and 13th C., and now
contain Renaissance and
Empire furniture. Openings
in the walls were made in

the 16th C. by the daughter
of Marshal de Montluc, the
general in command of the
Catholic armies during the
Wars of Religion. You reach
the courtyard via a pretty
humpbacked bridge.

Chassenon
3 miles (4.5 km)
E of Chabanais

In Roman times

Roman baths
16150 Chassenon
☎ 05 45 89 32 21
Chabanais Tourist Office
☎ 05 45 89 08 29
Open daily, June-15
Sept., 10am-noon and
2-7pm; Apr.-May and
15 Sept.-11 Nov.,
2-5pm. Guided tour.
Admission charge.

Spotcheck
F 4

Things to do
• Watersports on the
Lavaud lake
• Stay at the royal chateau
in Nieuil

Things to do with children
• Horse-riding and biking

Within easy reach
Confolens (p. 178)
La Rochefoucauld (p. 176)
Ruffec district (p.186)

Tourist Offices
Confolens:
☎ 05 45 84 22 22
Chabanais:
☎ 05 45 89 08 29
Montembœuf:
☎ 05 45 65 03 31
Roumazières-Loubert:
☎ 05 45 71 72 30

This Roman complex was
constructed in the 1st C.
from rocks created when a
meteorite fell to earth 200
million years previously.

The Château de Rochebrune is mirrored in its moat

The 300-acre (120 ha) site was enclosed by a wall and consisted of temples, a theatre and baths, which were at the eastern end. Local residents came here in large numbers to pray to the gods, restore their health and for entertainment. It may also have had a market-place. The **baths** (the only part open to the public) have underground rooms, pools, aqueducts, cold and hot rooms, all of which are well preserved. Some of the walls are 27 ft (8 m) high. The collections of objects from archaeological digs are also worth seeing.

Lavaud

4 miles (6 km)
S of Chabanais

Swimming and windsurfing

The Lavaud lake, on the borders of Haute-Vienne and the Charentes, covers a 100-acre (40-ha) area and has a water-sports centre where you can learn to windsurf, water-ski or sail a dinghy. You can also hire a pedalo or canoe, or just go for a swim. The nearby 445-acre (180-ha) lake is open to anglers. It's the ideal spot for a family day out and there are picnic areas all around the lakes, which were created when the river was dammed.

Exideuil-sur-Vienne

2½ miles (4 km)
W of Chabanais

Music at Whitsun

Festival de Chants et de Musiques du Monde
Exideuil-sur-Vienne
☎ 05 45 89 01 29

This festival is held every Whitsun (Pentecost) and brings together many different types of music and song. You'll see the village at its most lively and hear the sound of exotic musical instruments, such as the pan pipes, the sitar and African drums.

Nieuil

6 miles (10 km) NE of Chasseneuil-sur-Bonnière

Staying in a royal château

16270 Nieuil
☎ 05 45 71 36 38
Hotel-restaurant open late Apr. to early Nov.; La Grange aux Oies winter restaurant, open from mid-Dec. to mid-Apr.

This château was once a hunting lodge used by King François I, and it stands in 100 acres (40 ha) of grounds. Surrounded by a moat, it is now part of the prestigious **Relais et Châteaux** chain. In fact, it was the first château in France to be converted into a hotel. A weekend spent in these glorious surroundings, lazing by the pool, will cost from €122-260 a night for a double room. Even if you're not staying at the hotel, you can visit the grounds and art gallery (art-deco furnishings and old posters), which occupies the old stables. (Open late Apr.-early Nov. 2-7pm, in winter by appointment only, free admission).

Roumazières-Loubert

8 miles (13 km) NE of Chasseneuil-sur-Bonnière

Château de Peyras

16270 Roumazières-Loubert
☎ 05 45 71 25 25
Open daily, except Tues. 1 Apr.-30 Oct., 3-6.30pm. Closed during the *son et lumière*.
Free admission.

The Château de Peyras has dominated the Charente valley since the 13th C. It was the seat of the lords of Roumazières, and was designed as a fortress to protect the river crossing. The Black Prince and his army of 10,000 men passed by this castle on the way to the Battle of Poitiers in 1356.

The Château de Nieuil, now a luxury hotel

ON FOOT, ON HORSE-BACK, BY BIKE

There are plenty of **hiking, riding and cycling trails** through the lovely countryside of Charente-Limousine. The Tourist Offices publish comprehensive local guides, which suggest itineraries to suit every level of fitness. There are even guided walks with themes such as wild mushrooms or the flora and fauna of Roumazières-Loubert. As a rule, these routes take you through forests, streams and springs, and you can visit places of interest throughout the region.

Don't miss the 15th-C. detached building, whose timber frame looks just like an upturned boat. In July, a spectacular *son et lumière* performance is held here.

Learning about Charentes tiles

Two large tile-making factories can be found here due to the abundant deposits of clay. The factories can be visited if you call in advance to arrange a tour. This is the European capital of terracotta roof tiles. Today they are manufactured by machine and the firing is computer controlled. These industrialists

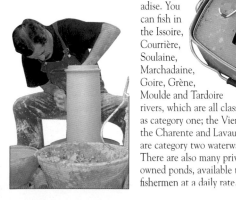

are heirs to a long tradition and still produce beautiful roof, floor and wall tiles.

Montembœuf
9 miles (15 km) NE of La Rochefoucauld

Tickling fish in Charente-Limousine

Information from the Confolens Tourist Office
☎ 05 45 84 22 22
Fédération de Pêche
60 Rue de Bourlion au Gond-Pontouvre,
☎ 05 45 69 33 91

The area, with its numerous waterways, is an angler's paradise. You can fish in the Issoire, Courrière, Soulaine, Marchadaine, Goire, Grène, Moulde and Tardoire rivers, which are all classified as category one; the Vienne, the Charente and Lavaud lake are category two waterways. There are also many privately owned ponds, available to fishermen at a daily rate.

Brigueuil
12 miles (20 km) NE. of Confolens

Walled town

Situated at a height of 1,122 ft (342 m), this former fortified town harbours the original 17th-C. walled city. The moment you enter the old town via the Pont-Levis, you are immediately immersed in a medieval world, created entirely from local stone. The imposing church, with its impressive Renaissance portal, was once used by the townspeople as a shelter during the numerous attacks on the town. When you leave, take the Péage gate which opens out onto a wonderful panorama of green woodland. From here you can explore the surrounding area which has a few treasures of its own, including a curious pyramid-shaped fountain.

The forest of Horte and the Tardoire valley
mills and chateaux galore

This lush district lying about 12½ miles (20 km) east of Angoulême, is crisscrossed by pretty rivers. Visit the feudal château at Villebois-Lavalette and make a detour to see the château at La Mercerie, a Versailles in miniature. Further north the valley of the Tardoire offers some wonderful canoeing trips. As for local attractions, you'll come across a château every mile and a mill every half-mile.

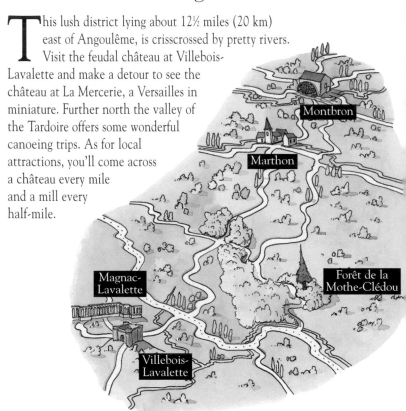

Montbron

Marthon

Forêt de la Mothe-Clédou

Magnac-Lavalette

Villebois-Lavalette

Villebois-Lavalette

16 miles (26 km)
SE of Angoulême
The feudal château
☎ 05 45 64 71 58
Open daily, 10am-noon
and 2.30-6pm,
May-Sept. (5pm from
Oct. to May)
Admission charge.
The Château of Villebois-
Lavalette dominates the
region from its hilltop. It was
built in the 10th C. by Élie
de Villebois, then extended
in the 12th and 13th C. by

the Lusignan family. Only
the 10th-C. chapel and outer
curtain wall, flanked by round
towers, still remain. In the
northern tower 12th-C.
latrines were built into the
thick walls. From the top of
the towers you'll get a
magnificent view over the
Dordogne valley.

300-year-old market halls
These market halls were built
in 1665 on the site of the
12th-C. covered market and
are the loveliest in the
region. They are decked with
flowers all summer. The oak
roofbeam rests on old and
worn stone
columns.

CANOEING ON THE TARDOIRE

Maison du Canoë
Montbron, Route de Vouthon (19 miles/30 km at the Angoulême Tourist Office)
☎ 05 45 23 93 58
The **Centre Départemental de Plein Air du Chambon** rents out kayaks and canoes on the Tardoire in July and August. The river has been widened to include canoe passes and fish ladders beside the mill dykes. For a lovely day out, boat down to the **Chambon Gorges**, passing mills and châteaux on the way. The trip includes a car to take you back to your starting point (€15 per person per day).

The market's sloping, uneven floor is covered in ancient tiles. This is certainly the place to shop every Saturday morning. You'll find local poultry, foie gras, honey and organic foods.

Magnac-Lavalette
16 miles (26 km)
SE of Angoulême
The Château de la Mercerie
Not open to the public.
Between 1930 and 1970, the Réthoré brothers squandered a small fortune in order to rebuild this little neo-Gothic château, which ended up looking like a Charentes version of Versailles palace. The château still remains unfinished, but the colonnaded façade in beautiful white limestone is an amazing

720 ft (220 m) wide and almost 50 ft (15 m) high. The walls are 13 ft (4 m) thick in places. The brothers are buried in the château.

Montbron
19 miles (30 km)
E of Angoulême
Visiting the miller
The Mills of Montbron
Information at the Montbron Tourist Office
☎ 05 45 70 81 87

Open daily, except Mon., 10am-noon and 2.30-5pm
Admission charge.
The Menet mill is one of the four 'living mills', with either millwheels or turbines, that have been restored to full working order. You can look around and buy wheat flour, buckwheat flour and walnut oil here. If you have always wanted to make your own bread you can take a course – it only lasts half a day – at the **Ecole de Pain du Moulin de Chabrot**.

Huile Vierge de Noix

Angoulême (p.170)
La Rochefoucauld (p. 176)
Aubeterre (p. 190)
Barbezieux (p. 196)

Spotcheck
E 5

Things to do
• Canoeing down the Tardoire river
• Shopping for food at the Mills of Montbron

Things to do with children
• Visiting the Clédou arboretum

Within easy reach
Angoulême (p.170)
La Rochefoucauld (p. 176)
Aubeterre (p. 190)
Barbezieux (p. 196)

Tourist Offices
Villebois-Lavalette:
☎ 05 45 64 71 58
Montbron:
☎ 05 45 23 60 09

La Mothe-Clédou
15 miles (23.5 km)
SE of Angoulême
A walk in the forest
Arboretum Jean-Aubouin du Clédou
Maison Forestière
☎ 05 45 23 00 15
Admission charge.
If you love exotic and rare plants and shrubs, don't miss this opportunity to see the botanical delights of the forest of La Mothe-Clédou. A special route designed by the Office National des Forêts (French forestry commission) makes it possible to study trees from 37 countries, including the giant sequoia (*Sequoia sempervirens*) and the Himalayan cedar. This educational tour lasts for 1½ hours and covers an area of over 14 acres (6 ha) that are specially laid out for the purpose.

Around Ruffec
Romanesque churches and the meandering Charente

In this land of greenery and rivers the charm of the Romanesque churches is equalled only by the elegance of the châteaux. Along the winding rivers of the Charente, Or or Péruse, you will find fortified villages, isolated abbeys and prehistoric sites. This countryside, with its many waterways, is a great favourite with anglers and canoeists.

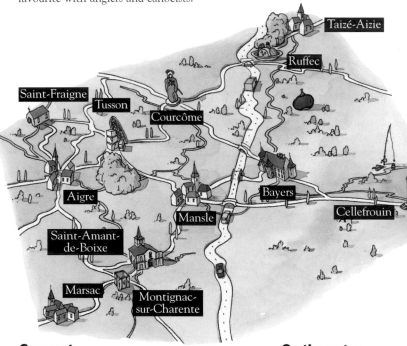

Taizé-Aizie

Ruffec

Saint-Fraigne

Tusson

Courcôme

Aigre

Bayers

Cellefrouin

Mansle

Saint-Amant-de-Boixe

Marsac

Montignac-sur-Charente

Gourmet shopping at Ruffec
Stop at Ruffec to discover a large range of delicious local foods. A market is held every Wednesday and Saturday morning and a very lively fair is held on the 13th and 28th of each month.

The wares on offer include farmhouse foie gras, *tourteau* (cheesecake), cheese tart and duck and goose *rillettes* (chitterlings).

On the water
The Charente river crosses the Ruffec district from Taizé-Aizie to Marsac. Its tributaries are full of fish – gudgeon, bleak, pike, eels and trout abound. When the season opens, holiday fishing licences (*carte de pêche vacances*) can be bought (€26 for two weeks).

Things to do

• Canoe rental at Mansle and at Montignac
• Rambling at Lichères and climbing the Roc de Rosny
• Fishing in the tributaries of the Charente

Things to do with children

• Exploring the Ruffec district on bicycle or horseback

Within easy reach

Angoulême (p. 170)
Melle district (p. 166)
Cognac (p. 200)
Charente-Limousine (p. 180)

Tourist Offices

Mansle:
☎ 05 45 20 39 91
Montignac:
☎ 05 45 22 71 97
Ruffécois:
☎ 05 45 31 05 42

At Mansle they can be obtained from the **Maison de la Presse**, **Le Penalty** bar and at **La Boîte à Pêche**. For a delightful way to explore the district, the **Club de Mansle** (canoeing centre, open 1 July-31 Aug; ☎ 05 45 22 26 68) and the **Club de Montignac** (Tourist Office ☎ 05 45 22 71 97) rent canoes by the day or by the week. And if you think holidays are a time to do nothing, you can swim and sunbathe at Amberac, Marsac or Montignac (near Saint-Amant-de-Boixe).

On foot, on horseback or by bicycle

Leave your car in one of the villages and explore the Ruffec district on foot, by bike or on horseback. If you're walking, take the GR 36 footpath, which spans the district from east to west. Many routes are suitable for families, and details are available at the tourist offices. At Mansle you can **rent bicycles** (**M. Rosellen** at La Gagnarderie; ☎ 05 45 20 36 33; about €13 a day for a mountain-bike, €8 for an ordinary bike). There are also many **equestrian centres** (ask for information at the Mansle Tourist Office: ☎ 05 45 20 39 91).

Courcôme
4 miles (7 km) SW of Ruffec
A pilgrimage for newly weds

The Romanesque church of Courcôme is one of the oldest in the Ruffec district. Some parts date from the 11th C., and the façade is 12th C. The capitals are decorated with the heads of imaginary beasts. Inside, you'll find a statue of the Virgin Mary which is greatly revered by the local people. According to tradition, newly wedded brides offer their wedding wreath or bouquet to the statue.

Taste the chestnuts
The red earth of Ruffec is covered in sweet chestnuts. If you want to enjoy them at their best, roast them the French way in a *diable*, an earthenware or cast-iron pot, which stands on three feet and has a long handle. The *diable* is put on the hob or over the flames. First, cut a cross in the skin of the chestnuts so that they do not burst in the heat. Once they are cooked, the French eat them hot, with jam or butter and accompanied by a glass of white wine.

and holding an overflowing wine glass in his hand, as his acolytes martyr St Fraigne. The fresco over the door illustrates the Apocalypse, and the one in the choir ceiling depicts the Last Supper. Ask for the keys at the town hall in Saint-Fraigne (☎ 05 45 21 37 67).

Bayers

8 miles (13 km)
S of Ruffec
The château
☎ 05 45 22 54 74
Guided tour all year round and daily 30 June-8 Sept., 2-6.30pm
Admission charge.
The château was essential for guarding the old ford over the Charente. It was built in the 12th and 15th C. and was the seat of an important estate which was owned by the La Rochefoucauld family. Note the building between the cylindrical tower and the gable-end overlooking the moats, the terrace (17th-18th C.), the walkway and the 12th-C. square castle keep with its flat buttresses.

Tusson

9 miles (15 km)
SE of Ruffec
A protected village
For the last 20 years Tusson has been adopted by the Marpen Club, an organisation that offers retraining courses to people who are out of work. The courses lead to a

certificate of competence in the building trades. If you wander through the village and admire the 12th- and 15th-C. houses, take a close look at the ones near the church. You will also see the stone-cutting sites and workshops for making stained glass. Include a visit to the **Musée des Arts et Traditions Populaires** where there are more than 200 exhibits illustrating agricultural life and crafts in the region.

(Daily, 10am-noon and 2.30-6pm; closed Tues. out of season. ☎ 05 45 31 17 47.) Finally, take a walk in the **medieval garden** (same opening hours as museum), which contains plants that were grown in the region from the 12th to the 15th C., including medicinal herbs.

Saint-Fraigne

13 miles (21 km)
SW of Ruffec
A contemporary sanctuary
Stop at the little church of Saint-Fraigne to admire the stained glass and frescoes created in the late 1940s by the painter and craftsman, Louis Mazetier. The stained glass illustrates the arrival of Christianity to the region, brought by the hermit, St Fraigne. See if you can spot Bacchus, sitting on a barrel

Cellefrouin

10 miles (17 km)
E of Mansle
Lanterns of the dead
The purpose of these monuments is not fully understood. Some believe they were designed to help travellers

GREEN TOURISM AT LICHÈRES

Lichères-la-Salle (3 miles (5 km) NE of Mansle) is a tourist centre for outdoor pursuits: it offers many hiking and rambling paths in the woodlands or along the Charente. For the more active the Roc de Rosny, has been adapted for **rock-climbing** (information at the Mansle Tourist Office: ☎ 05 45 20 39 91). Art-lovers should visit the **church of Saint-Denis**. It stands alone in the fields, a few hundred yards from the village and is a masterpieces of 12th-C. Romanesque art. Still at Lichères, take the **ferry** across the Charente. It is operated by ropes and was mainly used for moving cattle from one side of the river to the other.

who had lost their way, while others think the lamp on the top was to honour the dead. The Lanterne de Cellefrouin in the cemetery is one of the best examples. Around 40 ft (12 m) high, it consists of 8 columns on a plinth. The opening for the lamp is about 10 ft (3 m) up, and it was hoisted into position by a rope.

Montignac-sur-Charente

10 miles (16 km) N of Angoulême

Le Donjon

Montignac Tourist Office, Place du Docteur-Feuillet
☎ **05 45 22 71 97**
Open July-Aug. 3-7pm daily except Sun.; out of season on request at the Tourist Office.
☎ **05 45 22 71 97**
Free admission during exhibitions

The village of Montignac-sur-Charente is dominated by a 12th-C. castle keep and boasts a panoramic view over the Charente valley. To appreciate it to the full you should climb the narrow staircase to the top. The ruins of the medieval fortress, the 13th-C. towers and ramparts are also worth seeing.

Saint-Amant-de-Boixe

6 miles (9 km) S of Mansles

The abbey church

This abbey church, built between the 12th and the 15th C., is the largest religious building in the whole of the Charentes. The sculptures on the façade are largely inspired by those of the Angoulême cathedral and

include the apostles and other figures as well as animals. Inside, 14th-C. frescoes illustrate the childhood of Christ and the Last Supper.

The neolithic necropolis and the Forest of Boixe

3 miles (5 km) S of Mansle

The Boixe archeological site is one of the most interesting in the region. It took several digs to expose the tumulus. A corridor 27 ft (8 m) long, leads to a rectangular room whose pillars support a colossal stone slab measuring 13 ft (4 m) by 7 ft (2 m).

Aubeterre-sur-Dronne
picturesque medieval village

There is no doubt that Aubeterre is one of the prettiest villages in the Charentes. With its steep lanes, tiered houses, red-tiled roofs and flower-decked balconies, it looks like a village in the Pyrenees. Aubeterre was built in the Middle Ages on a hillside overlooking the Dronne, and harbours the finest underground church in Europe.

Musée du Papillon et des Arts Africain
Place Ludovic-Trarieux
☎ 05 45 98 64 58
Open from Easter to Sept. 9am-8pm; out of season by appointment and weekends 2-8pm.
Admission charge.
Albert Petit, who runs this museum, lovingly looks after the 12,000 butterflies and 6,000 other insects which he and his family have collected from Africa. 'Monsieur Papillon' (Mr Butterfly) also has a impressive collection of *Goliatus giganticus*, a gigantic beetle with huge claws, which deserves a place in the best horror films. For around €76 you can buy three or four of these little creatures together in a box. The museum also contains a display of some 600 examples of African art, including an 18th-C. box, slave bracelets and stones said to have magic healing powers, not forgetting the 3,000 Murano glass beads, dating from the 13th to the 18th C. which were used by early explorers as payment to African native bearers and traders. Every weekday morning in summer, the museum runs classes for children to show them how to catch butterflies in the surrounding countryside. Guided tours available in English.

River or beach?
Route de Ribérac.
A real beach with real sand, but the water is fresh, not salty. The Dronne spreads out into a lake and the banks have been adapted for bathing. A beach has been created with fine sand, which is replenished on a regular basis. It's an ideal place for all the family, both young and old.

The church of Saint Jacques
The church of Saint Jacques in the upper town is the other wonder of Aubeterre-sur-Dronne. The original church was destroyed in 1562 during the Wars of Religion and only its 12th-C. facade remains. The portal is so strongly influenced by Moorish architecture that you would think you were in Morocco. Look out for the signs of the zodiac in the lower section.

A journey to the centre of the earth

The 12th-C. church of Saint-Jean was carved entirely out of the hillside, and is one of the most spectacular sights in the Charentes. The 66-ft (20 m) high **underground nave** is unique in Europe. The baptismal font in the centre was cut into the rock between the 5th and the 10th C., and it allows for total immersion. Even more impressive is the necropolis, containing around 100 sarcophagi. Finally, there's an astonishing vaulted crypt, cut into the rock, beneath the church itself.

Place Trarieux

The Place Trarieux in the lower part of the town forms the bustling heart of the village. It is surrounded by ancient linden trees and in the centre stands a statue, erected by the inhabitants, in honour of **Ludovic Trarieux**, a local man and founder of the League of Human Rights. The square is very lively in the summer and is lined with shops selling locally made pottery, art galleries and bars. You're sure to love it.

Pottery workshops and shops

The narrow streets of Aubeterre are filled with potter's studios and shops. Make sure you shop around to compare the different wares and prices, and make your choices carefully as at the height of the season the prices can be very steep.

KELLOGG'S CORN FLAKES' CASTLE

This feudal château has largely been destroyed, but it retains apartments dating from the 14th and 17th C., as well as a square tower topped by a walkway and the vestiges of a curtain wall. Unfortunately, the château is not open to the public, because it's the property of the king of the toasted maize flake, the owner of Kellogg's Cornflakes.

Valley of the Seugne
on the edge of the Dordogne

The Seugne valley extends from Pons to Montguyon at the southern end of the Charente and borders the Gironde and the Dordogne. The region has the largest concentration of Romanesque churches in the département. Perversely, perhaps that's the reason why it produced Émile Combes (1835–1921), father of the separation of the Church and the State, who was nicknamed 'the devourer of nuns'!

Pons

*12¹/₂ miles (20 km)
SE of Saintes*
**Walking
through the town**
Pons stands on a plateau overlooking the valley of the Seugne. It is dominated by a massive **castle keep**, a masterpiece of Romanesque military architecture (open daily, 15 June-15 Sept., 10am-noon 3-7pm; out of season: 5.30pm). The town was the birthplace of Agrippa d'Aubigné and of the French prime minister Émile Combes. It was an important stop on the route to the shrine of St James of Compostela as can be witnessed by the pilgrims' hospice, which spans the road to Bordeaux. On leaving

Pons by the southern exit, stop at the Roman gate and take a look at the stone benches where pilgrims rested in the Middle Ages.

Jonzac

*12¹/₂ miles (20 km)
S of Pons*
**Old stones
at Jonzac**
Jonzac is the biggest town in the south of the département. It stands in the Seugne valley, on the river, and is actually

the combination of three separate villages: the Bourg du Château, the Bourg de l'Eglise and the Bourg des Carmes. The 15th-C. **château** with its round towers stands overlooking the Seugne. It now serves as the town hall. In the Bourg de l'Église, on the second of Jonzac's hills, look out for the **covered market** in typical Eiffel style, which was recently restored (market on Tues. and Fri.; small 'green' market on Sun. morning). Finally, on the left

bank of the Seugne you can enjoy a walk in the tranquil surroundings of the cloister in the **Carmelite convent**.

Mosnac-sur-Seugne
15 miles (24.5 km) S of Pons
Eating at the Moulin de Marcouze

☎ 05 4670 46 16
Open daily, June-Sept; closed early Oct. to end of March
Menus €24, €37, €65.
The **Moulin de Marcouze** is one of the best restaurants in the Charentes, serving food that is both local and traditional, but with a some refinements and original touches. You're advised to try one of the two specialities of the house: ravioli stuffed with *petits-gris charentais* (snails) and caviar and potato pie. There are also many other delicious

(and not quite as expensive) dishes, such as calf's sweet-breads with mustard and braised leg of lamb.

Montguyon
24 miles (38.5 km) S of Jonzac
Aire de Beau Vallon leisure centre
☎ 05 46 04 11 66
Open daily, 1 May-10 Sept. Bar open from 1 June.
Free admission.
The Aire de Beau Vallon is a leisure centre in the middle of a forest of martime pines; the perfect place for a family outing with young children. The lake has a miniature port, so that children can learn all about sailing in complete safety. You can go walking or horseriding through the forest, which has signposted paths. The three little sandy beaches are ideal for swimming and sunbathing.

International festival of song, dance and music
☎ 05 46 04 10 60
End of July-beginning of August
Admission charge.

Spotcheck
D 5

Things to do
• Gourmet shopping from a goose-breeder
• Attending the international festival of song, dance and music
• A meal at the Moulin de Marcouze

Things to do with children
• A day out at the Aire de Beau Vallon

Within easy reach
Cognac (p. 200)
Champagne Charentaise (p. 194)
Barbezieux (p. 196)
Aubeterre (p. 190)

Tourist Offices
Jonzac: ☎ 05 46 48 49 29
Pons: ☎ 05 46 96 13 31
Montguyon:
☎ 05 46 04 28 70

The Festival of Montguyon has been welcoming musicians and dancers from all over the world for the past 20 years. Although the music is important, this is mainly a dance festival. Performers come from Russia, the Marquesas islands, Mexico and Kenya, making it just as multi-cultural as its rival in Confolens. One-day courses are available that teach a variety of dances, including the Argentinian tango, the Flamenco, traditional African dances, and many more.

GOURMET SHOPPING AT A GOOSE-BREEDER
Élevage Manicot,
17520 Saint-Martial-sur-Né, 15 miles (24 km) S of Pons
☎ 05 46 49 52 72
Open daily, June-Sept., 9am-noon and 2-7pm, except Sun. and public holidays.
Breeding geese is an old family tradition here.

You can learn all about it at this farm, from the hatching of the goslings to the final canning process. You can also buy *confit*, chitterlings or traditional foie gras, the latter only being suitable for those who are not upset at the way the geese are force-fed.

Champagne charentaise
cognac country

The vines of the Grande Champagne form the best and most prestigious vineyards for making cognac. They cover the rolling hills between Cognac and Châteauneuf-sur-Charente. The region includes the valley of the Charente and the course of the Né. It is largely dependent on the production of cognac, and the many villages, inhabited mainly by bargemen, are evidence of the importance of this trade from the Middle Ages onwards.

Châteaubernard

1¼ miles (2 km)
S of Cognac

The Saint-Gobain glassworks

☎ 05 45 82 10 71
Tours in July-Aug.;
out of season group tours only. Booking at the Cognac Tourist Office,
☎ 05 45 82 10 71.
Admission charge.

The Saint-Gobain glassworks are the largest and most modern in the world. Nearly 2 million bottles a day are produced here to supply the markets for Cognac brandy, Bordeaux wines and Armagnac. The factory has three massive furnaces,

which can reach temperatures as high as 2,700 °F (1,500 °C) and can hold up to 500 tonnes of melted glass!

A view over the vineyard from the Château de Bouteville

4 miles (7 km) E of
Châteauneuf-sur-Charente

This 17th-C. château is now in ruins, apart from the central building, which is surrounded by round towers and deep moats. It was once owned by Count François de Montmorency, who was beheaded in 1627 for having defied Richelieu's ban on

fighting duels! These romantic ruins dominate the surrounding vineyards and forests and afford some wonderful views.

Mosnac

2½ miles (4 km) N of
Châteauneuf-sur-Charente

Musée Rêve-Auto-Jeunesse

☎ 05 45 62 54 64
Open daily, in season 9am-noon and 2-6pm, except Sun. Out of season, 2-6pm
Admission charge.

This is a museum of pedal-powered vehicles. **Madame Mas** is a passionate collector of little pedal cars and miniature motorised vehicles, which she has collected from all over France during the past 10 years or so. The collection now contains more than 200 models, including an electric Baby Bugatti, a petrol-engine Lotus, a Citroënette 5 HP, a wooden 1902 Panhard, a Dauphine, and an American Jeep. You will also see about 10 full-sized vehicles dating from 1900 to 1930, including a taxi from World War I, a 1908 Peugeot and a penny-farthing bicycle. A very original and fascinating museum!

Saint-Simon

6 miles (10 km) N of Châteauneuf-sur-Charente

Barges and bargemen

The story of Saint-Simon is closely linked to the building of lighters (flat-bottomed barges), which began in the Middle Ages. The barges plied the rivers, loaded with salt, wood and barrels of wine and cognac. The old houses of the bargemen had stone signs sculpted with a hammer and chisel. Saint-Simon cemetery is worth a detour. The tombs of bargemen are decorated with carvings of ropes, anchors and outlines of their craft. Look out for the lighterman's wall beside the river. It's covered with graffiti representing the boats.

Segonzac

10 miles (15.5 km) W of Châteauneuf-sur-Charente

La Cagouillarde restaurant

18 Rue Gaston-Briand, 16130 Segonzac
☎ 05 45 83 40 51

Open daily, except Sat. midday and Sun. evening. *Menus at €12, €18 and €23.*

This restaurant serves the finest local dishes, including stuffed *cagouilles* (snails) and grilled lamb cutlets served with *mojette* beans in walnut oil. The special menu of local dishes (*menu de terroir*) at €18 is highly recommended. It includes local ham served on a bed of potatoes baked in ashes, trout marinated in aniseed, warm goat's cheese salad and, to finish, a delicious vanilla ice-cream sundae garnished with grapes and sprinkled with cognac. The service is good, and the atmosphere is welcoming and friendly.

THE COGNAC UNIVERSITY

37 Rue Gaston Briand
16130 Segonzac
☎ **05 45 83 35 35**
Open daily, except Sat.-Sun., booking only.
Admission reserved for groups of more than six.
This serious international university of brandies and spirits has found a natural home in Segonzac, located at the heart of the Grande Champagne, where the best cognac grapes are grown. This is one of the best places to learn how to taste cognac. After a slide show explaining how the grapes are grown and how the cognac is made, marketed and sold, you sit at tasting desks to

taste five samples, representing 10 years of ageing. When you leave you'll be awarded a certificate by the university.

Spotcheck
E 5

Things to do

• Tasting brandies at the Cognac University in Segonzac
• Eating snails at La Cagouillarde

Things to do with children

• Visiting Le Musée Rêve-Auto-Jeunesse (museum of pedalled vehicles)

Within easy reach

Valley of the Seugne (p. 192)
Cognac (p. 200)
Barbezieux (p. 196)
Angoulême district (p. 174)

Tourist Offices

Châteauneuf-sur-Charente:
☎ **05 45 97 13 32**
Cognac: ☎ **05 45 82 10 71**
Segonzac: ☎ **05 45 83 37 77**

Barbezieux

from chapels, chateaux and abbeys
to the delights of the Charentes
countryside

Barbezieux nestles deep in the valleys of the Trèfle, the Condéon and the Beau, in the heart of the Petite Champagne. It is as famous for its châteaux, chapels and Romanesque abbeys as it is for its vines. You'll soon discover the many delights of the Charentes countryside as you wander through the vineyards and stroll beside the rivers.

Yviers

*3 miles (4.5 km)
W of Chalais*
**A monument
to Cheval,
the postman**
Maison de l'Insolite
☎ 05 45 98 02 65
Visits by appointment,
all year round.
This extraordinary edifice is
the work of **Lucien Favreau**,
a retired plasterer and a
companion of the Tour de
France (master craftsmen).
The building is rather a
touching piece of kitsch.
At first he designed it as a
mausoleum for his dog, to
which he was very attached.
However, he liked the
monument so much that he
simply carried on building.
The house, statues and tombs

are covered in paintings
depicting the life of the
owner, and on the façade
there's a dedication to
Cheval, the postman, whom
Lucien Favreau no doubt
considered his patron.

**An agricultural
show in miniature**
The **Comice Agricole**, an
agricultural show of the south
Charentes, is held on the first
weekend of September. This
trade show and exhibition
welcomes 150 exhibitors,
who display agricultural and

wine-making equipment,
livestock and crafts, and also
sell some delicious local foods.
The organisers devote a lot of
space to games, competitions
and shows, with a very full
programme of events, including guest appearances by
celebrities and even a Miss
Charentes beauty pageant.

Cressac-Saint-Genis

*12 miles (19 km)
E of Barbezieux*
**In the time of
the crusades**
Chapel of the Knights
Templar
**1 mile (2 km)
N of the village**
The keys of the chapel
are with Mme Labrousse,
by appointment.
☎ 05 45 64 08 74

THE HEAD OF ST MATHIAS

The church of Saint-Mathias de Barbezieux was built in the 11th C., rebuilt in the 13th C., and altered again after the Wars of Religion. At one time it was said to contain the relic of the head of St Mathias, and pilgrimages were made to the site until the custom fell into disuse in 1562 when the church was ransacked and the head stolen. Be sure to look out for the 13th-C. portal with its four vaults sculpted with foliage, and the statues of St Peter and St Mathias on the second floor of the 12th-C. bell tower.

The real treasure of this chapel are the 12th-C. frescoes. They represent many scenes from the Crusades, featuring Christian knights and Moslem horsemen. On the north wall you can see fragments illustrating the lives of the crusaders and Saracens in Palestine. At the top of the wall against a white background you can just make out the depiction of a cavalry charge against a retreating Moslem army. Below is the crusaders' camp, showing prisoners being exchanged for ransom money.

Blanzac

*11 miles (17 km)
E of Barbezieux*

In the footsteps of Alfred de Vigny

Manoir du Maine-Giraud (7 miles/3 km N of Bourg de Blanzac)
☎ **05 45 64 04 49**
Open daily, 9am-noon and 2-6pm.
Free admission.

The poet Alfred de Vigny lived here from 1827 to 1863, alternately producing poetry and cognac. The manor house consists of a single-storey raised house, flanked by one wing with a square tower. Access is through a 15th-C. tower, containing a stone spiral staircase. The dining room contains engravings, autographs and documents about the poet, and his study is located in the tower. The manor house is topped by a weather-vane with the initials AV. Although the current owners do not dally with poetry, they have continued to produce cognac. You can visit the *chais* and the distillery, and taste and buy some of the cognac.

Chalais

*19 miles (30 km)
SE of Barbezieux*

Lunch at the château

**Relais du Château
16210 Chalais**
☎ **05 45 98 23 58**

Spotcheck
D 5

Things to do

• Visiting Alfred de Vigny's home
• Attending the agricultural show
• Lunch at the château at Chalais

Within easy reach

Valley of the Seugne (p. 192)
Champagne Charentaise (p. 194)
Jarnac (p. 198)
Aubeterre (p. 190)

Tourist Offices

Barbezieux:
☎ 05 45 78 02 54
Chalais: ☎ 05 45 98 02 71
Segonzac: ☎ 05 45 83 37 77

Open daily, noon and evening, closed on Wed. *Menus from €14 to €32.*
You enter the château by a genuine drawbridge – one of the few still in operation in France. You then pass through a gatehouse into the courtyard. The panoramic view over the roofs of Chalais from the end of the terrace is magnificent. If you are hungry, why not try the restaurant that has opened in one of the wings of the château?

Jarnac
birthplace of François Mitterand

Jarnac has long been a town dedicated to brandy, and now it is also dedicated to the late François Mitterrand, who was born here. You'll find many treasures of Romanesque art, and the banks of the Charente offer wonderful walks. Like the late President of France, you can 'breathe the smell of the linden trees with passion'.

Mitterand's gifts
La Donation François Mitterrand
10 Quai de l'Orangerie
☎ 05 45 81 09 30
Open daily, July-Aug. 10am-noon and 2-7pm; April-Oct.2-6pm daily except Tues.
Admission charge.
The Donation François Mitterrand contains all the gifts that the President was given by heads of state. The two dragons, a gift from the King of Nepal are certainly the most beautiful. These frightening beasts of gilt and bronze were supposed to chase away evil spirits. Note the magnificently decorated vases, gifts from China and Japan, and which are a world apart from the far more ordinary vase that was a present from the Clintons.

Courvoisier
La Maison Courvoisier
2 Place du Château
☎ 05 45 35 56 16
Open Apr.-Oct., Mon.-Fri. (and at weekends., May-Sept. until 6pm), 9.30am-1pm and 2-6pm
Free admission.
This is one of the most famous producers of brandy. After visiting the *chais*, Napoleon decided that Courvoisier would become his sole supplier. The Maison Courvoisier decided to honour their prestigious patron with a museum. You'll find it located in the entrance lobby.

It contains hats and overcoats worn by the Emperor himself. You then go down to the *chais* and sit comfortably among the hundreds of casks of ageing brandy, where you'll be shown a video that tells you all about cooperage and distillation.

Capital architecture
Musée des Maquettes
10 Quai de l'Orangerie
☎ 05 45 81 38 88
Open daily, July-Aug. 10am-noon and 2-7pm; April-Oct. 2-6pm daily except Tues.
Admission charge.
The museum contains models of all the major architectural projects that were undertaken in Paris during François Mitterrand's two terms of office. The models of the Bibliothèque Nationale de France (national library) and the Cité des Sciences (scientific research establishment) are amazing. There are also displays and photographs tracing the major stages of the building of the Grande Arche de la Défense, the

Model of the Place de la Bastille and the new opera on the Quai de l'Orangerie

Spotcheck
D 5

Things to do

• Visit the Courvoisier firm
• See the gifts given to President Mitterrand by heads of state

Within easy reach

Cognac (p. 200)
Champagne Charentaise (p. 194)
Barbezieux (p. 196)

Tourist Office

Jarnac: ☎ 05 45 81 09 30

Opéra Bastille and the Institut du Monde Arabe. On the first floor there's a video room, screening exclusive interviews with President Mitterrand, in which he explains his views and choices of architects.

In the footsteps of Mitterrand

This walk begins at the birthplace of François Mitterrand at 22 Rue Abel Guy. It was in this typical house of the Saintonge province that Yvonne Mitterrand gave birth to her now famous son in October 1916. François was born in a room on the first floor. The house is still occupied so photography is not allowed. The local authorities of Jarnac have the intention of buying the house and turning it into a Mitterrand museum. The next stop on the itinerary is the Grand-Maisons cemetery. The old part of the cemetery consists mainly of vaults, many of which are richly decorated. The site of the Mitterrand family vault, which was restored and whitewashed on the death of the president, is pointed out by arrows at the entrance to the cemetery. There's a large vase in which pilgrims and admirers who come to visit his grave can place their tributes of red roses.

LE COUP DE JARNAC

In 1547, following an affront to a lady, the young Baron de Jarnac found himself forced to demand satisfaction from the Seigneur de la Châtaigneraie, right-hand man of King Henri II. La Châtaigneraie was a fearsome adversary, against whom Jarnac did not stand much of a chance. Wishing to die honourably, the young man took lessons from an old Italian master of arms, who taught him a secret trick. When his opponent raised his heavy two-handed sword, Jarnac thrust his rapier into the man's hamstring. Thanks to this technique, Jarnac emerged victorious from the duel, against all expectations. Since then the expression *coup de Jarnac* has entered the French language, meaning a cunning and decisive action.

Cognac
the home of brandy

With its ancient streets and mansions of the brandy merchants, Cognac is the jewel of the Charente. François I, king of France, was born here, and he gave the town its first letters patent. The 16th-C. mansions are evidence of its former prosperity, but today Cognac is still a thriving town with an international festival of detective films, which attracts thousands of fans every year.

blending techniques and free tastings. You can also buy brandy at the shop (from €8).

Wandering through the old town

The mansions owned by wealthy merchants are legion.

Visiting the cognac producers

The Cognac Tourist Office.
Admission charge.
It's impossible to visit Cognac without inspecting at least one of the big producers. **Hennessy** (☎ 05 45 35 72 68), **Martell** (☎ 05 45 36 33 33) and **Otard** (☎ 05 45 36 88 86) are the best known, and all offer guided tours that include demonstrations of

Be sure to see the **Hôtel de Rabayne**, decorated with a salamander, the insignia of François I. Rue Saulnier, site of the old salt port, contains the **Hôtel Brunet du Boccage** with its magnificent façade. In the Rue Grande the houses are built with blocks of stone on the ground floor and half-timbering on the upper floors. No. 7, the **Maison de la Lieutenance**, with its original sculptures on the façade, is the most famous of them all.

Château des Valois
Boulevard Denfert-Rochereau
☎ 05 45 36 88 88
Open daily, 9.30am-noon, 1.30-6.30pm in summer (Apr.-Oct.); out of season (Nov.-March) daily, 9.30am-noon and 2-6pm except weekends (last visit an hour before closing time).
Admission charge.
The 13th C. stones of this château witnessed the birth of François I, king of France. In 1795 Baron Otard bought the

'Paradise' in the Otard cellars

<small>FESTIVALS FOR ALL</small>

Three other festivals are held in Cognac. In August **Blues Passion** brings together amateur and professional musicians to play jazz, soul, reggae and blues from dusk until dawn. In early September the festival of the **Coup de Chauffe** (tall story) sees comedians and musicians invade the streets and the Parc François I; the festival ends with a firework display. In November the **Salon de la Littérature Européenne** is a convention of European readers and writers. Information from the Tourist Office ☎ 05 45 82 10 71.

château to make his cognac here. The château's old cellars are damp, which is excellent for ageing brandy. The visit passes by 'Paradise', where the oldest bottles are stored, but unfortunately, you are not allowed to go in.

Festival of detective films
23 Allées du Champ-de-Mars
☎ 05 45 35 60 00
Admission charge.
This festival is an extraordinary phenomenon. From early April this peaceful place is invaded by gangs of criminals, escaped convicts and psychopaths, who pour into the town and murder anyone who gets in the way. Fortunately, all this takes place on the cinema screen!

Folk art and Art Nouveau
Musée de Cognac
48 Boulevard Denfert-Rochereau
☎ 05 45 32 07 25
Open daily, except Tues., 10am-noon and 2-6pm (Oct.-May 2-5.30pm)
Admission charge.
This museum of folklore contains paintings, sculpture and art objects dating from the 13th C. to 20th C. The fine art section includes sculptures by Rodin, Flemish and Dutch painting as well as examples of Art Nouveau glass by Gallé and Lalique.

Spotcheck
D 5

Things to do
• Visiting the biggest cognac makers.
• Wandering through the old town
• Attending the detective film festival

Within easy reach
Saintes (p. 202)
Valley of the Seugne (p. 192)
Champagne Charentaise (p. 194)
Jarnac (p. 198)
Barbezieux (p. 196)

Tourist Office
Cognac:
☎ 05 45 82 10 71

A breath of fresh air
Cognac wanted to pay homage to its illustrious protector, king François I, so the **municipal park** was named after him. As you stroll around you'll see deer, swans and ducks. The park lies on the edge of a wood beside the Charente – a perfect place to relax, and you can even do a spot of fishing for gudgeon in the river. The beautiful lawns, banks of flowers, grottos, streams with little bridges, and the **gardens** make the park a delightful spot for romantic walks.

Saintes
crossroads of the Charentes

S aintes owes its name to the Celts of Santons, but the town was originally established by the Romans. It was the centre of river trade in wines and brandy, and remained the economic capital of the *département* of Charente-Maritime. Fairs are held every month, and you'll find a wealth of medieval buildings, but this lively old town is far from being stuck in the past.

Martyrdom in the 2nd C.
The church of Saint-Eutrope and its crypt
Rue Saint-Eutrope
☎ 05 46 74 23 82
Free admission.

The church owes its name to Bishop Eutropius who was sent by Pope Clement in the 2nd C. to convert the region to Christianity. After converting Eustelle, daughter of the governor of the town, his skull was split in two by an unfriendly local wielding an axe. The church was built by Benedictine monks in the early 15th C. and was long an important stop on the route to the shrine of **St James of Compostela**. Those who appreciate religious architecture should visit the **Abbaye-aux-Dames**. (☎ 05 46 97 48 48; summer: open daily 10am-12.30pm and 2-7pm; winter: open daily 2-7pm, Wed. and Sat. 10am-12.30pm and 2-7pm; admission charge.)

A fiery passion
Like his contemporaries, Michelangelo and Leonardo da Vinci, Bernard Palissy was an all-round genius. It was in Saintes in the 16th C. that he first became interested in the art of making ceramics. His quest for the secret of making glazes lasted for 20 years. When he was on the point of reaching success he began to run short of wood, so he burned his own furniture, as well as the floorboards. His coloured glazes and large plates decorated with animals and plants in relief made him famous. A statuette of the master stands beside the river Charente.

Non-stop concerts, from midday to midnight
Académies Musicales de Saintes
First two weeks in July.
☎ 05 46 97 48 48
Admission charge.

The Académies Musicales have acquired an international reputation, and have played with some of the most prestigious French and European orchestras. Their performances cover nearly 1,000 years of music. This is a unique opportunity to hear lovely music performed on period instruments. Concerts are held at the Abbaye-aux-Dames; token entry fee.

Fine art in a mansion
Musée du Présidial
2 Rue Victor-Hugo
☎ **05 46 93 03 94**
Open daily, except Mon. Summer: 10am-noon and 2-6pm; winter (Nov.-Apr.), 10am-noon and 2-5.30pm, Sun. open 2-6pm only
Admission charge; free on Sundays.
These collections are housed in a handsome 17th-C.

mansion in which Henri IV once stayed. They include paintings from the Flemish and Dutch schools (15th to 18th C.) and the French schools (17th and 18th C.). One room is dedicated to regional ceramics, including a few priceless works by Bernard Palissy. The museum is named after the president of the city of Saintes, the *présidial*, who chose this house as his residence in the 18th C.

River excursions
Information and booking at the Tourist Office.
☎ 05 46 74 23 82
Apr.-Sept.

Spotcheck
D 4

Things to do
• Taking a mini-cruise on the Charente
• Listening to concerts at the Académies Musicales

Within easy reach
Royan (p. 236)
Valley of the Seugne (p. 192)
Cognac (p. 200)
Saintonge (p. 204)

Tourist Office
Saintes: ☎ 05 46 74 23 82

In season, **Inter-îles** organises cruises along the Charente. The boats sail down river, north of Saintes to Port-d'Envaux. The river banks are lined with mansions belonging to the nobility and the homes of boat-owners, who built the lighters (flat-bottomed boats), used to transport brandy and salt from inland down the Charente to the estuary and the sea.

LA GALETTE SAINTONGEAISE

While you are in the Saintonge region, you must taste the local delicacy or try making it yourself. You will need 9 oz (250 g) flour, 4½ oz (125 g) softened butter, 3½ oz (100 g) icing sugar, ½ oz (15 g) diced candied angelica, ½ oz (15 g) baking powder, a pinch of salt, 1 tbsp cognac and 3 eggs. Combine the flour, salt, baking powder and angelica. Make a well in the centre and work the butter, eggs and cognac into the flour. Form into a ball and leave to rest for 1 hour. Roll out the ball to a thickness of ½ inch (1 cm). Brush with egg yolk mixed with 2 tbsp milk and make patterns with a fork. Bake for 15 minutes in a preheated oven at 400°F/200°C or Gas mark 6.

La Saintonge
Sleeping Beauty's castle

If Saintes has magnificent Romanesque churches, its immediate vicinity is a lush, green countryside with fairytale castles and picturesque villages built from the local limestone. The road along the Charente takes you through flower-filled villages and passes close to one of Europe's largest limestone quarries.

Saint-Porchaire

8 miles (13 km) NW of Saintes

Château de la Roche-Courbon

☎ 05 46 95 60 10

Open daily, 9.30am-noon and 2-6.30pm (6pm out of season).

The first place of interest is a fortress, originally built in the 15th C., then rebuilt in the 17th C. Its desolate air caused Pierre Loti to call it the **Castle of the Sleeping Beauty**. It was here that the writer had his first amorous adventure, with a mysterious gypsy who revealed 'the great secret of love and life' to him. Who knows, history might repeat itself for a modern-day visitor. At any event, you can wander through the romantic grounds and the raised garden.

La Chapelle-des-Pots

6¼ (10 km) E of Saintes

The ceramic museum

Open daily, 9am-12.30pm and 2-7pm all year.

Admission charge.

La Chapelle-des-Pots, as its name implies, has an ancient tradition of potting. In fact, the village has been making pottery since the 13th C. In the Middle Ages it exported its wares to northern Europe, and in the 18th C., exports went as far as the French colonies in North America. The museum contains a fascinating collection dating from the 13th C. to the present day, and includes a few Palissy-style pieces.

Crazannes

7½ miles (12 km) N of Saintes

Château de Crazannes

☎ 05 46 90 15 94

Open daily, July-Aug., 2.30-7pm; Apr.-June and Sept.-Oct, weekends public holidays.

Admission charge.

Don't expect to see an 11th-C. château, because the only remains are the Romanesque chapel and the castle keep. However, the place is still worth visiting. You can see the huge round tower of the keep and thick-walled dungeons where the bloodthirsty lord of the manor kept his unfortunate prisoners. The north front of the castle keep is beautifully carved, including a royal coat of arms over the entrance. It is fully furnished as the château is still lived in.

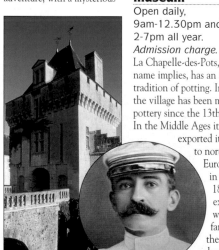

LIMESTONE LIKE NO OTHER

Limestone has been extracted from the Crazannes region at Port-d'Envaux, Saint-Savinien and Plassay for nearly 2,000 years. The stone is famous for its whiteness and its fine grain. It is as hard as concrete and resistant to damage by air, frost and rain. It has been used for important buildings in Saintes and the châteaux of Crazannes and La Roche-Courbon. The stone has been exported all over the world. In New York it supports the Statue of Liberty, in Belgium it was used to build churches in Ghent and Antwerp, and in Britain it covers the Thames Embankment in London.

Spotcheck
D 4

Things to do
• Visiting the Crazannes quarry

Things to do with children
• Be a sailor for a day at the Port de la Grenouilllette

Within easy reach
Saintes (p. 202)
Saint-Jean-d'Angély (p. 226)
Rochefort (p. 206)
Royan (p. 236)

Tourist Offices
Saintes:
☎ 05 46 74 23 82
Saint-Porchaire:
☎ 05 46 95 54 25
Saint-Savinien:
☎ 05 46 90 21 07

Look out for the enormous kitchen table, so huge that it had to be made on the spot.

The white gold of Crazannes
The Crazannes quarries
Access by autoroute A837 towards Saintes-Rochefort or D119,
☎ 05 46 91 48 82

Museum open 1 June-30 Sept., 9am-7pm; 1 Oct.-31 May, 10am-noon and 2-5pm.
Free admission.
One of the best limestones in Europe has been mined from the Crazannes quarries for nearly 2,000 years. Mining stopped after World War II, though the quarries were not exhausted. Since then, nature has reclaimed the land. The museum (free admission) is entirely devoted to Crazannes stone, and you will learn how it is extracted, cut and transported, as well as getting some insight into the lives of the quarrymen and the difficulties they have faced throughout the centuries. If you want to

know more, visit the **Maison de la Pierre de Crazannes**, in the village of Crazannes. (☎ 05 46 91 83 66, open during the season, daily except Mon., 2.15-6.15pm. Out of season, phone ahead. Admission charge.) It contains reconstructions of both a quarryman's and a stone merchant's home.

Saint-Savinien
12 miles (19 km) N of Saintes
Sailor for a day
Miniature Port of the Île de la Grenouillette
☎ 05 46 91 71 84
Open daily, July-Aug., 2-6pm; 21 March-15 Nov., Sun., public holidays, 2-6pm.
Only children are allowed on board these wonderful miniaturised ships and boats. They can choose from a

trawler, cargo boat, a Mississippi paddle-steamer and many more. A special pleasure boat has been converted so that children can steer it in safety and try a few manœuvres. Don't worry: the harbour master keeps a watchful eye out for any problems. A wonderful day out for the family, especially for any budding sailors.

Rochefort
former sea port

With one foot in the Charente river and the other in the marshes, Rochefort has managed to retain all the characteristics of a sea port from the era of the great explorers. Wander along the banks of the Charente and enjoy the discreet charm of this peaceful city, immortalised by the film, *Les Demoiselles de Rochefort* (1967).

Le Jardin des Retours

This garden beside the Charente is next to the royal ropeworks. The 'garden of returns' is where botanists used to store the plants they had collected from exotic places on their long voyages. Walk through the grounds to the banks of the Charente and enjoy the shade and tranquillity.

Maritime museum
Musée de la Marine, Place de la Galissonnière
☎ 05 46 99 86 57
Open daily, except Tues. and public holidays, 10am-noon and 2-7pm
Admission charge.
This museum, housed in the Hôtel de Cheusses, tells the

story of the naval dockyards, created by Colbert in the 17th C. You'll find model ships, sculptures and artefacts from the time when Rochefort was the most important naval dockyard in France. On the top floor there's an unusual display of ship's figureheads.

La Corderie Royale
Rue Audebert
☎ 05 46 87 01 90
Open daily, 9am-7pm in summer; 9am-6pm in winter
Admission charge.
The royal ropeworks was built in 1666 on the orders of Louis XIV. It was one of the largest factories of its kind in Europe in the 17th C. All the rigging for the great warships was made here, which explains the length of the building which has 500 doors and windows. Think of the poor cleaning women who had to

BIRDWATCHING

La Station de Lagunage, southwest of the town centre. Information at Espace Nature, Place Colbert
☎ 05 46 99 04 36
Open daily in the afternoon (15 July-15 Sept.) 2-6pm except weekends. Out of season, by appointment. Mon.-Fri. and occasional weekends. *Admission charge.*
This water treatment station is a wonderful place to take children to learn about wildlife. The waste water of Rochefort is treated in shallow basins, thus keeping the water clean enough for bathing and providing a desirable habitat for thousands of birds.

mop the 11,000 floor-tiles. Here you can learn about the history and adventures of tall ships. Local people in Rochefort like to explain that the ropeworks was the first 'vessel' to be built by the naval dockyards and that the building is actually floating on drained marshland. You can also visit the dockyard where the *Hermione*, La Fayette's frigate, was reconstructed.

Begonia greenhouse

Conservatoire du Bégonia,
La Prée Horticole
1 Rue Charles-Plumier
☎ 05 46 99 08 26
Open daily, Tues.-Sat., guided tours every hours from 2pm to 5pm *Admission charge.*
The 18th C. botanists who introduced the begonia into France created a new

tradition in Rochefort, that of horticulture. The **Conservatoire du Bégonia greenhouse** contains 1,500 species and varieties, brought from the Caribbean, Mexico, Malaysia and Africa by the chief curator, Michel Bégon, and his successors. Since he was in charge of the expeditions to bring back new plants, it's only natural that he gave his name to the most striking of new flowers, now known as the begonia. Red, orange and even white, this magnificent species will overwhelm you with its variety. Plants can be bought for around €3 a pot.

In the land of the 1,001 nights

La Maison de Pierre Loti,
141 Rue Pierre-Loti
☎ 05 46 99 16 88 ;
Booking at the Tourist Office
☎ 05 49 99 08 60
Open daily, 10am-5.30pm, (1 July-15 Sept.); out of season, open daily except Tues. and Sun. morning, 11am-4pm. *Admission charge.*
When you enter the house,

Spotcheck
C 4

Things to do
• Visit the begonia greenhouse
• Walk in the Jardin des Retours

Things to do with children
• Birdwatching

Within easy reach
Around Rochefort (p. 208)
Ile d'Oléron (p. 228)
The Fouras peninsula (p. 210)
Saintonge (p. 204)

Tourist Office
Rochefort:
☎ 05 46 99 08 60

you'll be taken on a fabulous journey to the land of 1,001 Arabian nights. The writer Pierre Loti collected an array of wonderful objects from all over the Orient. There's even a mosque and a Turkish drawing-room. Afterwards, you can prolong the pleasure by visiting the in-house cafe for a delicious cup of Turkish coffee.

Around Rochefort
between marsh and ocean

T he area between Rochefort and the Atlantic is marshland, a paradise for migrating and overwintering birds. Protected by the fort on the Île Madame and Fort Lupin, it is a land of contrasts where earth and water seem to be locked in an eternal struggle. Follow the Charente estuary and explore the country and typical villages.

Île Madame
6 miles (10 km)
W of Rochefort
A minute island
The Île Madame is the smallest of the islands of the Charentes and is accessible from land only at low tide over the Passe aux Bœufs (cattle ford). The early 18th-C. **fort** reinforced the system of defences in the Charente estuary and the Rochefort arsenal. In 1794 275 rebellious priests were starved to death and were buried on the spot where they died. A cross of pebbles marks their graves. The former salt marshes, which have now been drained, are an ideal stop for migrating birds.

Just off the island there is strange phenomenon: a spring of fresh water emerges from the sea-bed. A well collects the water, providing an invaluable resource for the tiny island.

Delicacies from the Charentes
Ferme-auberge Marine
☎ **05 46 83 43 47**
Reservations required.
Open daily, except Sun. evening, July-Aug.; except Wed., Sept-June.

This marine farm specialises in the cultivation of oysters and clams (€8 for 2¼ lb/ 1 kg). It also produces salt and delicious salted butter caramels. There's an inn attached to the farm where you can taste local dishes prepared by the proprietor (menus at €11, €15, €18 and €23). The Charentais menu, highly recommended, consists of oysters, stuffed clams, oyster profiteroles with samphire, farmhouse cheese and home-made desserts.

Port-des-Barques
6 miles (10 km)
W of Rochefort
A natural seawater pool
The Port-des-Barques peninsula, between the Charente and the Atlantic Ocean, is a wonderful place for observing wildlife. North of the village,

the seawater is held in a natural basin. It's a great place to swim and bathe in safety, with pleasantly warm water temperatures. When the tides are high, the sea covers this entire basin, but when it recedes it leaves behind a natural swimming-pool! Don't worry – there's a sluice-gate in operation all the time, which ensures that the water level can be changed, even when the tides are not high enough to cover the basin.

Soubise
¾ mile (1 km)
SW of Rochefort
Fort Lupin, a 17th-C. masterpiece

Fort Lupin, which stands on the left bank of the Charente estuary, is one of the best examples of the fortifications once used to defend the region. Unfortunately, it is private property and not open to the public. This 17th-C. fortress, built by the military engineer Vauban, is a classical masterpiece. The diamond-shaped castle keep is enclosed in a semi-circular battery, and is surrounded by

triangular moats on one side and by the river Charente on the other.

Tonnay-Charente
3½ miles (6 km)
E of Rochefort
A suspension bridge

This little village is worth a detour because of its port on the Charente, which is lined with houses, many of which date from the 18th C. But it is also famous for its

Spotcheck
C 4

Things to do
• Birdwatching at the Moëze Nature Reserve
• Eating seafood in the Île Madame

Things to do with children
• Bathing in a seawater pool

Within easy reach
Rochefort (p. 206)
Isle of Oleron (p. 228)
The Fouras peninsula (p. 210)

Tourist Offices
Rochefort:
☎ 05 46 99 08 60
Port-des-Barques:
☎ 05 46 84 80 01

magnificent suspension bridge, which is 670 ft (204 m) long and was built over the river in 1842. It is not open to vehicles. The piles of the bridge are arch-shaped, making it look like a cathedral in the air.

THE MOËZE NATURE RESERVE
Espace Nature

17780 Moëze
2 miles (3.5km) SW of Rochefort
☎ 05 46 99 04 36
Open July-Aug., Mon. and Thurs, 9am-5pm; out of season by appointment

The Moëze Nature Reserve in the western part of the Brouage marsh is one of the most important sanctuaries for migratory and overwintering waterfowl and waders. Small wading birds and ducks come to feed in the huge mudflats of the reserve. At the height of the season there are about 10,000 ducks, spoonbills and avocets. As

these water birds prefer short grass for nesting purposes, ponies and sheep are allowed to graze here freely.

Île d'Aix and the Fouras peninsula

hunting for shells and shellfish

The Fouras peninsula, 2½ miles (4 km) long, is sheltered by the islands of the Charentes archipelago. The Île d'Aix, accessible by boat, can be toured on foot, by bike or on horseback. With its landscape of coves, beaches, moors, rocky coasts and forests, it's a paradise for nature-lovers.

Swimming and fishing for shellfish on the Île d'Aix

The white houses of the village are laid out in a grid pattern, and in summer their gardens are full of bright holly-hocks. The Place d'Austerlitz, once a military parade ground, is planted with cypresses. It separates the village from the fortress on the shore. You'll find an attractive beach, the **Grande Plage**, extending along the western side of the island. If you prefer to hunt for shellfish, go to the **Plage aux Coquillages** (shell beach), which has clams, razor-shells and limpets. The **Soumard marsh**, in the centre of the island, is a favourite resting-place for wild geese, large ducks and grey herons.

Forts for Rochefort

The Fouras peninsula and island of Aix have no fewer than five forts built between the late 17th and early 19th C. to protect the mouth of the Charente and the Rochefort naval dockyard. The **Fort d'Enet** stands on a rock between the mainland and the island of Aix, and is accessible only on foot at low tide (from the Pointe de la Fumée at Fouras). The **Fort de la Rade** on the island of Aix

is surrounded by cypress trees that are hundreds of years old. **Fort Boyard**, between the islands of Aix and Oléron, is built on a sandbank.

Fort Vauban and the Musée de Fouras

Fouras Tourist Office
☎ 05 46 84 60 69
Fort:
Open daily 9am-8pm (open 3-6pm Sun. and public holidays in winter) *Free admission*
Museum:
Open daily 15 June-15 Sept. 3-6pm Out of season, Sun. and public holidays 3-6pm *Admission charge.*
Fort Vauban was built in the late 17th C. in front of the village of Fouras on the section of the peninsula

between the Pointe de la Nombraire and cove of La Coue. Its regional museum traces the history of Fouras. Exhibits include seabirds, models of fortifications and of ships, as well as head-dresses, traditional costumes, posters and paintings.

Musée Napoléon

Rue Napoléon, Île d'Aix
☎ 05 46 84 66 40
Open daily, except Tues., 1 Nov.-1 Apr. 9am-12.30pm and 2-5.30pm; Apr.-May-Oct.; 9.30am-12.30pm and 2-6pm; June-Sept., 9.30am-6pm
Admission charge.
This museum is housed in the former residence of the military governor of the island, which was built on Napoleon's orders. It was

here, in 1815, that Napoleon spent his last days on French soil, before handing himself over to the British. His room has been kept exactly as it was. There are also some excellent bronze busts of Napoleon and his generals, as well as a copy of the fateful letter of surrender to the British.

A taste of Africa

Musée Africain,
Rue Napoléon, Île d'Aix
☎ 05 46 84 66 40
Open daily, except Wed. Same opening times as Musée Napoléon but closed from noon to 1pm June-Sept.
Admission charge.
Baron Gourgaud, creator of the nearby Musée Napoléon, was also an African explorer. He made many trips to

South Africa and Kenya from where he brought back an interesting collection of artefacts and weapons. There are handsome painted or metal-covered wooden masks and intricately decorated ceremonial weapons that once belonged to the chiefs of African tribes. The largest item is a stuffed camel – brought back by Napoleon from his Egyptian campaign.

ON YOUR BIKE!

The island can only be reached by boat. Ferries run the whole year round from the Pointe de la Fumée. The crossing takes about 20 minutes (☎ 05 46 84 66 01; €9 return). Cars are forbidden on the island, so you can explore it by bike. To hire a bicycle, go to **Cycles Aix** (15 March-30 Sept.; ☎ 05 46 84 69 75), in the village (it will cost about €8 a day). A path leads all round the island from the Pointe Sainte-Catherine to the Cove of La Croix, via the Pointe de Coupedont, at the eastern tip of the island.

La Rochelle
Atlantic port

La Rochelle, the regional capital, has many claims to fame. It was a free Huguenot city, proud of its privileges, but lay in ruins in 1628 after the long royalist siege. Its fortunes were revived thanks to its brisk trade with the New World. Today the city not only has a magnificent architectural heritage, but is once again a thriving port, as befits a city with such a long history of trading.

In the steps of Christopher Columbus

Musée du Nouveau Monde, 10 Rue Fleuriau
☎ 05 46 41 46 50
Open daily except Tues.
10.30am-12.30pm and 1.30-6pm;
Sun. and public holidays 3-6pm
Admission charge.
This museum is housed in an 18th C. mansion and traces the history of the trading links between La Rochelle and America, including the slave trade. It includes some quite unpleasant reminders of this terrible trade, such as a gigantic whip of hippopotamus hide, over 40 in (1 m) long. There are also maps, letters granting slaves their freedom and a surprising painting by Kessel depicting a scene with cannibals. You can also see a display of photographs taken by Curtis, an anthropologist who defended the rights of the native Americans. These priceless documents show native American chiefs in ceremonial dress.

Perfume flasks

Musée du Flacon à Parfum,
33 Rue du Temple
☎ 05 46 41 32 40
Open daily, Mon. 3-7pm,
Tues.-Sat. 10.30am-7pm;
July-Aug. open on Sun. 3-6pm
Admission charge.

Huge tanks and spectacular fish, children adore it! Visit La Rochelle Aquarium and discover new marine species.

Spotcheck
C 3

Things to do
• Visiting the Quartier du Gabut
• Take a ride on a yellow bicycle
• Shop for speciality food at the Épicerie
• Attending the Francofolies

Things to do with children
• See the fish in the Aquarium

Within easy reach
Aiguillon Bay (p. 150)
Island of Ré (p. 218)
Surgères (p. 224)
Châtelaillon-Plage (p. 222)

Tourist Office
La Rochelle:
☎ 05 46 41 14 68

The museum is on the first floor of a perfumery and contains some magnificent examples of the art of the perfume bottle, including early 20th C. examples. All the famous French perfumers are represented – Guerlain, Dior, Lanvin, Hermès, etc. The most interesting items include *Aphrodite de Cnide*, a flask in the shape of a face, which Baccarat manufactured from a drawing by Dali, and some beautiful Bohemian crystal flasks by Lancôme.

The Aquarium
Port des Minimes
☎ 05 46 34 00 00
Open daily: July-August 9am-11pm; Apr.-May-June-Sept. 9am-7pm; Oct.-March 10am-noon and 2-7pm
Admission charge.
Discover the world of under-water flora and fauna in this aquarium. You will particularly enjoy the guided tour, which is embellished with fascinating facts and stories about the underwater world. Did you know, for example, that it is

the male seahorse who incubates the eggs, not the female; that the porcupine fish swells itself up to frighten away its enemies; or that after they have eaten, gigantic moray eels are cleaned by shrimps and gleaner fish, who nibble up the scraps of food they have left behind?

SHOPPING FOR SPECIALITY FOODS
L'Épicerie, 22 Rue Saint-Sauveur
☎ 05 46 41 74 99
Open daily except Sun. afternoon and Mon. 9am-1pm and 3-7pm; July-August open daily 9am-8pm

Gourmets will enjoy finding original and unusual foods here. The people that run the shop are from Normandy and Brittany, and offer all the traditional foods of the region but have also managed to unearth some culinary innovations. You'll find angelica jam, mustard with samphire, sea salt flavoured with herbs, and hot pepper mayonnaise with seaweed and samphire, chitterlings and duck liver with cep and an oyster terrine from Kerouets. They also sell Troussépinette, a Vendéen liqueur based on blackthorn shoots (€10), and Pineau des Charentes.

IN THE MARKET

Place du Marché
Open daily, 7am-1pm
The market is a popular local meeting place. You'll find all the regional specialities here: *farci charentais* (minced pork and vegetables), *petit fagot* (preserved pig's liver), *cagouilles à la charentaise* (snails) and succulent tripe, of which the best is at Établissements Camus, in the centre of the market. Fish dishes include *mouclade* (mussels), tuna in Sauce Mirielle and plaice in Sauce Mareyeur. Be sure to try the goat's cheeses with such unusual names as *taupinière charentaise* (Charente molehill).

a great deal of graffiti, half of which is now protected. On the second floor on the left, look out for one of the lovely engravings, which represents the Port of La Rochelle, the towers of La Chaîne and Saint-Nicolas as well as a ship on the high seas. Climb to the top for a view over the city – you'll certainly be rewarded for your efforts!

Prisoner graffiti
Tour de la Lanterne, at the tip of the ramparts, Rue Sur-les-Murs
☎ 05 46 41 56 04
Open daily except Tues. from 1 Apr.-30 Sept. 10am-7pm; out of season 10am-12.30pm and 2-5.30pm.
Admission charge.
This tower was built in the second half of the 15th C. and served as a naval landmark, a beacon and eventually as a prison – first for pirates and enemy seamen, then for the persecuted Protestants, and finally for members of the clergy during the Revolution. The occupants of the tower left behind

The Protestant Museum
2 Rue Saint-Michel
☎ 05 46 50 88 03
Open daily, 1 July-15 Sept., 2.30-6pm, except Sun.; out of season, by appointment.
Admission charge.
This museum is devoted to the history of the Reformation, especially its effects on La Rochelle, Aunis and Saintonge, as told through engravings, medals, documents and various artefacts. Also on display are dozens of old bibles written in all the European languages, including examples printed

in La Rochelle in 1606 and 1616. One interesting reminder from this 'wilderness' period of clandestine Protestant religious meetings is a collapsible portable pulpit which could be used to hold a service and, if

necessary, allow a quick getaway for the preacher and brethren.

International film festival

La Coursive, 4 Rue Saint-Jean du Pérot
☎ 05 46 51 54 00
Admission charge.
This annual international film festival is held in late June and early July and exhibits feature films from all over the world. There are special exhibits concentrating on a particular actor or director, and tributes to a number of contemporary figures. The festival ends with an all-night screening of films with a particular theme. If you are a true cinephile, buy a non-transferrable pass for the whole festival. Otherwise, a card admitting you to 20 films should be enough.

A walk in the park

Parc Charruyer
Free admission
The Parc Charruyer links the **Port de la Pallice** and the **Vieux Port**, with the river running through it. It's planted throughout with elms and has a botanical garden full of rare and exotic plants.

Although the park is only yards from the sea, as you watch the swans and ducks cavorting on the water, you could easily believe you were in the country.

The Quartier du Gabut

The Quartier du Gabut lies between the deepwater harbour and the trawler basin, its main feature being brightly painted little wooden huts. Made by local fishermen, these were coated with pitch and painted with whatever colours remained at the bottom of the paint pot. In the late 1980s the huts were renovated and the district's special character was recognised.

Walking through the old town

The streets named Admyrault, Saint-Jean and Réaumur contain some lovely old mansions. The streets of Saint-Yon, Chaudrier and Dupaty are completely lined with arcades, so it's an ideal place for a shopping trip if you're unlucky enough to have some bad weather during your holiday. Look at the inner courtyard of no. 26

Rue Dupaty, and admire this handsome mansion with its huge Renaissance windows, grand staircase and balconies. The preceding house, no. 24, is the Hôtel Marchegay, which dates from the second

half of the 18th C. It's always worth peeping through the doors into the courtyards to glimpse their elegant interiors.

Musée des Beaux-Arts

28 Rue Gargoulleau
☎ **05 46 41 64 65**
Open daily, 2-5pm, except Tues. and public holidays
Admission charge.
Although this museum of fine art is small, it's well worth a visit. The main attraction is an extraordinary series of 58 prints by Georges Rouault entitled *Miserere* and evoking the dialogue between man and Christ. There are also paintings by Eugène Fromentin, a local painter of international repute, whose inspiration is mainly oriental. His works include *The Arab Horsemen* and *Attack on a Caravan*. The painter whom the Impressionists most hated,

Bouguereau, was also from La Rochelle. His work is represented here with the painting *Océanide*, which shows a naked woman lying on a river bank.

The Temple of Wine

Le Taste Vin,
22 Rue du Temple
☎ **05 46 41 02 78**
Open daily, during season, 9.30am-7.30pm; out of season 9.30am-12.30pm and 3-7.30pm, closed Sun.
Free admission.
This vintner is to be found inside a wonderful vaulted cellar and is a paradise for lovers of good wine and cognacs. All the great clarets

are represented, given the proximity of Bordeaux, but so are the local wines of the Charentes, including Rosé-des-Dunes and Moulin-de-Mérienne (€5 a bottle of red, 100% Merlot grapes). Try the **passion** cocktail (€10) or some of the liqueurs.

Hôtel de Ville

Place de la Mairie
☎ **05 46 51 51 51**
Guided tour,
July-Aug., daily, 3pm and 4pm; Sept.-Jun, daily, 3pm; all year long, weekends and school holidays, 3pm.
Admission charge.
There are very few mayors in France who can claim to have such a magnificent town hall as this one.

What's more, it has been used as a town hall for 600 years. There's a surrounding Gothic style crenellated wall, which protects the 16th-C. Renaissance façade. Take your time wandering through the gallery beneath the main building and admire the remarkable coffered ceiling. Inside, in the mayor's parlour, look out for the handsome carved wooden table with its cracked marble top into which, according to legend, Jean Guiton, mayor of the town, plunged his dagger while swearing an oath never to capitulate during the siege of 1627, which nearly brought the town to its knees.

Musée d'Orbigny-Bernon
2 Rue Saint-Côme
☎ 05 46 41 18 83
Open daily, 10am-noon and 2-6pm, except Tues., Sun. morning, and public holidays
Admission charge.
This museum has porcelain, pottery and enamels from the region and is considered one of the finest collections in France. It's one of the best places to see work by Bernard Palissy, including a superb 16th-C. charger, decorated with a serpent, crayfish and shells. The second floor boasts some magnificent 18th-C. examples of Chinese and Japanese porcelain, as well as sumptuous, richly embroidered mandarin's robes.

All aboard!
**Musée Maritime,
Bassin des Chalutiers**
☎ 05 46 28 03 00
Open daily, Apr.-Sept., 10am-7pm, Oct.-Apr., 2-6.30pm Closed mid-Nov to mid-Jan.
Admission charge.

At last a maritime museum that features water and is built on a grand scale. The trawler basin contains various types of boats, including wooden tuna-boats and frigates. Don't miss *France 1*, the last French weather frigate – it's 263 ft (80 m) long. Everything is open to the public, from the engine room to the captain's bridge. Another important ship is the *Joshua*, Bernard Moitessier's famous red ketch, in which he made several round-the-world voyages single-handed.

THE YELLOW BICYCLES

These little yellow bicycles have made La Rochelle famous since 1974, and are much appreciated by tourists. 350 bikes are available free of charge to visitors. The yellow bicycles can be found at the **Place de Verdun** (daily, Mon.-Sat., 7.30am-7pm, Sun., 1-7pm; July-Aug. until 7.30pm) and **Quai Valin** (daily, July-Aug., 9am-7pm; May-Sept., 9am-12.30pm and 1.30-7pm).

An excellent network of cycle paths make cycling by far the safest and most pleasant way to explore the city. Starting from the town centre, cycle to the Bay of Port-Neuf and the trading port; then carry on until you come to the bridge leading to the Île de Ré.

Île de Ré
a taste of the Mediterranean

O ver the centuries the islets of Loix, Saint-Martin, Ars and Les Portes, joined together to form the Île de Ré. Its Mediterranean climate and the bridge linking it to the mainland make it one of the principal tourist destinations in the region. Ré is an island of contrasts and tradition – you'll love its sandy beaches, whitewashed houses with brightly coloured shutters and gardens full of hollyhocks, its landscape filled with myrtle and rosemary, and its salt marshes and vineyards.

The bridge to the Île de Ré

Ré has not been a real island since 1988, its inhabitants preferring this gigantic reinforced concrete bridge, 2 miles (3 km) long and 100 ft (30 m) high, to the old-fashioned ferries that used to link them with the mainland. The toll bridge was built by the huge construction firm of Bouygues, and gave

rise to a series of law suits. Holiday-makers pay a high price for the convenience – a round-trip ticket on the toll bridge costs €16.50 for a car in summer and €9 out of season.

Pedal power rules

The bicycle is king on the Île de Ré. Abandon your car and explore the villages and marshland by bike. **Cycland**

rents bicycles all over the island, which means that you can get your bike repaired at many places all around the island (**Ars**, on the harbour, ☎ 05 46 29 47 17; **La Couarde**, 56 Grande Avenue, ☎ 05 46 29 06 09; **Saint-Martin**, Impasse de Sully, ☎ 05 46 09 08 66; **Saint-Clément**, 10 Rue du Centre, ☎ 05 46 29 29 08). Discover the salt marshes and oyster-beds by taking the Chemin des Marais from Saint-Martin to Portes-en-Ré 12¹⁄₂ miles (20 km) away. For a lovely route through the forest, take the Chemin de la Forêt de Saint-Clément to Portes-en-Ré, through the public forest of Lizay 3³⁄₄ miles (6 km) away.

LOCAL WINES

Coopérative des Vignerons de l'Île de Ré
Route de Sainte-Marie
☎ 05 46 09 23 09
Open daily, July-Aug., except Sun., 9am-noon and 2.30-7pm; out of season, daily, except weekends, 9am-noon and 2-6pm. *Free admission.*

The heat is often oppressive on the Île de Ré, so find a shady spot and indulge in a refreshing glass of the famous Rosé-des-dunes wine. The Coopérative des Vignerons de l'Île de Ré also offers other local wines of the Charentes such as

Royal Blanc, a delicious blend of Colombard, Sauvignon and Chardonnay grape varieties (around €3 a bottle), and Le Gouverneur (Cabernet-Sauvignon and Merlot grapes), aged in oak casks (around €3 a bottle). You will also find red and white Pineau des Charentes, cognac and some good sparkling wines.

Spotcheck
B 3

Things to do
- Explore the island by bike
- Taste the local wines
- Birdwatching

Things to do with children
- Exploring Noah's Ark
- Swimming at the Plage des Prises

Within easy reach
Aiguillon Bay (p. 156)
La Rochelle (p .212)
Châtelaillon-Plage (p. 222)

Tourist Offices
Ars-en-Ré:
☎ 05 46 29 46 09
Le Bois-Plage:
☎ 05 46 09 23 26
Saint-Clément-des-Baleines:
☎ 05 46 29 24 19
Saint-Martin-en-Ré:
☎ 05 46 09 20 06

Saint-Martin-de-Ré

Saint-Martin has been the main town on the island since the Middle Ages. In the 17th C. Vauban built huge fortifications that were large enough to protect the entire population, including

their livestock, should they be attacked. The citadel was turned into a prison in the 18th C. and is still in use today. Although it is not open to the public, it can be approached by the path along the coast that runs by the small fortified port.

Beaches and dunes at Bois-Plage

The exceptional whiteness of the sand is bound to impress. There are 6¼ miles (10 km), of beaches and dunes along the whole of the south coast of the island, from the **Anse du Martray** to La Noue.

NOAH'S ARK

L'Arche de Noé,
¼ mile (500 m)
from the Phare des
Baleines (lighthouse)
☎ **05 46 29 23 23**
Open daily, June-Aug.,
10.30am-6pm, Apr.-
May-Sept., 2-6pm
Open in Oct., Sun.,
2-6pm
Admission charge.
Noah's Ark is an extra-
ordinary combination
of zoo, botanical
garden, oceanographic
museum, shell
museum, butterfly and
insect farm as well as
being a museum of the
history of the prison
on the Île de Ré.
Everyone will find
something of interest

in this ambitious
enterprise. After
wandering through
the botanical garden,
with its hundreds of
different species,
plunge into the parrot
jungle, which contains
hundreds of parrots
and parakeets display-
ing the most incredible
colours. Then explore
the depths of the
Pacific Ocean and
the Red Sea before
coming back to the
surface to admire the
thousands of insects
and butterflies in
the museum.

It's paradise for wind-
surfers, shrimpers and
shellfish-gatherers and
a wonderful place for
a family holiday.
The **Plage
des Prises**,
near the
Henri IV
wood in the
Anse du
Martray, is one
of the best

beaches on the island and is
the most sheltered.

Ars-en-Ré

In the W of the island
A bell-tower as a beacon

You can't miss the church of
Saint-Étienne. With its tall
black-and-white painted
bell-tower, used as a beacon
for ships, it dominates the
whole commune. Strangely,
the handsome Romanesque
portal through which you
enter is sunk about 33 in
(85 cm) into the ground.
In summer climb to the top of
the bell-tower (open daily,
10am-12.30pm) to get a
superb view of the forest of
La Combe à Eau and the
oyster-beds at Fiers d'Ars.

La Pointe des Baleines

Western tip of the island
The Phare des Baleines
(lighthouse) was built in
1855 to replace the 17th-C.

watchtower that stands a
few yards away. It is 180 ft
(55 m) high and offers a
beautiful view of the coast
of the Vendée, the Breton
Straits and the marshland
with its oyster-beds. The
spiral staircase has 250 stone
steps, and when you look
down from the top, it resembles the inside of snail shell.
The point and the lighthouse
were named after the whales
that could be seen offshore
many years ago.

Saint-Clément-des-Baleines

In the W of the island
Thousands of birds

**Bird Sanctuary of
Lilleau des Niges,
2 miles (3 km) S of
the Portes-en-Ré.
Apply first to the
Maison des Marais,
Saint-Clément-des-
Baleines**
☎ **05 46 29 50 74**

Open daily, 18 June–17 Sept., 10am–12.30pm and 3-7pm; out of season, booking; guided tours
Admission charge.
The bird sanctuary at Lilleau des Niges was created by the Ligue pour la Protection des Oiseaux and covers 540 acres (220 ha) of the Fiers d'Ars. It is a resting place, nesting site and overwintering site for thousands of birds, of more than 300 species. There are barnacle geese, shelducks, oyster-catchers, redshanks and the magnificent white-spotted bluethroat, sometimes known as the 'nightingale of the marshes'.

Loix
W of the island
The spirit of salt
La Maison du Sel, Rue de Sully
☎ 05 46 29 03 83
Open daily, 10.30am–1pm and 2.30-6.30pm from 15 June to 15 Sept.
Free admission.
This exhibition was created by an association of workers on the salt marshes who wanted to promote the salt marshes and revive their use. There are two shops, one of

which is situated at the Phare des Baleines. From here you can buy a wide choice of salt-related products, including coarse sea salt for cooking, salt with herbs, salted butter caramels and, to replace your shower gel, bath salts (box of 18 caramels, €5, pot of mustard with salt, €2.50). These products make excellent gifts, some quite unusual, and are never too expensive.

Les Portes-en-Ré
W of the island
Delicious food
Auberge de la Rivière, 27 Avenue des Salines
☎ 05 46 29 54 55
Open daily, June-Sept., closed Tues. evening and Wed. out of season
Menus at €18, €24, €29 and €53.

The Auberge de la Rivière is located in a sheltered spot behind some trees, at the entrance to the village of Portes-en-Ré. You couldn't choose a better place to discover the fish and seafood

of Ré. Specialities of the house include fillet of sea bream with saffron and clam sauce, langoustine canneloni and cream of lobster. There are home-made desserts, including a memorable chocolate pudding. The chef buys all his ingredients from the market and local fishermen, to make sure that his patrons have the best and freshest food on the island.

Châtelaillon-Plage
golden sands and swimming

Châtelaillon was officially classified as a resort in 1926. It stretches along the Atlantic coast south of La Rochelle. The golden sands, nearly 2 miles (3 km) long, make it a family resort *par excellence*. The brightly coloured villas, typical of early 20th-C. French seaside architecture contribute to the charm of this lovely holiday town.

La Grande Plage

The beach at Châtelaillon is without doubt the safest on the Atlantic coast. The tourists have made it a family beach *par excellence*! You may be interested to know that 28,252,000 cu. ft (800,000 m³) of extra sand were required to make it what it is today. The result is 2 miles (3 km) of golden sandy beaches to enjoy. The waves are small and there are no breakers. The shore slopes gently beneath the waves, making it very safe for children. There are life-guards, too, along the whole length of the beach for added peace of mind. It should be noted that naturists are not welcome at this family beach.

The shellfish-farmers' village

Village des Boucholeurs. Guided tours during the season. Information at the Tourist Office.
☎ 05 46 56 26 97

Although Châtelaillon is mainly a tourist resort, it has retained some of its fishing grounds. In the southern part of the town, the Village des Boucholeurs contains brightly coloured fishing huts and oyster-beds. Between sun-bathing sessions you could discover how mussels and oysters are farmed by taking a tractor ride along the beach. A tour of the oyster- and mussel-beds is a lovely 1¼ mile (2 km) trip at low tide.

Fort Saint-Jean

Fort Saint-Jean is one of the few remaining vestiges from the era before the seaside resort came into being in the early 20th C. This impressive fortress is surrounded by a curtain wall 2,000 ft (600 m)

The oyster-beds in the shellfish farming village

THE TOWN WITH 750 VILLAS

Châtelaillon's reputation does not derive solely from its lovely sheltered beach. It has been a resort since the early 20th C., when the middle classes started to build villas so they could enjoy the sea air and bathing. Every Wednesday at 11am in season (admission charge), the Tourist Office organises a guided tour of the town and its beautiful villas. The **Villa des Dunes**, on the seafront, is the most famous, with its red and beige façade which is typical of French seaside architecture of the period.

Spotcheck
C 4

Things to do
• Fishing for shellfish
• Birdwatching

Things to do with children
• Bathing on the Grande Plage

Within easy reach
La Rochelle (p. 212)
Surgères (p. 224)
Fouras peninsula (p. 210)

Tourist Office
Châtelaillon-Plage:
☎ 05 46 56 26 97

long and flanked by 14 towers. It dominates its surroundings from the top of the 115 ft (35 m) high castle keep. Unfortunately, the fort is now privately owned and is not open to the public. However, you can get quite near it, and take an enjoyable walk around its walls.

Shellfish fishing
At low tide the sea reveals sand and rock-pools that are teeming with life, such as little shellfish – limpets, clams and winkles – and shrimps, prawns and crabs. You are only allowed to fish between sunrise and sunset, and at Châtelaillon the rules are even stricter than elsewhere. The quantities removed must not exceed 11 lb (5 kg), and the *piochon* (a wooden stick with a metal

blade on the end to break up the sand and dislodge shell-fish) is the only implement allowed. At high tide, you can fish with a rod and line on the dyke and in the harbour for sea bream, red and grey mullet and eels, but you must have a fishing permit.

Yves
3 miles (5 km)
S from Châtelaillon-Plage
Birdwatching
Réserve Naturelle du Marais d'Yves
Open daily, July-Aug., 10am-noon and 3-6pm; booking out of season
☎ 05 46 82 12 44
The nature reserve of the Marais d'Yves covers nearly 494 acres (200 ha) of the marsh and dunes as well as a huge lagoon on which dozens of

species of birds come to rest. Depending on the season, you will be able to spot wild geese, shelduck, herons, storks, spoonbills and a variety of large and small wading birds. There are two hides from which you can watch buzzards flying overhead, as well as the numerous noisy geese. If you're lucky, you may even see a marsh fox. Don't be surprised to come across some long-horned cattle. They are used as ecological lawn-mowers to keep the grass in the marshes short to encourage nesting birds.

Surgères
butter, cream and cheese

The beautiful Hélène de Surgères, whose praises were sung by Ronsard, was born in this town in the heart of the plain of Aunis. After long being dedicated to making brandy, in the late 19th C., Surgères became the capital of the butter and dairy industry. Walk around the medieval walls, explore the church, or stroll along the banks of the Gères to get a feel for the town.

THE CREAM OF BUTTERS

École Nationale des Industries Laitières et Agroalimentaires (ENILA),
Route de La Rochelle
☎ 05 46 27 69 00
Open daily, Sept.-June, Mon.-Fri., 8am-noon and 2-5.30pm; closed July and Aug.
Surgères' reputation is based on its dairy industry and the quality of its butter. The national dairying school at Surgères has a shop that sells an impressive selection of butters, including raw churned butter, pasteurised butter, lightly salted butter and sweet butter – something for every taste. You'll also find cheeses made from goat's and cow's milk, produced by apprentice dairy workers.

Wandering through Surgères
Enjoy a walk with a romantic atmospheric by wandering around the old medieval fortress. It has 20 round towers and a 7-acre (3 ha) park planted with ancient chestnut and walnut trees. In the heart of all this greenery stands the 12th-C. **church of Notre-Dame**, one of the handsomest Romanesque churches in the region. Look out for the two equestrian statues framing the central window of the very wide and imposing façade. Behind the church, follow the well-signposted path that takes you on a circular walk along the banks of the Gères, the river from which Surgères derives its name.

At the market
The **Grande Foire** de Surgères, the local market, is held on the third Tuesday of

the month, between 6am and 3pm. It's worth making the effort to visit the town when this market is being held. The less important weekly markets are held on Tuesdays, Thursdays and Saturday mornings. The fair and the market are both held in the Halles, the recently restored market-hall. You can buy all the local foods of the region: Charentais *rillon* (sausage), *galette à l'angélique* (angelica-flavoured cake), *farci charentais* (minced pork with vegetables) etc.

Somewhere to eat

Le Vieux Puits,
6 Rue Paul-Bert
☎ 05 46 07 50 83

Closed Sun. evening and Thur. evening; mid-Sept.-mid-Oct.
Menus at €15, €21 and €29.
Le Vieux Puits is one of the best restaurants in the region, famous for its fish dishes. Here, fish and meat are combined in the same dishes: chicken breast stuffed with mussels, fillet of veal with crayfish, and salad of mussels with warm goat's cheese are just some of the delicious and inventive local dishes on offer.

Lozay
10 miles (15 km)
SE of Surgères
Romanesque art on the motorway
Aire-jardin de la Saintonge Romane, Lozay. Access via the A10 or the D107

Free admission from sunrise to sunset.
You're not dreaming, this layby on the Lozay motorway is a garden dedicated to the best examples of Romanesque art in Saintonge. There are models and reproductions of capitals, modillions and portals of the loveliest Romanesque churches of the region. They include the façade of the church at Echebrune, a bestiary, monumental sculptures and the apse of the church at Aulnay. It's an excellent way of learning about the medieval art treasures of the region. Don't miss the medieval herb garden where such medicinal herbs as marjoram, melissa and marsh-mallow are grown just as they were in the 12th C. You can also pick up information guides here, telling you where to find the other Romanesque sites in the region.

Saint-Jean-de-Liversay
14 miles (22.5 km)
NW of Surgères
Say it with flowers
Serre de la Pierrière, Josée and Lionel Guillon
Rue de la Plaine,

Spotcheck
C 4

Things to do

• Discovering Romanesque art on the motorway
• Shopping at the market or the fair
• Tasting butter made by apprentice dairy workers

Within easy reach

Châtelaillon-Plage (p. 222)
Rochefort (p. 206)
Saint-Jean-d'Angély (p. 226)
Niort (p. 158)

Tourist Office

Surgères: ☎ 05 46 07 20 02

17570 Saint-Jean-de-Liversay
☎ 05 46 01 88 78
Open daily from Thur. to Sat., 3-6pm
The Guillon family have a 5-acre (2 ha) nursery where they specialise in growing gladioli (about €5 for a bunch of 10 blooms) and marguerites (about €3 a bunch). Unlike other cut flowers, these keep well for 10 days if the water is changed daily. You will also find other flowers, such as antirrhinum and zinnias in a variety of colours.

Saint-Jean d'Angély and the valley of the Boutonne

Romanesque art and vineyards

Saint-Jean-d'Angély stands on the right bank of the river Boutonne, a few miles from the city of Saintes. It, too, is an historic town, with a peaceful way of life. With its Romanesque art treasures, cognac vineyards and the locally bred *baudet de Poitou*, there's plenty for the visitor to enjoy.

A walk in the town

You'll find architectural heritage at the corner of every street in Saint-Jean-d'Angély. Begin your exploration of the old town by looking at the façade of the Gothic abbey church, which was never completed. Continue past the 16th-C. **Fontaine du Pilori**, erected thanks to a subscription from the local inhabitants who preferred it to the pillory that had previously stood under their windows! The Tour de l'Horloge (clock tower), which contains the *sin*, a huge bell,

the symbol of the freedom of the commune, is another of the town's attractions, as are the many 18th-C. mansions.

The royal abbey of Saint-Jean-d'Angély

This magnificent abbey was founded by Pépin, Duke of Aquitaine, when a human head was brought back to him from the Far East and presented to him in the same way as that of John the Baptist. The head became a precious relic and made the abbey famous until the day it was destroyed by fire. Before that time

pilgrims on their way to the shrine of St James of Compostela would make a detour to visit the abbey of Saint-Jean d'Angély. Later, a visit from Louis XIV and valuable manuscripts by Pascal, held in the library, restored the abbey's prestige.

Migron

12½ miles (20 km) SE of Saint-Jean-d'Angély
The Ecomusée du Cognac

Logis des Bessons
☎ 05 46 94 91 16
Open daily, 9.30am–12.30pm and 2.30-6pm.
Guided tours in July-Aug. 3.30pm
Free admission.
At the Logis des Bessons the production of brandy has been passed down from father to son since 1850. The Tesseron family will take

you on a guided tour of the distillery and show a video about 'the cognac adventure'. You'll learn all about double distillation, blending and ageing. The Musée des Arts et Traditions du Vigneron Charentais has five pictures of the life of a grape grower

THE DONKEY SANCTUARY
La Tillauderie, 6¼ miles (10 km) W of Dampierre-sur-Boutonne
☎ 05 46 24 07 72
Open daily, July-Aug., 10am-7pm; May-June and Sept., 10am-noon and 2-6pm
Admission charge.
This national donkey sanctuary and breeding centre stands on the edge of the forest of Chizé. Its mission is to preserve the *baudet du Poitou* breed. You can watch these cuddly animals and stroke them. There are guides to show you around and you can see an exhibition about the various breeds of donkeys and how they are raised. Children tend to get so attached to these lovely, placid creatures that you may have difficulty explaining why you can't take one home with you!

in the 19th C. Finally, there is a tasting and an opportunity to buy the cognac itself.

Dampierre-sur-Boutonne
11 miles (18 km) NE of Saint-Jean-d'Angély
Château de Dampierre
Open daily, June-Sept., 10am-6.30pm, Oct.-Nov. and March-May, Sun. and public holidays, 2-5pm
☎ 05 46 24 02 24
Admission charge.
The 16th- C. Château de Dampierre, standing on an island in the middle of the Boutonne, is the loveliest château in the region. The main building consists of two galleries with three-centered basket arches, which give it an Italianate air. The 93 coffers in the ceiling of the upper gallery are sculpted with symbols, quotations and figures relating to Catherine de Medici. The furnishings include a French 17th-C. ebony cabinet inlaid with precious woods and ivory, as well as tapestries from Flanders and Aubusson.

Aulnay-de-Saintonge
10½ miles (17 km) NE of Saint-Jean-d'Angély
Church of Saint-Pierre d'Aulnay
The church stands in the cemetery and looks wonderful

Spotcheck
D 4

Things to do
• Tasting cognac at the Écomusée in Migron
• Walking through the old town of Saint-Jean d'Angély

Things to do with children
• Visit to the donkey sanctuary

Within easy reach
Surgères (p. 224)
Rochefort (p. 206)
La Saintonge (p. 204)

Tourist Offices
Aulnay-de-Saintonge:
☎ 05 46 33 14 44
Saint-Jean-d'Angély:
☎ 05 46 32 04 72

in the setting sun. It is remarkable for the sculptures that adorn the west and south portals, including a bestiary, the four horsemen of the Apocalypse and classic themes of Romanesque art in Saintonge – the struggle between vice and virtue, the wise and foolish virgins, and signs of the zodiac with a depiction of seasonal labour. Inside there are carvings of elephants and lions on the capitals of some of the columns.

Île d'Oléron
golden sands, forests, salt marshes and vineyards

O léron is one of the most beautiful of the Charentes islands. It has long, sandy beaches to the west and north, with a low-lying coastline in the east where the salt marshes have been converted into oyster-beds. Inland, you'll find vineyards and white-painted villages adorned with mimosa, oleander and tamarisk.

Tasting the wines of Oléron

Coulon et Fils Saint-Gilles (at the NW exit from Saint-Pierre d'Oléron) ☎ 05 46 47 02 71

North of Saint-Pierre-d'Oléron, vineyards cover the countryside. Oléron produces Vin de Pays Charentais, cognac and Pineau-des-Charentes. When you visit the wine-makers you will find wines with the appellation *vin de pays Charentais de l'Île d'Oléron*, which allows the wine-makers to distinguish their superior wine from a mere Vin de Pays Charentais. They offer three types of white wine, but first taste the Colombard, a dry and fruity wine, which is a perfect match for the wonderful seafood found on the island (around €3 for a 12 fl oz/75 cl bottle).

A walk in the forest

The forest of Oléron covers 4,942 acres (2,000 ha) at the southern tip of the island, within the commune of Saint-Trojan. It is planted with maritime pines and oaks, and has many footpaths. The Vigne Américaine footpath starts at the parking area of Gatseau bay, and goes deep into the forest, leading to the Bris forest pass, which in turn leads to the large beach in the

CYCLING ROUND THE ISLAND

The best way to discover the island is by bicycle, even though the distances may be fairly long. Several shops have got together to rent bicycles. This means that if your bike needs repairing, you can get help all over the island; you don't have to go back to the place where you originally rented it. **Cycles J. Demion, Le Port, Saint-Trojan-les-Bains,** ☎ 05 46 76 02 63. is just one such address. It will cost around €46 for a week or €11 a day for a mountain-bike and €27 a week or €7 a day for a standard bike.

west. It will take at least 90 minutes to cover the 2 miles (3.5 km). The Maumusson path leads through the forest to the southern tip of the island. It will take 2¼ hours to reach the end, the Pertuis de Maumusson, a distance of nearly 3 miles (4.5 km).

Unusual cycling tours

Saint-Pierre-d'Oléron Tourist Office
☎ 05 46 47 11 39
15 June-15 Sept.
Admission charge.
The **Deux Roues pour une Île Association** offers special tours of the island by bike, guided by one of the local inhabitants. For the bravest, the **Circuit des Cabanes** (the hut tour), some 16 miles (25 km) long, will take you into the heart of the marshes along the Chenal d'Arceau, which is covered with oyster-beds. Gourmets are advised to take the **Circuit des Légendes**. After tasting Pineau-des-Charentes or cognac, you can sample locally made beer and honey produced by Jean-Luc Métayer, before having refreshments at the Quatre-Moulins stop. There are other special tours, concentrating on wine and salt with rather romantic French names, such as *Pédal au fil de l'eau*, literally

meaning 'pedalling beside the water'. Information is available from the island's tourist offices, but it is up to you to rent your bicycle.

Beaches out of sight

Saint-Trojan has the largest beaches on the island. There are stretches of golden sand all along the east of the commune (**Petite Plage, Plage du Soleil** and **Plage de Gatseau**), as well as around the headland in the south of the island (**Pertuis de Maumusson** and **Grande Plage**). The central part of the Grande Plage is reserved for naturists. However, if you want to keep your costume on and relax on a really pleasant beach, the Plage de Gatseau comes highly recommended.

Saint-Denis-d'Oléron

The lighthouse and the Pointe du Chassiron

☎ 05 46 47 86 70
Open daily, June-Sept., 10am-noon and 2-7pm (out of season 5pm)
Free admission.
The Pointe de Chassiron at the northern tip of the island has a wonderful panorama. As soon as there is a little wind, huge white rollers with

foaming tops cut deeper into the cliffs. The trees are bent and twisted with branches facing inland because of the action of the wind. At low tide an old semicircular fish-trap can be seen at the base of the cliff. If you want to get

Spotcheck
B 4 - C 4

Things to do
• Exploring the island by bike
• Swimming at the beaches
• Tasting the island wines

Things to do with children
• Visiting the lighthouse
• Cycling through the bird marshes

Within easy reach
Châtelaillon-Plage (p. 222)
Fouras peninsula (p. 210)
Rochefort (p. 206)
Marennes (p. 232)
Arvert peninsula (p. 234)

Tourist Offices
Saint-Denis-d'Oléron:
☎ 05 46 47 95 53
Saint-Pierre-d'Oléron:
☎ 05 46 47 11 39
Saint-Trojan-les-Bains:
☎ 05 46 76 00 86

a better view and have the energy, then climb the 224 steps of the black-and-white Chassiron lighthouse (open 10am-noon and 2-7pm).

Saint-Trojan-les-Bains
Take the train
Avenue du Débarquement
☎ 05 46 76 01 26
Find out about the timetables, which vary with the tides.
Admission charge.

The Saint-Trojan **tourist train** crosses the south of the island diagonally through the forest and along the bay of Gatseau, ending its run at the coastal dunes and the Maumusson beach. The best time to take the train is at

sunset, when you can travel between the dunes and the forest, listening to the story of *The Shipwrecked Mariners of Pertuis* and the *Submerged Bell-tower*, related by a local poet (8.30pm in Aug., 9pm in July).

Le Grand-Village-Plage
Port des Salines
Rue des Anciennes-Salines
☎ 05 46 75 82 28
Free admission to the site; admission charge for the museum.
This is the only salt marsh on the island that is still being worked. The village, with its brightly coloured fishing huts, has a few displays for tourists. You will learn all about oyster-farming, boat-building and the famous fish-traps that are placed out at sea. Also look out for the black-and-

white photographs of the salt marsh workers and oyster-farmers of the past. Two footpaths (about 1 hour), lead around the salt marshes.

You can also rent a rowing boat for an hour (about €6) and tour the marshes from the water.

Le sel d'Oléron
Le Grand-Village-Plage, Port des Salines
☎ 05 46 75 82 28

One of the wooden huts in the village serves as a shop – selling a variety of local foods. The salt marsh workers pack their own salt, so try the table salt with four seaweeds (*aux quatre algues*) and samphire, a green plant that grows in the salt marshes and that can be cooked like French beans. It is also sold pickled in vinegar like gherkins (€3 for 1¼ lb (500 g) fresh samphire, €5 for a 10 oz (350 g) jar of pickled samphire).

Le Château-d'Oléron
The defences of the citadel
Parking at the citadel
☎ 05 46 47 66 07
Admission charge.
The citadel is the historic capital of the island and has ramparts, moats and fortified gates. It was a 17th-C. stronghold, which formed part of the defence system along the western coast.

It was created by the military engineer Vauban on the orders of Louis XIV to protect the mouth of the Charente and the port of Rochefort. For those who prefer to take things easy, a train runs around the citadel and the oyster port (departure from the parking area of the citadel, from Easter to October 10am-6pm.)

Boyardville
By boat to Fort Boyard
Les Vedettes Oléronnaises,
Place du Marché
☎ **05 46 76 09 50**
Open daily, Apr.-Sept., depending on the tide
Unfortunately, the legendary Fort Boyard, owned exclusively by the France 2 television channel, is not open to the public, but you can get quite close to this imposing building from the sea. The fort was part of the defence system built to protect the mouth of the Charente and the port of Rochefort, but until quite recently it was used mainly as a prison. Pleasure boats offer cruises from the Port of Boyardville to the island of Aix, passing just below Fort Boyard.

Dolus-d'Oléron.
Birdwatching
Les Grissotières
☎ **05 46 75 37 54**
Open daily, July-Aug., 10am-8pm; June and Sept., 10am-1pm and 2-7pm; Apr.-May, except Sat., 10am-1pm and 2-7pm; Oct.-March, daily except Sat., 2-6pm.
Admission charge.
The Marais aux Oiseaux (bird marsh) is a park where both wild and domesticated animals can be observed.

It covers an area of some 24 acres (10 ha) and is regularly visited by migrating birds. The tour begins at the farm which is home to the domesticated animals. You then climb to the top of the observatory, which will give you the best view of the wildlife. There are spoonbills, wild geese, egrets, fallow deer and hinds, and if you're lucky you may even catch sight of the only kingfisher on the marshes, who has a habit of perching on the information signposts.

Marennes
oysters and oyster farming

Marennes, once an island in the gulf of Saintonge, is now part of the mainland, lying on the right bank of the river Seudre. Oyster-farming has gradually replaced salt extraction, and Marennes has become one of the leading oyster-breeding sites in France, farming the famous Marennes-Oléron oysters.

Jewel of the Saintonge

Château de la Gataudière, La Gataudière
☎ 05 46 85 01 07
Open daily, March-Nov. 10am-noon and 2-6pm, Sun. 2-5.30pm
Admission charge.
This 18th-C. château has been dubbed 'the jewel of the Saintonge'. It was the work of François Fresnau, the engineer and botanist who first discovered the hevea, the rubber tree from Guyana. Before entering the main building, take a look at the façade, which is decorated with representations of oysters, salt and bunches of grapes – the region's source of wealth. Inside, the Louis XIII furnishings, carved stonework, grand reception room, and the dining room with its wood panelling and brocade-lined walls are a reminder of the château's former glory.

A bell-tower as lighthouse

Église Saint-Pierre-de-Sales, at Marennes
Admission charge.
The Gothic bell tower of the church of Saint-Pierre-de-Sales was once used as a

lighthouse, with lamps on the platform to guide ships in the Seudre estuary to the Marennes channel. Climb up to the ledge, which is open during the season. (July.-Aug., 10am-12.30pm and 2-7pm; information at the Marennes Tourist Office: ☎ 05 46 85 04 36.) The view is unique.

Boating through oyster country
Bassin de Marennes-Oléron, Port-Cayenne, Marennes
☎ 05 46 85 20 85
Boat tours Apr.-June and Sept., 2.30pm; July.-Aug., 10.30am, 2.30pm, 3.30pm, 4.30pm, 5.30pm
Admission charge.
There are pleasure boat tours of the Marennes-Oléron area, which will take you up the Cayenne canal and lead to the beds where the famous oysters are fattened. The boat then continues by making a tour of the whole basin, and you get a superb view of the Île d'Oléron, the Straits of Maumusson and Ronce-les-Bain on the opposite bank of the Seudre. At low tide the boats take a different route to show the oyster-beds, which are uncovered by the receding waters, and you'll learn all about their breeding and cultivation. Take a warm sweater or fleece as it can get quite chilly.

THE CITADEL OF BROUAGE
Brouage Tourist Office
4 miles (6.5 km)
NE of Marennes
☎ 05 46 85 19 16
Free admission.
Brouage is a delightful village, now encircled by marshes. Not so long ago, it was a flourishing port with a brisk trade in salt. It was the birthplace of Samuel Champlain, who discovered Canada. In the 16th C., Brouage was sheltered by massive fortifications, which were also used as prisons for aristocrats and recalcitrant priests during the French Revolution. You can still visit the underground harbours that linked the main square with the sea, and were vital for the defence system.

Bourcefranc-le-Chapus
3 miles (5 km)
NW of Marennes
A fort in the water
☎ 05 46 85 07 59
By boat in July-Aug., 10am-6.30pm, by foot 20-30 June and 1-15 Sept.
Admission charge.

Fort Chapus was built in 1691 on the orders of Louvois, Louis XIV's minister. It stands on an islet ¼ mile (500 m) from the mainland and is accessible via a ford when the tide is low enough. Inside the fort and its keep, there's an interesting exhibition about the breeding and cultivation of oysters and mussels. Climb to the top of the keep and admire the sea view. You'll find that the bridge and island of Oléron are on the ocean side, while the oyster-beds, salt-marshes and canals are all on the landward side, looking towards Marennes. You will be able to identify all the landmarks because each section of the walkway has a map.

Saint-Sornin
6.5 miles (10.5 km)
NE from Marennes
Angling and vineyards
The village of Saint-Sornin stands on a promontory in the gulf of Santon, overlooking a huge marshland, used for grazing, angling and hiking. The Tour de Broue, a square 12th- C. tower, protects the surrounding land from which the sea retreated some centuries ago. Since then, vines have encroached on the salt-marshes, which produce a good local wine (p. 72).

Spotcheck
C 4

Things to do
• Taking a boat trip through oyster country and learning about oyster farming
• Walking around the citadel of Brouage

Within easy each
Rochefort (p. 206)
Île d'Oléron (p. 228)
Arvert peninsula (p. 234)
La Saintonge (p. 204)

Tourist Offices
Brouage:
☎ 05 46 85 19 16
Bourcefranc-le-Chapus:
☎ 05 46 85 07 00
Marennes:
☎ 05 46 85 04 36

The Arvert peninsula
la Côte Sauvage

To the west of Royan the Arvert peninsula is planted with maritime pines, which gradually give way to little villages of oyster-farmers in the Seudre estuary. Beyond these pines that protect the hinterland from being smothered by the sand dunes, lies the Côte Sauvage (savage coast), with its huge white sandy beaches and powerful breakers.

La Palmyre
9 miles (15 km)
NW of Royan
Visit the zoo
Zoo de La Palmyre
☎ 05 46 22 46 06
Open daily, 9am-7pm;
out of season, 9am-noon
and 2pm-6pm
Admission charge.
The **Zoo de la Palmyre** is by far the best zoo in France, and is a

wonderful place for a family outing. It will take at least 3 hours to cover the 35 acres (14 ha) of the zoo and see the 1,600 animals and birds that live there. They include polar bears, African gorillas and Siberian tigers as well as rhinoceroses, wallabies and elephants.

Saint-Sulpice-de-Royan
4 miles (6.5 km)
N of Royan
Local wines
Wine-makers of the
Côtes de Saintonge
Shop open daily,
9am-12.30pm
and 2-6pm,
This is a good place to know about if you don't want to die of thirst during your holidays, enabling you to discover the many wines made in the Charentes district. The wine-makers market their Vins de Pays Charentais most keenly. The most highly recommended are the white wines made from the Sauvignon and Colombard grape varieties, which cost approximately €3 a bottle, and the Équinoxe Cognac, which was created especially to be drunk with soda-water as an apéritif. Don't forget to try the white or rosé Rayon d'Or, a brand of Pineau-des-Charentes, both of which are famous. Also, remember that the French recommend that Pineau should be drunk from a tulip-shaped glass, so as to preserve its bouquet.

Forêt de la Coubre

9 miles (15 km)
NW of Royan
Pony-trekking on the peninsula
Écurie Tournebride
10 Route de Coux,
à Arvert
☎ 05 46 36 18 96
Open daily, July-Aug.,
9am-8pm
Admission charge.

THE OYSTER ESTUARY

The Seudre estuary contains little villages of oyster-farmers. The long channels between the beds are lined with brightly painted huts. At La Tremblade, Arvert, Chaillevette, Mornac-sur-Seudre and Étaules you can taste the famous Marennes-Oléron oysters. Take a walk beside the channel of La Tremblade and stop at the **Escale de l'Huître**, which is owned by Monsieur Razé. Here you can taste his famous oysters, fattened for five months according to very strict rules (**Établissements Razé**, La Grève, 16 miles (25 km) N of Royan, ☎ 05 46 36 23 45, open daily from 9am to 7pm). You can also take a boat trip on *La Seudre,* which tours the Marennes-Oléron basin, the Straits of Maumusson, the southern end of the Île d'Oléron, and the oyster ports.

The charms of the Arvert peninsula can best be appreciated from horseback. The Tournebride stables offers various pony-trekking routes, depending on your level of horsemanship and your preferences. You can ride out into the forest, at the southern tip of the peninsula, or beside the oyster-beds and oyster channels to Mornac-sur-Seudre (it will take about 7 hours to cover the 19-22 miles (30-35 km). Riding along the beaches of the Côte Sauvage at sunset is a memorable experience.

Mornac sur Seudre

6 miles (10 km)
N from Royan
A charming village
This is a lovely village for a family day out. Wander through the lanes of Mornac-sur-Seudre and admire its white-painted cottages with brightly coloured woodwork. This little oyster-farming port has become home to many painters and potters. Don't miss **Mélo-Coton** (9 Rue du Port, ☎ 05 46 22 66 38, open 1 Apr.-30 Sept., 10.30am-12.30pm and 3-7pm) where unique knitwear is made from fishing line yarn. At no. 20 in the same street, Chantal Lavaud makes

Spotcheck
C 4

Things to do
• Walking in the oyster estuary
• Visit the charming village of Mornac-sur-Seudre

Things to do with children
• Visit the zoo of La Palmyre
• Pony-trekking in the forest of La Coubre

Within easy reach
Île d'Oléron (p. 228)
Marennes (p.232)
Saintonge (p. 204)
Royan (p. 236)

Tourist Offices
Mornac-sur-Seudre:
☎ 05 46 22 61 68
Royan: ☎ 05 46 05 04 71

Saintonge earthenware of great originality. (Open all year round, 10.30am-12.30pm and 3-6.30pm. ☎ 05 46 22 62 81.)

Royan
fine, sandy beaches

Royan has been a well-known seaside resort since the late 19th C., although it has changed a great deal since then. It was completely rebuilt in the 1950s – and not always in the best of taste. Yet Royan has retained much of its original charm, and its many beaches, which in this part of the world are known as *conches*, have only helped to enhance its reputation!

The fish auction
**Port de Pêche,
Quai des Sabliers
☎ 05 46 38 61 86**
This is the place where all the fish caught on the Royan coast are bought and sold. The auction is reserved for the trade and is not open to the public, but you can watch it from two staircases that lead to a large window overlooking the centre isle. Sea bream, plaice, sole, turbot and prawns are sold by the tonne! It's an impressive sight and very noisy. The catches are sold to the highest bidder or the person who shouts loudest as soon as the boats dock.

The church of Notre-Dame
This is one church in the region that has nothing Romanesque about it. Carpet bombing by the Allies during World War II completely destroyed the original church and it was replaced by a tall

concrete structure erected in the late 1950s. You'll love or hate the nave, which is 150 ft (45 m) high, and the vaulting, which is as high as that of Notre-Dame in Paris. The façade is currently cracking dangerously!

An unusual lighthouse
Le Phare de Cordouan
Access by boat from Royan. Tours from Easter to September
Admission charge.
The **Cordouan lighthouse** is one of the oldest in France, having been built in the late 16th C., and is one of the rare lighthouses still occupied by a lighthouse-keeper. It lies 6 miles (10 km) off the coast of Royan. Some 220 ft (67 m) tall, its light can be seen from 28 miles (45 km) away, so it is pretty impressive. On the first floor there are apartments with black-and-white marble floors. You may need to summon the energy to climb the 290 steps to the top, but when you get there the view over the Gironde estuary, the Pointe de la Coubre and the coast of Arvert is worth the effort. A boat ride will take you to out the lighthouse:
Royan Croisières, Quai Vosport (opposite the sailing school), 17200 Royan,
☎ 05 46 06 42 36.

Le Gua
6 miles (10 km) N of Royan
Musée de la Poche de Royan
☎ 05 46 22 89 90
Open daily, July-Aug., 10am-7pm; out of

season, 10am-noon and 2-6pm.
Admission charge.
This museum traces the little known story of the **Royan Pocket** (*Poche*). Towards the end of World War II, several thousand German soldiers

THE BEACHES

Royan is one of France's leading seaside resorts. The **Grande Conche** beach is 2,000 ft (600 m) long and is a paradise for bathers. The little **Conche Foncillon** beach, near the marina and those of the **Chay** (a seawater treatment centre) and the **Pigeonnier** are ideal for families. Finally, the, **Conche de Pontaillac**, at the western tip of the town, is quieter and more select. These smaller beaches are more sheltered from the wind and don't get as crowded as the Grande Conche because they are not as well known.

still controlled the Gironde estuary and the island of Oléron, preventing the Allies from landing in the region. In August 1944,

instead of bombing the this area, the British released 1,700 tonnes of bombs on Royan. As a result, the town was razed to the ground, while the enemy forces remained intact. The 'Pocket' was not liberated until 1 May 1945, a few days before the Armistice. The museum contains a reconstruction of a beach 330 ft (100 m) long, with bunkers and an impressive array of

Spotcheck
C 5

Things to do

- Bathing at the beach
- A sea trip to the Cordouan lighthouse
- Wine tasting at the Chateau de Didonne

Within easy reach

Arvert peninsula (p. 234)
Saintes (p. 202)
Talmont (p. 238)

Tourist Office

Royan: ☎ 05 46 05 04 71

weapons, tanks, motorcycles and amphibian vehicles. The spectacular exhibition covers some 16,146 sq ft (1,500 m²).

Semussac
6 miles (10 km)
S of Royan
Wine tasting at the Château de Didonne

☎ 05 46 06 49 89
Open daily, July-Aug., 8am-8pm; Out of season, groups only, phone for information
At the Château de Didonne they make every effort to demonstrate the delights of the local wines of the Charentes, as well as cognac and Pineau. After being shown round the cellars by the proprietor, visitors can sample the wines and buy them if they like. Be sure to try the Colombard white wine and the **Prince de Didonne house cognac**, which ranges in quality from three-star to X.O.

Walls of cognac-filled oak vats in the cellars of Prince de Didonne at Semussac

Talmont and the Gironde estuary
sandy beaches and pine forests

Talmont is a picturesque little village, with whitewashed cottages surrounded by hollyhocks and tamarisks. The white cliffs of the Gironde estuary have been eroded by the waves and have produced fine sandy beaches. This landscape is dotted with fishing huts on stilts and forests of oak and maritime pine.

Meschers
3 miles (5 km)
NW of Talmont
The Régulus caves
Boulevard de la Falaise
☎ 05 46 02 52 29
Open daily, Feb-Nov,
10am-6pm
Admission charge.
There's a wonderful view over the Gironde estuary from here. These caves have a fascinating history. They have been inhabited for thousands of years and there is ample evidence of their occupation. They were used at various times by pirates, brigands and wreckers.

During the religious wars persecuted Protestants held services here. In the 19th C. they provided shelter for fishermen and for the homeless. Since then, the caves have been left to the sightseers, although there is a lingering air of piracy about them.

Saint-Dizant-du-Gua
14 miles (23 km)
SE of Talmont
The blue fountains
Château de Beaulon
☎ 05 46 49 96 13
Open daily, June-Sept.,
9am-noon and 2-6pm,
Sun., and public holidays;
Oct.-May., 9am-noon and
2-6pm, except weekends.
Admission charge.
The 15th-C. Château de Beaulon (not open to the public) served as a palace for

the bishops of Bordeaux in the 17th C. The grounds are laid out as a park with flowers and trees, and also contain the 'blue fountains', ponds fed by underground springs that are an extraordinary blue colour thanks to microscopic algae in them. The château is known for its vineyard. In the nearby commune of Lorignac, nearly 2 miles (3 km) to the N, look out for the **distillery** with its traditional copper stills. Fine fruity brandies and Pineau are made here.

A PILGRIMS' CHURCH

Talmont was once a stop on the pilgrim route to the shrine of St James of Compostela. This magnificent 11th-C. **Church of Sainte-Radegonde**, on the Gironde estuary, stands at the edge of a cliff that has been eroded away by the waves and now looks as if it is on the point of tumbling into the water. The charm of this gem of Roman-esque art lies in its compact shape and precarious balance between land and sea. It looks particularly striking when viewed at sunset.

Barzan

*2½ miles (4 km)
E of Talmont*
The Fâ Mill
☎ 05 46 90 43 66
Open daily, July-Aug. 10am-1pm and 2-7pm; April-June and Sept., 2-6pm; Oct.-March, weekends and school holidays, 2-5pm. *Admission charge.*
This 16th-C. mill has lost its sails, but at 120 ft (36 m) high and 16 ft (5 m) in diameter, it's still an impressive sight. The promontory on which it proudly stands has a Roman temple that once stood in the centre of a town of 20,000 inhabitants, making it at least as important as Saintes. Incredible archaeological treasure lurks a few feet below ground, just waiting to be unearthed.

Mortagne-sur-Gironde

*8 miles (13 km)
SE of Talmont*
Hermitage near the sea
Ermitage Saint-Martial
☎ 05 46 90 60 01 or 05 46 90 62 95
Daily guided tours in season, 11am-6.30pm, Out of season, by appt. *Free admission, but a contribution is appreciated.*
From the Middle Ages to the French Revolution, pilgrims bound for the shrine of St James of Compostela stopped here before taking the ferry across the Gironde. They stayed at the hermitage near the sea, which is cut out of the rock and consists of four cavities, used as a kitchen, hall, refectory and dormitory. There's also a 9th-C. chapel.

Saint-André-de-Lidon

*11 miles (18 km)
NE of Talmont*
The Chaillaud botanical gardens

☎ 05 46 90 08 10
Park open daily 9am-7pm, cellar open in season 9am-7pm, Oct.-March by appointment only
Free admission.
The Deau family own the Chaillaud estate and offer visitors the delights of a botanical garden, as well as the opportunity to taste an

Things to do
• Visiting the pilgrims' church beside the sea
• Tasting cognac in the Parc du Chaillaud
• Discovering the Régulus caves

Within easy reach
*Royan (p. 236)
Valley of the Seugne (p.192)
Saintes (p. 202)*

Tourist Offices
Meschers:
☎ 05 46 02 70 39
Talmont: ☎ 05 46 90 16 25

excellent old cognac or seductive Pineau-des-Charentes. These bottles of cognac have the elegance of perfume flasks. The Cognac XO n°8, is 20 years old and the Extra Éternité has been aged in oak casks for 50 years. The estate is surrounded by a colourful botanical garden that stretches out into the countryside and nearby forest. There are 600 varieties of flowers, shrubs, perennials and rose bushes, all of which appear to flourish here.

Photo credits

Inside the book

All the photographs in this guide were taken by **Hervé Lenain, Hémisphères**, with the exception of those on the following pages:

Bruno Barbier, Hémisphères: p. 7 (b.r.); p. 26 (u.); p. 41 (b.); p. 132 (u.); p. 137 (b.); p. 206 (c.).
Stéphane Frances, Hémisphères: p. 5 (u.r.); © 'Les Garçons'; p. 44 (u.); p. 130 (u.r.); p. 153 (u.); p. 183 (u.r.); p. 196 (u.); p. 231 (b.). **Patrick Frilet, Hémisphères**: p. 10 (b.); p. 16 (u.); p. 82 (c.r., b.); p. 100 (b.); p. 145 (u.); p. 156 (u.). **Bertrand Gardel, Hémisphères**: p. 38 (b.); p. 100 (u.); p. 204 (u.); p. 211 (b.). **Bertrand Gardel/Bertrand Rieger**: p. 11 (u.r.); p. 22 (b.); p. 25 (c.r.); p. 27 (c.); p. 30 (u., b.r.); p. 39 (b.); p. 40 (u.); p. 68 (u.); p. 72 (u.); p. 79 (b.); p. 81 (u., b.); p. 82 (u.); p. 89 (b.); p. 103 (u.); p. 109 (u.); p. 111 (b.l.); p. 112 (c.l.) p. 116 (u.); p. 117 (c.r., b.r.); p. 119 (c.r.); p. 122 (b.); p. 138 (u.); p. 139 (c.l.); p. 144 (b.); p. 147 (b.l.); p. 151 (b.); p. 157 (b.c.); p. 159 (b.); p. 162 (u.); p. 164 (u.l.); p. 165 (u., b.r.); p. 166 (u.); p. 168 (u.); p. 169 (b.l.); p. 170 (u.); p. 171 (c.); p. 173 (u.r.); p. 179 (c.); p. 182 (u.c.); p. 184 (b.); p. 185 (b.); p. 186 (b.); p. 191 (b.); p. 194 (u.); p. 199 (b.); p. 201 (u.r.); p. 203 (b.); p. 208 (b.); p. 210 (u.); p. 212 (c.r.); p. 213 (b.); p. 216 (c.); p. 223 (b.); p. 224 (u.); p. 225 (c., b.); p. 228 (u.); p. 233 (u.); p. 234 (c.); p. 237 (u., b.l.). **Laurent Giraudou, Hémisphères**: p. 125 (b.); p. 172 (u.); p. 179 (b.). **Gil Giulio, Hémisphères:** p. 5 (u.l.); p. 7 (c.l.); p. 8 (u.); p. 33 (u.r.); p. 103 (b.r.); p. 113 (b.); p. 148 (u.). **Philippe Guignard, Hémisphères**: p. 8 (c.l.); p. 32 (c.); p. 231 (u.); p. 233 (c.). **Bertrand Rieger, Hémisphères:** p. 123 (c.r.); p. 209 (b.l.). **Louis Sassi, Hémisphères:** p. 111 (c.r.); p. 156 (c.). **Annette Soumillard, Hémisphères**: p. 148 (c.). **Pawel Wysocki, Hémisphères:** p. 9 (c.r.); p. 142 (b.r.); p. 143 (b.l.); p. 146 (u.); p. 162 (b.); p. 183 (c.r.). **Pawel Wysocki/Stéphane Frances, Hémisphères :** p. 4 (u.); p. 8 (c.r.); p. 45 (b.); p. 79 (c.); p. 96 (b.); p. 133 (b.); p. 144 (u.); p. 193 (b.l.); p. 201 (c.l.); p. 204 (b.l.); p. 206 (b.r.); p. 212 (u.); p. 218 (b.). **Jacques Debru:** p. 5 (c.l.); p. 8 (b.); p. 17 (c.r.); p. 19 (b.); p. 34 (b.); p. 35 (b.); p. 39 (c.r.); p. 42 (u.); p. 68 (b.); p. 69 (c.); p. 73 (u.r.); p. 74 (u., c.r.); p. 80 (c.); p. 84 (u., b.); p. 88 (b.); p. 89 (c.r.); p. 92 (b.); p. 93 (b.); p. 99 (u.); p. 103 (c.r.); p. 108 (u.); p. 110 (u.); p. 114 (u.); p. 115 (u.); p. 119 (u.); p. 120 (u.); p. 121 (b.l.); p. 127 (c.l.); p. 134 (u.); p. 142 (c.); p. 149 (u.); p. 159 (c.); p. 200 (b.c.); p. 239 (b.). **Bernadette Matthysse:** p. 154 (u.). **Jacana:** p. 18 (u.). **Photothèque Hachette (droits réservés):** p. 43 (c.); p. 44 (c., b.); p. 45 (u., c.); p. 54 (u., c.); p. 55 (c.r.); p. 56 (c.); p. 57 (u., c.r., b.); p. 58 (u., c.); p. 59 (b.); p. 204 (b.r.). **Droits réservés:** p. 17 (u.); © **Fédération Française de naturisme:** p. 34 (c.); p. 35 (u.). © **Établissement Rondinaud:** p. 42 (c., b.); p. 43 (u., b.). © **Collection *Les Cahiers du Cinéma*:** p. 206 (u.).

This guide was written by Christine Legrand and Bertrand Lauzanne-Maigret, with additional help from Frédéric Olivier, Françoise Picon and Aude Sarrazin.

Illustrations: Pascal Gindre

Illustrated maps: Renaud Marca

Cartography: © Idé-Infographie (Thomas Grollier)

Translation and adaptation: Chanterelle Translations, London (Josephine Bacon)

Additional design and editorial assistance: Lydia Darbyshire, Jane Ellis and Christine Bell

Project manager: Liz Coghill

We have done our best to ensure the accuracy of the information contained in this guide. However, addresses, telephone numbers, opening times etc. inevitably do change from time to time, so if you find a discrepancy please do let us know. You can contact us at: george.philip@philips-maps.co.uk or write to us at Philip's, address below.

Hachette UK guides provide independent advice. The authors and compilers do not accept any remuneration for the inclusion of any addresses in these guides.

Please note that we cannot accept any responsibility for any loss, injury or inconvenience sustained by anyone as a result of any information or advice contained in this guide.

First published in the United Kingdom in 2000 by Hachette UK
Second impression with revisions 2003

Distributed in the United States of America by Sterling Publishing Co., Inc. 387 Park Avenue South, New York, NY 10016-8810

A CIP catalogue for this book is available from the British Library

ISBN 1 84202 009 9

Hachette Travel Guides, c/o Philip's, a division of Octopus Publishing Group Ltd, 2–4 Heron Quays, London E14 4JP

Printed in Slovenia by DELO tiskarna by arrangement with Prešernova družba

Handy words and phrases

Over the next few pages you'll find a selection of very basic French vocabulary and many apologies if the word you are looking for is missing. For those struggling with French menus, there is more help at the back of the book in the detailed menu decoder.

Let us begin, however, with a very basic guide to some French grammar: All French nouns are either masculine or feminine and gender is denoted as follows: 'the' singular is translated by le (m), la (f) or l' (in front of a word beginning with a vowel or mute 'h'; 'the' plural = les (whatever gender and in front of a vowel or mute 'h'). 'A' = un (m), une (f) (no exceptions for vowels or mute 'h').

There are two forms of the word 'you' – tu is 'you' in the singular, very informal and used with people you know, vous is 'you' in the singular but is used in formal situations and when you don't know the person, vous is also the plural form. Young people often address each other as 'tu' automatically, but when in doubt and to avoid offence, always use 'vous'.

Adjectives agree with the gender of the accompanying noun. For a singular masculine noun there is no change to the adjective, but to indicate the masculine plural, an 's' is added to the end of the adjective; an 'e' is usually added for a feminine noun and 'es' for the plural. If you are not very familiar with French don't worry too much about gender agreement when talking (unless you wish to perfect your pronunciation, as 'e' or 'es' usually makes the final consonant hard), we have used feminine versions where applicable simply to help with the understanding of written French. These are either written out in full or shown as '(e)'. Finally, if you do not know the right French word try using the English one with a French accent – it is surprising how often this works.

The verb 'to be'

I am	je suis
you are (informal/singular)	tu es
he/she/it is	il (m)/elle (f)/il est*
we are	nous sommes
you are (formal/plural)	vous êtes
they are	ils (m)/elles (f) sont*

When you are in a hurry gender can complicate things – just say le or la, whichever comes into your head first and you will sometimes be right and usually be understood.

* The most common forms use the masculine: 'it is' = il est, 'they are'= ils sont. C'est = 'that is' or 'this is', and is not gender specific.

Essential vocabulary

Yes/No	Oui/Non
OK	D'accord
That's fine	C'est bon
Please	S'il vous plaît
Thank you	Merci
Good morning/Hello	Bonjour (during the day)

Good evening/night/Hello	Bonsoir (during the evening)
Hello/Goodbye (very informal)	Salut
Goodbye	Au revoir
See you soon	A bientôt
Excuse me	Excusez-moi
I am sorry	Je suis désolé (m)/désolée (f)
Pardon?	Comment?

Handy phrases

Do you speak English?	Parlez-vous anglais?
I don't speak French	Je ne parle pas français
I don't understand	Je ne comprends pas
Could you speak more slowly please?	Pouvez-vous parler moins vite s'il vous plaît?
Could you repeat that, please?	Pouvez-vous répéter, s'il vous plaît?
again	encore
I am English/Scottish/ Welsh/Irish/American/ Canadian/Australian/ a New Zealander	Je suis anglais(e)/écossais(e)/ gallois(e)/irlandais(e)/américain(e)/ canadien(ne)/australien(ne)/ néo-zélandais(e)
My name is …	Je m'appelle …
What is your name?	Comment vous appelez-vous?
How are you?	Comment allez-vous?
Very well, thank you	Très bien, merci.
Pleased to meet you	Enchanté(e).
Mr/Mrs	Monsieur/Madame
Miss/Ms	Mademoiselle/Madame
How?	Comment?
What?	Quel (m)/Quelle (f)?
When?	Quand?
Where (is/are)?	Où (est/sont)?
Which?	Quel (m)/Quelle (f)?
Who?	Qui?
Why?	Pourquoi?

Essential words

good	bon/bonne
bad	mauvais/mauvaise
big	grand/grande
small	petit/petite
hot	chaud/chaude
cold	froid/froide
open	ouvert/ouverte
closed	fermé/fermée
toilets	les toilettes/les w.c.
women	dames
men	hommes
free (unoccupied)	libre
occupied	occupé/occupée
free (no charge)	gratuit/gratuite
entrance	l'entrée
exit	la sortie
prohibited	interdit/interdite
no smoking	défense de fumer

Time and space

....

PERIODS OF TIME

a minute	une minute
half an hour	une demie-heure
an hour	une heure
a week	une semaine
fortnight	une quinzaine
month	un mois
year	un an/une année
today	aujourd'hui
yesterday/tomorrow	hier/demain
morning	le matin
afternoon	l'après-midi
evening/night	le soir/la nuit
during (the night)	pendant (la nuit)
early/late	tôt/tard

TELLING THE TIME

What time is it?	Quelle heure est-il?
At what time?	A quelle heure?
(at) 1 o'clock/2 o'clock etc.	(à) une heure/deux heures etc.
half past one	une heure et demie
quarter past two	deux heures et quart
quarter to three	trois heures moins le quart
(at) midday	à midi
(at) midnight	à minuit

Getting around

....

by bicycle	à bicyclette/en vélo
by bus	en bus
by car	en voiture
by coach	en car
on foot	à pied
by plane	en avion
by taxi	en taxi
by train	en train

IN TOWN

map of the city	un plan de la ville
I am going to ...	Je vais à ...
I want to go to ...	Je voudrais aller à ...
I want to get off at ...	Je voudrais descendre à ...
platform	le quai
return ticket	un aller-retour
single ticket	un aller simple
ticket	le billet
timetable	l'horaire
airport	l'aéroport
bus/coach station	la gare routière
bus stop	l'arrêt de bus
district	le quartier/l'arrondissement
street	la rue
taxi rank	la station de taxi
tourist information office	l'office du tourisme
train station	la gare
underground	le métro

bag/handbag	le sac/le sac-à-main
case	la valise
left luggage	la consigne
luggage	les bagages

DIRECTIONS

Is it far?	Est-ce que c'est loin?
How far is it to …?	Combien de kilomètres d'ici à …?
Is it near?	Est-ce que c'est près d'ici?
here/there	ici/là
near/far	près/loin
left/right	gauche/droite
on the left/right	à gauche/à droite
straight on	tout droit
at the end of	au bout de
up	en haut
down	en bas
above (the shop)	au-dessus (du magasin)
below (the bed)	au-dessous (le lit)
opposite (the bank)	en face (de la banque)
next to (the window)	à côté (de la fenêtre)

DRIVING

Please fill the tank (car)	Le plein, s'il vous plaît
car hire	la location de voitures
driver's licence	le permis de conduire
petrol	l'essence
rent a car	louer une voiture
unleaded	sans plomb

In the hotel

•••

I have a reservation	J'ai une réservation
for 2 nights	pour 2 nuits
I leave …	Je pars …
I'd like a room	Je voudrais une chambre
Is breakfast included?	Le petit-déjeuner est inclus?
single room	une chambre à un lit
room with double bed	une chambre à lit double
twin room	une chambre à deux lits
room with bathroom	une chambre avec salle de bains
and toilet	et toilette/W.C.
a quiet room	une chambre calme
bath	le bain
shower	la douche
with air conditioning	avec climatisation
1st/2nd floor etc.	premier/deuxième étage
breakfast	le petit-déjeuner
dining room	la salle à manger
ground floor	le rez-de-chaussée (RC)
key	la clef
lift/elevator	l'ascenseur

PAYING

How much?	C'est combien, s'il vous plaît?/ Quel est le prix?
Do you accept credit cards?	Est-ce que vous acceptez les cartes de crédit?
Do you have any change?	Avez-vous de la monnaie?

(in) cash	(en) espèces
coin	le pièce de monnaie
money	l'argent
notes	les billets
price	le prix
travellers' cheques	les chèques de voyage

Eating out

••

If you are having trouble understanding the rather complicated-looking
menu which is put before you, then turn to p.x for the menu decoder.
In the meantime, the following phrases should be useful when you are
trying to communicate with the waiter or waitress.

GENERAL

Do you have a table?	Avez-vous une table libre?
I would like to reserve a table	Je voudrais réserver une table.
I would like to eat	Je voudrais manger
I would like something to drink	Je voudrais boire quelque chose
I would like to order, please	Je voudrais commander, s'il vous plait
The bill, please	L'addition, s'il vous plait
I am a vegetarian	Je suis végétarien(ne)

MEALS AND MEALTIMES

breakfast	le petit-déjeuner
cover charge	le couvert
dessert	le dessert
dinner	le dîner
dish of the day	le plat du jour
fixed price menu	la formule/le menu à prix fixe
fork	la fourchette
knife	le couteau
lunch	le déjeuner
main course	le plat principal
menu	le menu/la carte
(Is the) service included?	Est-ce que le service est compris?
soup	la soupe/le potage
spoon	la cuillère
starter	l'entrée/le hors-d'oeuvre
waiter	Monsieur
waitress	Madame, Mademoiselle
wine list	la carte des vins

COOKING STYLES

baked	cuit/cuite au four
boiled	bouilli/bouillie
fried	à la poêle
grilled	grillé/grillée
medium	à point
poached	poché/pochée
rare	saignant
steamed	à la vapeur
very rare	bleu
well done	bien cuit

MEAT, POULTRY, GAME AND OFFAL

bacon	le bacon
beef	le boeuf
chicken	le poulet
duck	le canard

frogs' legs	les cuisses de grenouilles
game	le gibier
ham	le jambon
kidneys	les rognons
lamb	l'agneau
meat	la viande
pork	le porc
rabbit	le lapin
salami style sausage (dry)	le saucisson-sec
sausage	la saucisse
snails	les escargots
steak	l'entrecôte/le steak/le bifteck
veal	le veau

FISH AND SEAFOOD

cod	le cabillaud/la morue
Dublin bay prawn/scampi	la langoustine
fish	le poisson
herring	le hareng
lobster	le homard
mullet	le rouget
mussels	les moules
oysters	les huîtres
pike	le brochet
prawns	les crevettes
salmon (smoked)	le saumon (fumé)
sea bass	le bar
seafood	les fruits de mer
skate	le raie
squid	le calmar
trout	la truite
tuna	le thon

VEGETABLES, PASTA AND RICE

cabbage	le chou
cauliflower	le chou-fleur
chips/french fries	les frites
garlic	l'ail
green beans	les haricots verts
leeks	les poireaux
onions	les oignons
pasta	les pâtes
peas	les petits pois
potatoes	les pommes-de-terre
rice	le riz
sauerkraut	la choucroute
spinach	les épinards
vegetables	les légumes

SALAD ITEMS

beetroot	la betterave
cucumber	le concombre
curly endive	la salade frisée
egg	un oeuf
green pepper/red pepper	le poivron/poivron rouge
green salad	la salade verte
lettuce	la laitue
tomato	la tomate

FRUIT

apple	la pomme
banana	la banane

blackberries	les mûres
blackcurrants	les cassis
cherries	les cerises
fresh fruit	le fruit frais
grapefruit	le pamplemousse
grapes	les raisins
lemon/lime	le citron/le citron vert
orange	l'orange
peach	la pêche
pear	la poire
plums	les prunes/les mirabelles (type of plum)
raspberries	les framboises
red/white currants	les groseilles
strawberries	les fraises

DESSERTS AND CHEESE

apple tart	la tarte aux pommes
cake	le gâteau
cheese	le fromage
cream	la crème fraîche
goat's cheese	le fromage de chèvre
ice cream	la glace

SUNDRIES

ashtray	un cendrier
bread	le pain
bread roll	le petit pain
butter	le beurre
crisps	les chips
mustard	la moutarde
napkin	la serviette
oil	l'huile
peanuts	les cacahuètes
salt/pepper	le sel/le poivre
toast	le toast
vinegar	le vinaigre

DRINKS

beer	la bière
a bottle of	une bouteille de
black coffee	un café noir
coffee	un café
with cream	un café-crème
with milk	un café au lait
a cup of	une tasse de
decaffeinated coffee	un café décaféiné/un déca
espresso coffee	un express
freshly-squeezed lemon/ orange juice	un citron pressé/une orange pressée
a glass of	un verre de
herbal tea	une tisane/infusion
with lime/verbena	au tilleul/à la verveine
with mint	à la menthe
with milk/lemon	au lait/au citron
milk	le lait
(some) mineral water	de l'eau minérale
orange juice	un jus d'orange
(some) tap water	de l'eau du robinet
(some) sugar	du sucre
tea	un thé
wine (red/white)	le vin (rouge/blanc)

Shopping (also see 'Paying')

•••

USEFUL SHOPPING VOCABULARY

I'd like to buy...	Je voudrais acheter…
Do you have...?	Avez-vous …?
How much, please?	C'est combien, s'il vous plaît?
I'm just looking, thank you	Je regarde, merci.
It's for a gift	C'est pour un cadeau.

SHOPS

antique shop	le magasin d'antiquités
baker	la boulangerie
bank	la banque
book shop	la librairie
cake shop	la pâtisserie
cheese shop	la fromagerie
chemist/drugstore	la pharmacie
clothes shop	le magasin de vêtements
delicatessen	la charcuterie
department store	le grand magasin
gift shop	le magasin de cadeaux
the market	le marché
newsagent	le magasin de journaux
post office	la poste/le PTT
shoe shop	le magasin de chaussures
the shops	les boutiques/magasins
tobacconist	le tabac
travel agent	l'agence de voyages

expensive	cher
cheap	pas cher, bon marché
sales	les soldes
size (in clothes)	la taille
size (in shoes)	la pointure
too expensive	trop cher

TELEPHONING

telephone/phone booth	le téléphone/la cabine téléphonique
phone card	la carte téléphonique
post card	la carte postale
stamps	les timbres

Months of the year

•••

January	janvier
February	février
March	mars
April	avril
May	mai
June	juin
July	juillet
August	août
September	septembre
October	octobre
November	novembre
December	décembre

a year	un an/une année
a month	un mois

Days of the week

....

Monday	lundi
Tuesday	mardi
Wednesday	mercredi
Thursday	jeudi
Friday	vendredi
Saturday	samedi
Sunday	dimanche

Colours

....

black	noir/noire
blue	bleu/bleue
brown	brun/brune
green	vert/verte
orange	orange
pink	rose
red	rouge
white	blanc/blanche
yellow	jaune

Numbers

....

enough	assez
zero	zéro
one; first	un/une; premier/première
two/second	deux/deuxième
three/third	trois/troisième
four/fourth	quatre/quatrième
five/fifth	cinq/cinquième
six/sixth	six/sixième
seven/seventh	sept/septième
eight/eighth	huit/huitième
nine/nineth	neuf/neuvième
ten/tenth etc	dix/dixième etc
eleven	onze
twelve	douze
thirteen	treize
fourteen	quatorze
fifteen	quinze
sixteen	seize
seventeen	dix-sept
eighteen	dix-huit
nineteen	dix-neuf
twenty	vingt
twenty-one	vingt-et-un
twenty-two/three etc	vingt-deux/trois etc.
thirty	trente
forty	quarante
fifty	cinquante
sixty	soixante
seventy	soixante-dix
eighty	quatre-vingts
ninety	quatre-vingt-dix
hundred	cent
thousand	mille

Menu decoder

À point medium rare
Abats offal
Abricot apricot
Acarne sea-bream
Affiné(e) improve, ripen, mature (common term with cheese)
Africaine (à l') african style: with aubergines, tomatoes, ceps
Agneau lamb
Agrumes citrus fruits
Aigre-doux sweet-sour
Aiguillette thin slice
Ail garlic
Aile (Aileron) wing (winglet)
Aïoli mayonnaise, garlic, olive oil
Algues seaweed
Aligot purée of potatoes, cream, garlic, butter and fresh Tomme de Cantal (or Laguiole) cheese
Allemande (à l') German style: with sauerkraut and sausages
Alsacienne (à l') Alsace style: with sauerkraut, sausages and sometimes foie gras
Amande almond
Amandine almond-flavoured
Amer bitter
Américaine (à l') Armoricaine (à l') sauce with dry white wine, cognac, tomatoes, shallots
Amuse-gueule appetizer
Ananas pineapple
Anchoiade anchovy crust
Anchois anchovy
Ancienne (à l') in the old style
Andouille smoked tripe sausage
Andouillette small chitterling (tripe) sausage
Aneth dill
Anglaise (à l') plain boiled
Anguille eels
Anis aniseed
Arachide peanut
Arc-en-ciel rainbow trout
Artichaud artichoke
Asperge asparagus
Assaisonné flavoured or seasoned with; to dress a salad
Assiette (de) plate (of)
Aubergine aubergine, eggplant
Aumônière pancake drawn up into shape of beggar's purse
Auvergnate (à l') Auvergne style: with cabbage, sausage and bacon
Avocat avocado pear
Baba au rhum sponge dessert with rum syrup
Baguette long bread loaf
Baie berry
Baigné bathed or lying in
Banane banana
Bar sea-bass
Barbeau de mer red mullet
Barbue brill

Basilic basil
Basquaise (à la) Basque style: Bayonne ham, rice and peppers
Baudroie monkfish, anglerfish
Bavette skirt of beef
Béarnaise thick sauce with egg yolks, shallots, butter, white wine and tarragon vinegar
Béchamel creamy white sauce
Beignet fritter
Belle Hélène poached pear with ice cream and chocolate sauce
Berrichonne bordelaise sauce
Betterave beetroot
Beurre (Échiré) butter (finest butter from Poitou-Charentes)
Beurre blanc sauce with butter, shallots, wine vinegar and sometimes dry white wine
Beurre noir sauce with brown butter, vinegar, parsley
Bière à la pression beer on tap
Bière en bouteille bottled beer
Bifteck steak
Bigarade (à la) orange sauce
Bisque shellfish soup
Blanc (de volaille) white breast (of chicken); can also describe white fish fillet or white vegetables
Blanchaille whitebait
Blanquette white stew
Blé corn or wheat
Blettes swiss chard
Blinis small, thick pancakes
Boeuf à la mode beef braised in red wine
Boeuf Stroganoff beef, sour cream, onions, mushrooms
Bombe ice-cream
Bonne femme (à la) white wine sauce, shallots, mushrooms
Bordelaise (à la) Bordeaux style: brown sauce with shallots, red wine, beef bone marrow
Boudin blanc white coloured sausage-shaped mixture; pork and sometimes chicken
Boudin noir black pudding
Bouillabaisse Mediterranean fish stew and soup
Bouillon broth, light consommé
Bouquet garni bunch of herbs used for flavouring
Bourguignonne (à la) Burgundy style: red wine, onions, bacon and mushrooms
Bourride creamy fish soup with aioli
Brandade de morue salt cod
Bretonne sauce with celery, leeks, beans and mushrooms
Brioche sweet yeast bread
Brochet pike
Brochette (de) meat or fish on a skewer
Brouillé scrambled
Brûlé(e) toasted
Bruxelloise sauce with asparagus, butter and eggs

Cabillaud cod
Cacahouète roasted peanut
Cacao cocoa
Café coffee
Caille quail
Cajou cashew nut
Calmar (Calamar) inkfish, squid
Campagne country style
Canard duck
Caneton (Canette) duckling
Cannelle cinnamon
Carbonnade braised beef in beer, onions and bacon
Carré chop
Casse-croûte snack
Cassis blackcurrant
Cassolette small pan
Cassoulet casserole of beans, sausage and/or pork, goose, duck
Cèpe fine, delicate mushroom
Cerise (noire) cherry (black)
Cerneau walnut
Cervelas pork garlic sausage
Cervelle brains
Champignons (des bois) mushrooms (from the woods)
Chanterelle apricot coloured mushroom
Chantilly whipped cream with sugar
Charcuterie cold meat cuts
Charcutière sauce with onions, white wine, gherkins
Chasseur sauce with white wine, mushrooms, shallots
Chateaubriand thick fillet steak
Chaussons pastry turnover
Chemise (en) pastry covering
Chicon chicory
Chicorée curly endive
Chipiron *see* calmar
Choix (au) a choice of
Chou (vert) cabbage
Choucroute souring of vegetables, usually with cabbage (sauerkraut), peppercorns, boiled ham, potatoes and Strasbourg sausages
Chou-fleur cauliflower
Chou rouge red cabbage
Choux (pâte à) pastry
Ciboule spring onions
Cidre cider
Ciboulette chive
Citron (vert) lemon (lime)
Citronelle lemon grass
Civet stew
Clafoutis cherries in pancake batter
Clou de girofle clove (spice)
Cochon pig
Cochonailles pork products
Cocotte (en) cooking pot
Coeur (de) heart (of)
Coing quince
Colin hake
Compote stewed fruit
Concassé(e) coarsely chopped
Concombre cucumber
Confit(e) preserved or candied
Confiture jam
Confiture d'orange marmalade
Consommé clear soup

Coq (au vin) chicken in red wine sauce
Coque (à la) soft-boiled or served in shell
Coquillage shellfish
Coquille St-Jacques scallop
Coriandre coriander
Cornichon gherkin
Côte d'agneau lamb chop
Côte de boeuf side of beef
Côte de veau veal chop
Côtelette chop
Coulis de thick sauce of
Courge pumpkin
Couscous crushed semolina
Crabe crab
Crécy with carrots and rice
Crème cream
Crème anglaise light custard sauce
Crème brûlée same, less sugar and cream, with praline (*see* Brûlée)
Crème pâtissière custard filling
Crêpe thin pancake
Crêpe Suzette sweet pancake with orange liqueur sauce
Cresson watercress
Crevette grise shrimp
Crevette rose prawn
Croque Monsieur toasted cheese or ham sandwich
Croustade small pastry mould with various fillings
Croûte (en) pastry crust (in)
Cru raw
Crudité raw vegetable
Crustacés shell fish
Cuisse (de) leg (of)
Cuissot (de) haunch (of)
Cuit cooked
Datte date
Daube stew (various types)
Daurade sea-bream
Décaféiné decaffeinated coffee
Dégustation tasting
Diane (á la) pepper cream sauce
Dieppoise (à la) Dieppe style: white wine, cream, mussels, shrimps
Dijonaise (à la) with mustard sauce
Dinde young hen turkey
Dindon turkey
Dorade sea-bream
Doux (douce) sweet
Échalotte shallot
Écrevisse freshwater crayfish
Émincé thinly sliced
Encre squid ink, used in sauces
Endive chicory
Entrecôte entrecôte, rib steak
Entremets sweets
Épaule shoulder
Épice spice
Épinard spinach
Escabèche fish (or poultry) marinated in court-bouillon; cold
Escalope thinly cut (meat or fish)
Escargot snail
Espadon swordfish
Estouffade stew with onions, herbs, mushrooms, red or white wine (perhaps garlic)
Estragon tarragon

Farci(e) stuffed
Farine flour
Faux-filet sirloin steak
Fenouil fennel
Fermière mixture of onions, carrots, turnips, celery, etc.
Feuille de vigne vine leaf
Feuilleté light flaky pastry
Fève broad bean
Ficelle (à la) tied in a string
Ficelles thin loaves of bread
Figue fig
Filet fillet
Financière (à la) Madeira sauce with truffles
Fines de claire oyster (*see* Huîtres)
Fines herbes mixture of parsley, chives, tarragon, etc.
Flageolet kidney bean
Flamande (à la) Flemish style: bacon, carrots, cabbage, potatoes and turnips
Flambée flamed
Flamiche puff pastry tart
Foie liver
Foie de veau calves liver
Foie gras goose liver
Fond d'artichaut artichoke heart
Fondu(e) (de fromage) melted cheese with wine
Forestière bacon and mushrooms
Four (au) baked in the oven
Fourré stuffed
Frais fresh or cool
Fraise strawberry
Fraise des bois wild strawberry
Framboise raspberry
Frappé frozen or ice cold
Friandise sweets (petits fours)
Fricassée braised in sauce or butter, egg yolks and cream
Frisé(e) curly
Frit fried
Frites chips/French fries
Friture small fried fish
Fromage cheese
Fromage de tête brawn
Fruit de la passion passion fruit
Fruits confits crystallised fruit
Fruits de mer seafood
Fumé smoked
Galette pastry, pancake or cake
Gamba large prawn
Ganache chocolate and crème fraîche mixture used to fill cakes
Garbure (Garbue) vegetable soup
Gâteau cake
Gauffre waffle
Gelée aspic gelly
Genièvre juniper
Gésier gizzard
Gibelotte *see* Fricassée
Gibier game
Gigot (de) leg of lamb; can describe other meat or fish
Gingembre ginger
Girofle clove
Glacé(e) iced, crystallized, glazed
Glace ice-cream
Gougère round-shaped, egg and cheese choux pastry

Goujon gudgeon
Goujonnettes (de) small fried pieces (of)
Gourmandises sweetmeats; can describe fruits de mer
Graisse fat
Gratin browned
Gratin Dauphinois potato dish with cheese, cream and garlic
Gratin Savoyard potato dish with cheese and butter
Gratiné(e) sauced dish browned with butter, cheese, breadcrumbs, etc.
Gravette oyster (*see* Huîtres)
Grenouille (*cuisses de grenouilles*) frog (frogs' legs)
Gribiche mayonnaise sauce with gherkins, capers, hardboiled egg yolks and herbs
Grillade grilled meat
Grillé(e) grilled
Griotte (Griottine) bitter red cherry
Gros sel coarse rock or sea salt
Groseille à maquereau gooseberry
Groseille noire blackcurrant
Groseille rouge redcurrant
Gruyère hard, mild cheese
Hachis minced or chopped-up
Hareng herring
    à l'huile cured in oil
    fumé kippered
    salé bloater
    saur smoked
Haricot bean
Haricot blanc dried white bean
Haricot vert green/French bean
Hollandaise sauce with butter, egg yolk and lemon juice
Homard lobster
Hongroise (à la) Hungarian style: sauce with tomato and paprika
Huile oil
Huîtres oysters
    Les claires: the oyster-fattening beds in Marennes terrain (part of the Charente Estuary, between Royan and Rochefort, in Poitou-Charentes).
    Flat-shelled oysters: *Belons* (from the river Belon in Brittany)
    Gravettes: from Arcachon in the South West); both the above are cultivated in their home oyster beds.
    Marennes are those transferred from Brittany and Arcachon to *les claires*, where they finish their growth.
    Dished oysters (sometimes called *portugaises*): these breed mainly in the Gironde and Charentes estuaries; they mature at Marennes.
    Fines de claires and *spéciales* are the largest; *huîtres de parc* are standard sized. All this lavish care covers a time span of two to four years.
Hure (de) head (of); brawn, jellied
Île flottante unmoulded soufflé of beaten egg with white sugar
Imam bayeldi aubergine with rice, onions, and sautéed tomatoes
Infusion herb tea
Italienne (à l') Italian style: artichokes, mushrooms, pasta

Jalousie latticed fruit or jam tart
Jambon ham
Jambonneau knuckle of pork
Jambonnette boned and stuffed (knuckle of ham or poultry)
Jarret de veau stew of shin of veal
Jarreton cooked pork knuckle
Jerez sherry
Joue (de) cheek (of)
Julienne thinly-cut vegetables: also ling (cod family)
Jus juice
Lait milk
Laitue lettuce
Lamproie eel-like fish
Langouste spiny lobster or crawfish
Langoustine Dublin Bay prawn
Langue tongue
Lapereau young rabbit
Lapin rabbit
Lard bacon
Lardons strips of bacon
Laurier bay-laurel, sweet bay leaf
Léger (Légère) light
Légume vegetable
Lièvre hare
Limaçon snail
Limande lemon sole
Limon lime
Lit bed
Lotte de mer monkfish, anglerfish
Loup de mer sea-bass
Louvine (Loubine) grey mullet, like a sea-bass (Basque name)
Lyonnaise (à la) Lyonnais style: sauce with wine, onions, vinegar
Mâche lamb's lettuce; small dark green leaf
Madeleine tiny sponge cake
Madère sauce *demi-glace* and Madeira wine
Magret (de canard) breast (of duck); now used for other poultry
Maïs maize flour
Maison (de) of the restaurant
Maître d'hôtel sauce with butter, parsley and lemon
Manchons see Goujonnettes
Mangetout edible peas and pods
Mangue mango
Manière (de) style (of)
Maquereau mackerel
Maraîchère (à la) market-gardener style; velouté sauce with vegetables
Marais marsh or market garden
Marbré marbled
Marc pure spirit
Marcassin young wild boar
Marché market
Marchand de vin sauce with red wine, chopped shallots
Marengo tomatoes, mushrooms, olive oil, white wine, garlic, herbs
Marennes (blanches) flat-shelled oysters (*see* Huîtres)
Marennes (vertes) green shell oysters
Marinières see Moules
Marmite stewpot
Marrons chestnuts

Médaillon (de) round piece (of)
Mélange mixture or blend
Ménagère (à la) housewife style: onions, potatoes, peas, turnips and carrots
Mendiant (fruits de) mixture of figs, almonds and raisins
Menthe mint
Merguez spicy grilled sausage
Merlan whiting (in Provence the word is used for hake)
Merlu hake
Merluche dried cod
Mesclum mixture of salad leaves
Meunière sauce with butter, parsley, lemon (sometimes oil)
Meurette red wine sauce
Miel honey
Mignon (de) small round piece
Mignonette coarsely ground white pepper
Mijoté(e) cooked slowly in water
Milanaise (à la) Milan style: dipped in breadcrumbs, egg, cheese
Mille-feuille puff pastry with numerous thin layers
Mirabeau anchovies, olives
Mirabelle golden plums
Mitonée (de) soup (of)
Mode (à la) in the manner of
Moelle beef marrow
Moelleux au chocolat chocolate dessert (cake)
Montmorency with cherries
Morilles edible, dark brown, honeycombed fungi
Mornay cheese sauce
Morue cod
Moule mussels
Moules marinières mussels cooked in white wine and shallots
Mousseline hollandaise sauce with whipped cream
Moutarde mustard
Mouton mutton
Mûre mulberry
Mûre sauvage (de ronce) blackberry
Muscade nutmeg
Museau de porc (de boeuf) sliced muzzle of pork (beef) with shallots and parsley with vinaigrette
Myrtille bilberry (blueberry)
Mystère a meringue desert with ice-cream and chocolate; also cone-shaped ice cream
Nature plain
Navarin stew (usually lamb)
Navets turnips
Nid nest
Noilly sauce based on vermouth
Noisette hazelnut
Noisette sauce of lightly browned butter
Noisette (de) round piece (of)
Noix nuts
Noix de veau topside of leg (veal)
Normande (à la) Normandy style: fish sauce with mussels, shrimps, mushrooms, eggs and cream
Nouille noodle
Nouveau (Nouvelle) new or young

Noyau sweet liqueur from crushed stones (usually cherries)
Oeufs à la coque soft-boiled eggs
Oeufs à la neige see Île flottante
Oeufs à la poêle fried eggs
Oeufs brouillés scrambled eggs
Oeufs cocotte eggs cooked in individual dishes in a bain-marie
Oeufs durs hard-boiled eggs
Oeufs moulés poached eggs
Oie goose
Oignon onion
Ombrine fish, like sea-bass
Onglet flank of beef
Oreille (de porc) ear (pig's)
Oreillette sweet fritter, flavoured with orange flower water
Origan oregano (herb)
Orléannaise Orléans style: chicory and potatoes
Ortie nettle
Os bone
Osso bucco à la niçoise veal braised with orange zest, tomatoes, onions and garlic
Pain bread
Pain complet/entier wholemeal
Pain de campagne round white loaf
Pain d'épice spiced honey cake
Pain de mie square white loaf
Pain de seigle rye bread
Pain grillé toast
Pain doré/Pain perdu bread soaked in milk and eggs and fried
Paleron shoulder
Palmier palm-shaped sweet puff pastry
Palmier (coeur de) palm (heart)
Palombe wood pigeon
Palomête fish, like sea-bass
Palourde clam
Pamplemousse grapefruit
Panaché mixed
Pané(e) breadcrumbed
Papillote (en) cooked in oiled paper or foil
Paquets (en) parcels
Parfait (de) mousse (of)
Paris-Brest cake of choux pastry, filled with butter cream, almonds
Parisienne (à la) leeks, potatoes
Parmentier potatoes
Pastèque watermelon
Pastis (sauce au) aniseed based
Pâte pastry, dough or batter
Pâte à choux cream puff pastry
Pâte brisée short crust pastry
Pâté en croûte baked in pastry crust
Pâtes fraîches fresh pasta
Pâtisserie pastry
Paupiettes thin slices of meat or fish, used to wrap fillings
Pavé (de) thick slice (of)
Pavot (graines de) poppy seeds
Paysan(ne) (à la) country style
Peau (de) skin (of)
Pêche peach
Pêcheur fisherman
Pèlerine scallop
Perche perch
Perdreau young partridge

Perdrix partridge
Périgourdine (à la) goose liver and sauce Périgueux
Périgueux sauce with truffles and Madeira
Persil parsley
Persillade mixture of chopped parsley and garlic
Petit gris small snail
Pétoncle small scallop
Picholine large green table olives
Pied de cheval large oyster
Pied de mouton blanc cream coloured mushroom
Pied de porc pig's trotter
Pigeonneau young pigeon
Pignon pine nut
Piment (doux) pepper (sweet)
Pintade (pintadeau) guinea fowl (young guinea fowl)
Piperade omelette or scrambled eggs with tomatoes, peppers, onions and sometimes ham
Piquante (sauce) sharp tasting sauce with shallots, capers and wine
Pissenlit dandelion leaf
Pistache green pistachio nut
Pistou vegetable soup bound with pommade (thick smooth paste)
Plateau (de) plate (of)
Pleurote mushroom
Poché(e), pochade poached
Poêlé fried
Poire pear
Poireau leek
Pois pea
Poisson fish
Poitrine breast
Poitrine fumée smoked bacon
Poitrine salée unsmoked bacon
Poivre noir black pepper
Poivron (doux) pepper (sweet)
Polonaise Polish style: with buttered breadcrumbs, parsley, hard-boiled eggs
Pomme apple
Pommes de terre potatoes
  château roast
  dauphine croquettes
  frites chips
  gratinées browned with cheese
  Lyonnaise sautéed with onions
  vapeur boiled
Porc (carré de) loin of pork
Porc (côte de) loin of pork
Porcelet suckling pig
Porto (au) port
Portugaise (à la) Portuguese style: fried onions and tomatoes
Portugaises oysters with long, deep shells (see Huîtres)
Potage thick soup
Pot-au-feu clear meat broth served with the meat
Potimarron pumpkin
Poularde large hen
Poulet chicken
Poulet à la broche spit-roasted chicken
Poulpe octopus
Poussin small baby chicken

Pré-salé (agneau de) lamb raised on salt marshes
Primeur young vegetable
Profiterole puffs of *choux* pastry, filled with custard
Provençale (à la) Provençal style: tomatoes, garlic, olive oil, etc.
Prune plum
Pruneau prune
Quenelle light dumpling of fish or poultry
Queue tail
Queue de boeuf oxtail
Quiche lorraine open flan of cheese, ham or bacon
Raclette scrapings from specially-made and heated cheese
Radis radish
Ragoût stew, usually meat but can describe other ingredients
Raie (bouclée) skate (type of)
Raifort horseradish
Raisin grape
Ramier wood pigeon
Rapé(e) grated or shredded
Rascasse scorpion fish
Ratatouille aubergines, onions, courgettes, garlic, red peppers and tomatoes in olive oil
Réglisse liquorice
Reine-Claude greengage
Rémoulade sauce of mayonnaise, mustard, capers, herbs, anchovies
Rillettes (d'oie) potted pork (goose)
Ris d'agneau lamb sweetbreads
Ris de veau veal sweetbreads
Riz rice
Robe de chambre jacket potato
Rognon kidney
Romarin rosemary
Rôti roast
Rouget red mullet
Rouget barbet red mullet
Rouille orange-coloured sauce with peppers, garlic and saffron
Roulade (de) roll (of)
Roulé(e) rolled (usually crêpe)
Sabayon sauce of egg yolks, wine
Sablé shortbread
Safran saffron
Saignant(e) underdone, rare
St-Jaques (coquille) scallop
St-Pierre John Dory
Salade niçoise tomatoes, beans, potatoes, black olives, anchovies, lettuce, olive oil, perhaps tuna
Salade panachée mixed salad
Salade verte green salad
Salé salted
Salmis red wine sauce
Salsifis salsify (vegetable)
Sandre freshwater fish, like perch
Sang blood
Sanglier wild boar
Saucisse freshly-made sausage
Saucisson large, dry sausage
Saucisson cervelas saveloy
Sauge sage
Saumon salmon
Saumon fumé smoked salmon

Sauvage wild
Scipion cuttlefish
Sel salt
Soja (pousse de) soy bean (soy bean sprout)
Soja (sauce de) soy sauce
Soubise onion sauce
Sucre sugar
Tapenade olive spread
Tartare raw minced beef
Tartare (sauce) sauce with mayonnaise, onions, capers, herbs
Tarte open flan
Tarte Tatin upside down tart of caramelized apples and pastry
Terrine container in which mixed meats/fish are baked; served cold
Tête de veau vinaigrette calf's head vinaigrette
Thé tea
Thermidor grilled lobster with browned béchamel sauce
Thon tuna fish
Thym thyme
Tiède mild or lukewarm
Tilleul lime tree
Tomate tomato
Topinambour Jerusalem artichoke
Torte sweet-filled flan
Tortue turtle
Tournedos fillet steak (small end)
Touron a cake, pastry or loaf made from almond paste and filled with candied fruits and nuts
Tourte (Tourtière) covered savoury tart
Tourteau large crab
Tranche slice
Tranche de boeuf steak
Traver de porc spare rib of pork
Tripoux stuffed mutton tripe
Truffade a huge sautéed pancake or galette with bacon, garlic and Cantal cheese
Truffe truffle; black, exotic, tuber
Truite trout
Truite saumonée salmon trout
Turbot (Turbotin) turbot
Vacherin ice-cream, meringue, cream
Vapeur (à la) steamed
Veau veal
Veau pané (escalope de) thin slice of veal in flour, eggs and breadcrumbs
Venaison venison
Verveine verbena
Viande meat
Vichyssoise creamy potato and leek soup, served cold
Viennoise coated with egg and breadcrumbs, fried (usually veal)
Vierge literally virgin (best olive oil, the first pressing)
Vierge (sauce) olive oil sauce
Vinaigre (de) wine vinegar or vinegar of named fruit
Vinaigrette (à la) French dressing with wine vinegar, oil, etc.
Volaille poultry
Yaourt yogurt

VACANCES

Alsace	1 84202 167 2
The Ardèche	1 84202 161 3
The Basque Country	1 84202 159 1
Brittany	1 84202 007 2
Catalonia	1 84202 099 4
Corsica	1 84202 100 1
The Dordogne & Périgord	1 84202 098 6
French Alps	1 84202 166 4
Languedoc-Roussillon	1 84202 008 0
Normandy	1 84202 097 8
Poitou-Charentes	1 84202 009 9
Provence & the Côte d'Azur	1 84202 006 4
Pyrenees & Gascony	1 84202 015 3
South West France	1 84202 014 5

A GREAT WEEKEND IN ...

Focusing on the limited amount of time available on a weekend break, these guides suggest the most entertaining and interesting ways of getting to know the city in just a few days.

Amsterdam	1 84202 145 1
Barcelona	0 54008 323 2
Berlin	1 84202 061 7
Brussels	1 84202 017 X
Budapest	0 54008 270 0
Dublin	1 84202 096 X
Florence	0 54008 322 4
Lisbon	1 84202 011 0
London	1 84202 168 0
Madrid	1 84202 095 1
Naples	1 84202 016 1
New York	0 54008 321 6
Paris	1 84202 001 3
Prague	1 84202 000 5
Rome	1 84202 169 9
Seville	0 54008 275 9
Stockholm	0 54008 318 6
Venice	1 84202 018 8
Vienna	1 84202 026 9

ROUTARD

Indulge your taste for travel with the ultimate food, drink and accommodation guides for the independent traveller.

Andalucia & Southern Spain	1 84202 028 5
Athens & the Greek Islands	1 84202 023 4
Belgium	1 84202 022 6
California, Nevada & Arizona	1 84202 025 0
Canada	1 84202 031 5
Cuba	1 84202 062 5
Ireland	1 84202 024 2
North Brittany	1 84202 020 X
Paris	1 84202 027 7
Provence & the Côte d'Azur	1 84202 019 6
Rome & Southern Italy	1 84202 021 8
Thailand	1 84202 029 3